Shakespeare and Film

A NORTON GUIDE

Shakespeare and Film

A NORTON GUIDE

Samuel Crowl
Ohio University

W. W. Norton & Company
New York   London

W. W. Norton & Company has been independent since its founding in 1923, when William Warder Norton and Mary D. Herter Norton first published lectures delivered at the People's Institute, the adult education division of New York City's Cooper Union. The Nortons soon expanded their program beyond the Institute, publishing books by celebrated academics from America and abroad. By mid-century, the two major pillars of Norton's publishing program—trade books and college texts—were firmly established. In the 1950s, the Norton family transferred control of the company to its employees, and today—with a staff of four hundred and a comparable number of trade, college, and professional titles published each year—W. W. Norton & Company stands as the largest and oldest publishing house owned wholly by its employees.

Copyright © 2008 by W. W. Norton & Company, Inc.

Editor: Julia Reidhead
Associate Editor: Erin Granville
Managing Editor, College: Marian Johnson
Associate Managing Editor, College: Kim Yi
Copy Editor: Patterson Lamb
Production Manager: Diane O'Connor
Manufacturing by Courier Company
Book design by Anna Oler

Library of Congress Cataloging-in-Publication Data

Crowl, Samuel.
    Shakespeare and film : a Norton guide / Samuel Crowl.—1st ed.
        p.   cm.
    Includes bibliographical references and index.
    ISBN 978-0-393-92765-8 (pbk.)
    1. Shakespeare, William, 1564–1616—Film and video adaptations.   2. English drama—Film and video adaptations.   3. Film adaptations—History and criticism.   I. Title.
    PR3093.C747   2008
    791.43'6 — dc22   2007021115

W. W. Norton & Company, Inc., 500 Fifth Avenue, New York, N.Y. 10110
www.wwnorton.com
W. W. Norton & Company Ltd., Castle House, 75/76 Wells Street, London W1T 3QT

1 2 3 4 5 6 7 8 9 0

For my Shakespeare professors at Hamilton College
and Indiana University:

Edwin Barrett and C. L. Barber

and

For my Shakespeare students at Ohio University

"Look here upon this picture, and on this . . ."

Contents

Acknowledgments

I want to thank Julia Reidhead, senior editor and vice president of W.W. Norton, for first suggesting this project to me in the busy book exhibit room of the Shakespeare Association of America meeting in New Orleans in April of 2004. Julia has gently but persistently pushed and prodded me to make this a better, more useful guide at every stage in its development. She also realized the dream of a small-town lad from the Midwest, who grew up reading *The New Yorker*, to be taken for drinks at the Algonquin Hotel by his editor. I would also like to thank Erin Granville, associate editor at Norton, who has improved this book on every page by her fine editorial hand, her intelligent sense of structure and organization, and her probing questions about some of my assumptions.

The editors of the Ohio University Press and the *Shakespeare Bulletin* have graciously allowed me to incorporate brief revised versions of material that first appeared in books, essays, and reviews written for their audiences. I owe a huge, and continuing, debt of gratitude to my Shakespeare-on-film colleagues for over thirty years of invigorating conversation and debate about the accomplishment of Laurence Olivier, Orson Welles, Akira Kurosawa, Franco Zeffirelli, Kenneth Branagh, and others in successfully translating Shakespeare into film. Those colleagues include Jack Jorgens, Kenneth Rothwell, H. R. Coursen, Russell Jackson, Courtney Lehmann, José Ramón Diaz Fernández, Kathy Howlett, John Ford, Anthony Davis, Sarah Hatchuel, and Mark Thornton Burnett. Professor Douglas Lanier of the University of New Hampshire made generous and telling suggestions for the improvement of this guide from approach to structure, and I thank him for the care he devoted to the manuscript.

My understanding of the potentials and perils in translating Shakespeare from the page to the screen was greatly enriched by the faculty participants in the two workshops in Teaching Shakespeare on Film Ken Rothwell and I led at the 2004 Shakespeare Association of America meeting and the Ohio high school teachers who participated in the summer workshop on the same subject. Herb Coursen and I led later that year in Athens for Ohio University's Ping Institute for the Teaching of the Humanities. Those teachers raised the key issues about Shakespeare on film that I have tried to incorporate into this guide. As always, a number of friends, colleagues, and students participated in the ongoing conversation about Shakespeare and film as this guide was taking shape and I want to mention just a few who have to stand for many: Stuart and Anne Scott, Sam Crowl and Terry Kelleher, Barb and Peter Thompson, Charlie and Claire Ping, Miranda Crowl and Bill Pistner, Ed and Carolyn Quattrocchi, Brad and Chris Lafferty, Jen and Geoff Wiswell, Doug and Scott Roberts, David J. Skal, Michael Kaiser, Alex Baker, and Jen Walker.

I am grateful to Ohio University's College of Arts and Sciences for a research grant that allowed me to employ Michael Drew as a research assistant on this project. Michael was instrumental in preparing the guide's film glossary and filmography. The former (Ken Daley) and current (Joe McLaughlin) chairs of the English department were creative in their support for this book and were especially savvy about arranging my teaching schedule to provide optimum expanses of time free for writing over the past two years. Once again, Patty Colwell flawlessly took my text from fountain pen to computer screen. Professor Susan Crowl brought her musical expertise to bear on the sections in the guide dealing with film scores and was particularly helpful in dealing with Dmitri Shostakovich's scores for Kozintsev's Shakespeare films and Patrick Doyle's for Branagh's. Thanks also to Jeff Harmison for helping me master the frame grab software.

Finally, this book is dedicated to the two professors, Edwin Barrett and C. L. Barber, who shaped my response to Shakespeare in the drama of the classroom and in the art of criticism and to the many students at Ohio University with whom I have wandered in Shakespeare's realms of gold, on the page, on the stage, and on the screen, over the past four decades.

Shakespeare on Film and Television

I taught my first course on Shakespeare on Film in the spring of 1973. Such courses were rare then, as 16mm film versions of Shakespeare's plays were hard to locate and expensive to rent, and the study of Shakespeare on screen had not yet become recognized or even acknowledged by traditional Shakespearean scholars as a legitimate field of inquiry. In the past three decades, performance, including Shakespeare on film, has become one of the leading areas of focus in Shakespeare studies. The development of the videotape and the DVD, coupled with the renaissance of the Shakespeare film genre in the 1990s, has led to the incorporation of Shakespeare films into the classroom study of Shakespeare in high schools, colleges, and universities across the country. The new technology has created a vast library of Shakespeare films and television productions available for use by teachers and professors, so that many of us now assign films in our courses as readily as we include leading critical essays and books on Shakespeare.

Shakespeare and Film: A Norton Guide is intended to speak to the growing audience of students studying Shakespeare on film and television, either in the traditional Shakespeare survey course or in offerings devoted exclusively to Shakespeare on film. The scholarly study of Shakespeare on film has been a remarkable recent growth industry, with five or six new books or collections of essays appearing every year since the early 1990s. These books and essays boldly follow an expansionist agenda, both in defining the Shakespeare film genre and theorizing its place in the global entertainment economy. What the field has lacked is a comprehensive guide to Shakespeare and film focused specifically on the use of the Shakespeare film in the undergraduate classroom. This book was conceived and written to address that need.

Organization

Shakespeare and Film: A Norton Guide is divided into two parts, each consisting of five chapters. The chapters in Part I present the student with an overview of the history of Shakespeare on film and television from the silent era to the present; a detailed look at the six major directors (Laurence Olivier, Orson Welles, Kenneth Branagh, Akira Kurosawa, Grigori Kozintsev, and Franco Zeffirelli) most responsible for shaping the form and content of the Shakespeare film; a brief history and analysis of the ways in which Shakespeare has been adapted for television; and an examination of the remarkable renaissance of the Shakespeare film genre in the 1990s. These chapters provide the critical and historical context to equip students with a more comprehensive understanding of the genre than might be gained solely from an exposure to several Shakespeare films in the standard Shakespeare survey course.

Part II provides avenues of exploration for students in thinking and writing about Shakespeare on film in a more systematic manner. The chapters in this section remind students that Shakespeare films spring from specific cultural and historical contexts; they must forge a complex relationship with dense and layered texts created for another medium (the stage); they need to discover or invent film equivalents for conventions common to Shakespeare's theater; they strive to create a film grammar and rhetoric to express Shakespeare's rich language in visual images and patterns; and they undertake through technical means (camera work, music, and editing) to express ideas and images alive in Shakespeare's text and their cinematic transformation by the film director.

In these chapters I provide examples of the ways in which Shakespeare films reflect the cultural moment of their production and the particular cinematic style of their directors. These films translate Shakespeare's verbal images into visual ones; they adapt stage conventions like the soliloquy to the conventions of film; they establish certain shots or sequences as a means of defining a particular director's personal signature in capturing Shakespeare on film. I also explore television's capacity for producing Shakespeare and the strengths and weaknesses it brings to the process of moving Shakespeare from the page to stage to screen. My hope is that students will find that these examples stimulate their thinking about film, television, and Shakespeare, and encourage them to build on my suggestions in seeking out meaningful approaches of their own to this material. Film is an independent art form, and students need to appreciate that the best Shakespeare films are rarely those that cling to a fidelity model in their translation of Shakespeare from stage to screen.

I have drawn my examples from a full range of over forty sound Shakespeare films and television productions, from the 1935 Warner Brothers *A Midsummer Night's Dream* to Michael Radford's *The Merchant of Venice* (2004), but I have concentrated intentionally on those film and television versions of Shakespeare's plays most likely to be used in traditional survey courses devoted to Shakespeare, versions directed by Laurence Olivier, Orson Welles, Franco Zeffirelli, Peter Hall, Kenneth Branagh, Michael Almereyda, Baz Luhrmann, Trevor Nunn, Richard Eyre, Jonathan Miller, Jane Howell, Michael Hoffman, Richard Loncraine, and Julie Taymor.

The Shakespearean Spin-off Film or Adaptation

Though the Shakespeare spin-off film has become an increasingly attractive and prolific genre in our time—one, *Shakespeare in Love,* even won the Academy Award for Best Picture in 1998—I have left a discussion of these films out of this guide for several reasons. I am a believer in the "big tent" approach to Shakespeare on film and television and want the scholarly field to claim as wide a landscape as possible in considering the myriad ways Shakespeare is adapted by and absorbed into popular culture. However, I have learned in conversations with fellow Shakespeare professors across the country that few spin-off films are ever included in the standard Shakespeare survey course, as there is rarely enough time to include even an appropriate selection of the best of the traditional Shakespeare films or television productions. In fact, most film and television productions are likely to find their way into the Shakespeare survey via the film clip rather than through the showing of full-length productions. I have also discovered that the spin-off film, especially the high-school teen flick variety so conspicuous in our own time, including *10 Things I Hate about You* (1999), *O* (2001), and *She's the Man* (2006), or darker, more mature films, like

My Own Private Idaho (1991), *The King Is Alive* (2000), or *Scotland, Pa.* (2001), have their greatest impact when they are discovered by our students on their own. Then students bring the enthusiasm of their find to the classroom and experience the thrill of ownership of Shakespeare and the myriad ways he is at work in their world as well as in the college classroom. In addition, these films are most likely to be included in specialized courses like Shakespeare and Popular Culture or Shakespeare and Hollywood and thus lie just outside the purview of this guide.

Keys to Filmmaking

There are six key elements in the making of a film: script, direction, camera, acting, music, and editing. The script or screenplay is not just the dialogue spoken in the film but a thorough description of each shot, scene, and sequence of the film. Unlike play scripts, screenplays are likely to change—sometimes radically—as the shooting of the film progresses. The screenplay for a Shakespeare film is of particular importance because it derives from an established text in the canon of dramatic literature. Words reign on Shakespeare's stage; he packs everything into the language. As method actors from Marlon Brando to Al Pacino have learned, you have to play the text in Shakespeare, not the subtext. Film, however, is dominated by the visual image; words matter, but the image reigns. The director is the key figure in movie-making, and it is his vision and imagination that drives the film. The director of the Shakespeare film must find an interesting and effective balance between word and image. He is ultimately responsible for melding all of the film's disparate elements into an artistic whole (or into powerful fragments if he is working from a postmodern aesthetic).

The camera is the single most important technological tool in filmmaking, and understanding its contributions to the visual narrative is of prime importance to students. Acting is the most immediately identifiable element in a movie, but it is not the work of the actor alone as each performance is refined by how a scene is arranged by the director, shot by the camera, and ultimately linked with other scenes in the editing room. Music plays a much larger role in film rhetoric than it does on the stage. The film score introduces and subsequently tracks character, underlines emotion, creates tension, and sweeps along under the action, often without our conscious awareness of how it is doing its work. The editing process is where all the elements of the film are brought together and linked in the pace and rhythm established by the director. The student of Shakespeare on film needs to be alert to these crucial areas of filmmaking, and Chapter 6 of this guide will revisit many of these elements in the context of specific Shakespeare films and television productions.

Television

Television does not possess the technical resources of film. Shakespeare productions shot in a television studio are recorded by three or four bulky, floor-bound cameras and the occasional handheld camera. Film is shot in bits and pieces with the opportunity to make multiple takes of a particular shot or scene. Because of the availability of actors, location shooting, and high production costs, films are rarely shot in sequence and are put together only in the final editing process. Television Shakespeare is generally shot in sequence with the director cutting the production as the performance unfolds by switching the shot being recorded from one camera to another. The student does not have to master any basic television vocabulary except to note when the shot is moving from one camera to another and how far the camera is from the actors at any given moment.

The basic television shot is medium **close-up**, with the camera focusing on the actor from the waist up. Television exists in a space between stage and film. Students will quickly see that televised Shakespeare relies more on the script and the actor to tell the story than on camera and editing. For instance, in Lady Macbeth's famous sleepwalking scene, film has the capacity to cut back and forth between her face and her hands as she tries to rub out that damned spot and cleanse her mind of Duncan's murder. The same scene, recorded by television, is more likely to have Lady Macbeth's face and hands present in the frame at the same moment. Even though it might seem unrealistic, as we rarely wash our hands raised up in front of our face, an effective television shot might have Lady Macbeth rubbing her hands in front of her face so that the camera shoots her psychological torment through the action that expresses her trauma.

The Film Clip

I try to include as many full-length films and television productions in my Shakespeare course as time will allow so students can fully enter the world of each performance and judge it both on its own merits and as a reflection and comment on its Shakespearean source. Another and perhaps more widespread approach is for the professor to show several brief film clips of the same speech or scene from a variety of film and television productions of the play. This allows students a wonderful comparative perspective on the variety of ways different productions realize the same textual material.

Even brief clips can be read (like isolated passages from novels) so that they reveal a great deal about the approach and style the director has taken to the Shakespearean material. Students exposed only to brief clips from films like Olivier's *Hamlet* (1948) or Welles's *Othello* (1952) or Luhrmann's *William Shakespeare's Romeo + Juliet* (1996) will find substantial information in both the first and second half of this guide that will help them place those brief moments in the broader context of the entire film and the director's general style when translating Shakespeare from text to screen. Film clips provide exposure to a range of approaches to realizing Shakespeare on film and television and can be the basis for interesting papers of a comparative nature on the way a character (Iago, for instance, or Ophelia) is created by the combination of acting and camera work, or the way a single speech (Hamlet's "To be or not to be" soliloquy, for example) reveals the film's technical approach to the Shakespearean soliloquy, the actor's interpretation of the character, and the director's visual conception of the text.

The Fidelity Model

Though it may seem counterintuitive to the Shakespeare student and scholar, the fidelity model has rarely been a successful approach to creating an interesting, lively, and intelligent Shakespeare film. As subsequent chapters in this guide will explore, movies have their own conventions, and one of them is length. There are worthy exceptions, of course, but most commercial films are between ninety and one hundred fifty minutes long. Woody Allen comedies are on the short end of that range, while Peter Jackson epics push the longer end. Only a few Shakespeare plays (*The Comedy of Errors*, *A Midsummer Night's Dream*, and *Macbeth*) are short enough to be squeezed into the conventional film time frame. Shakespeare's texts have to be reimagined as screenplays, and that almost automatically means that the text will be trimmed, often by 50 percent or more.

The director wants to make an artistically and commercially successful film, and to do so he needs to translate his vision of Shakespeare's text into an art form that is significantly different from the theatrical space for which Shakespeare conceived his plays. This requires imagination and intelligence and skill. He has to translate Shakespeare into the language of film and that means the language of image and action. Simply filming the text is not a viable option. Students should not complain about what has been "left out" of a Shakespeare film but concentrate instead on what has been left in and the reasons why. The wonderful thing about Shakespeare in performance, whether on stage or screen, is the infinite variety of approaches that a single Shakespearean text can inspire. Much like critical readings of Shakespeare, none of those performances or readings are the text; they are versions of it and they are more or less successful depending on the intelligence, wit, and talent of the director, his technical crew, and the actors.

Scholarship

There has been an explosion of scholarship on Shakespeare and film in the past thirty years. That productivity has not been matched in the critical attention devoted to Shakespeare on television, which remains a field of inquiry still waiting to be defined and explored. The bibliography for this guide contains the major book-length studies and collections of critical essays devoted to Shakespeare on film. Here I will attempt to provide a brief narrative of the scholarly development of the field.

Shakespeare on film now has a journal (*Shakespeare Bulletin*), a historian (Kenneth Rothwell), a bibliographer (José Ramón Díaz Fernández), a pioneering critic (Jack Jorgens), and a host of contemporary critics and theoreticians spanning the full range of formalist and postmodern approaches to the subject. Jack Jorgens and other early critics (primarily Michael Anderegg, Lorne Buchman, John Collick, H. R. Coursen, Samuel Crowl, Anthony Davies, Peter S. Donaldson, Barbara Hodgdon, Bernice Kliman, Luke McKernan and Olwen Terris, Barry Parker, Ace Pilkington, and Kenneth Rothwell) provided the essential critical and scholarly groundwork for the emerging field by publishing book-length critical studies and filmographies.

Critics like Buchman, Coursen, Crowl, Davies, Donaldson, and Hodgdon began to stake out the methodological boundaries or divisions of the enterprise, with approaches as varied as the psychoanalytic (autobiography as key to directorial strategies), the intertextual (dialogue between stage and film productions), the formal (reading films with the tools of the New Criticism), materialist (marketplace and means of production), cultural studies (resonances with the film's historical moment), and popular studies (Shakespeare and the mass media). These older critics were soon joined by younger voices like those of Judith Buchanan, Stephen Buhler, Mark Thornton Burnett, Richard Burt, Sarah Hatchuel, Kathy Howlett, Douglas Lanier, and Courtney Lehmann extending the boundaries of the field into film theory, mass media, pop culture, and politics.

Besides the scholarly monograph, several influential collections of essays were published in the 1990s and continued to appear on an almost yearly basis in the new century. The most prominent of these collections were *Shakespeare and the Moving Image* (1994), *Screen Shakespeare* (1994), *Shakespeare, the Movie* (1997), *Shakespeare on Film: New Casebooks Series* (1998), *Shakespeare, Film, and Fin de Siècle* (2000), *The Cambridge Companion to Shakespeare on Film* (2000; second edition, 2007), *Spectacular Shakespeare* (2002), *Reel Shakespeare* (2003), *Shakespeare, the Movie II* (2003), *A Concise Companion to Shakespeare on Screen (2005)*, and *Screening Shakespeare in the Twenty-First Century* (2006). These collections were augmented by special issues of literary and film journals devoted to essays on Shakespeare and film including *Literature/Film Quarterly* (1992, 1994, 1997, 2000, 2001, 2002, 2004), *Post Script* (1997, 1998), *Shakespeare Quarterly* (2002), and *Cineaste* (1998).

Increasingly, the essays in these volumes have concentrated on the films of the past two decades when the genre experienced a remarkable revival sparked by the commercial success of Kenneth Branagh's *Henry V* (1989) and *Much Ado about Nothing* (1993) and Baz Luhrmann's *William Shakespeare's Romeo + Juliet* (1996). The books, essay collections, and special journal issues mentioned in this section will provide the student with a wide array of critical and theoretical approaches to Shakespeare on film in general and to the analysis of many individual Shakespeare films.

Taxonomy: Theatrical, Realistic, Filmic, and Hybrid

The great variety of Shakespeare films makes it inviting to attempt to define and classify them into distinct groupings based on shared qualities. The student may find such definitions and distinctions helpful, but it is wise to note that few Shakespeare films fit purely or perfectly into any one group. Most Shakespeare films have attributes drawn from a variety of categories even if they finally fit most comfortably into a single one. Jack Jorgens recognized this when he developed one of the first taxonomies for the Shakespeare film. Jorgens was concerned only with Shakespeare films that used Shakespeare's text (Olivier, Welles, Zeffirelli) or a translated version of it (Kozintsev) or a version that followed the plot of Shakespeare's play but with dialogue not directly linked to Shakespeare's (Kurosawa). He divided those films into three categories: the **theatrical**, the **realistic**, and the **filmic**. He argued that Olivier's Shakespeare films fit most comfortably within the first category, Zeffirelli's in the second, and Welles's in the third. He also found that because most popular Hollywood films belong to the second category, cinematic realism was the major movie mode and most Shakespeare films fell into that category.

Jorgens articulated his groupings in his 1977 book *Shakespeare on Film*, and in general they have stood the test of time. In her recent *Shakespeare, From Stage to Screen* (2004), Sarah Hatchuel basically accepts Jorgens's categories and expands them only in the direction of the Shakespearean adaptation or spin-off film. Shakespeare films, like all three of Olivier's, often follow a path from stage to screen and thus reveal their theatrical roots. Other Shakespeare films, picking up on film's ability to create a stunning visual spectacle, easily settle into the realistic mode. Still others, like Welles's *Othello*, Kozintsev's *Hamlet* (1964), and Kurosawa's *Throne of Blood* (1957), translate their Shakespearean material into great visual cinema poems where image trumps text. I would add a fourth category to Jorgens's trio: the **hybrid**.

The hybrid consists of films that find their inspiration as much from other, conventional Hollywood films and film genres as they do from their Shakespearean source material. Many of the Shakespeare films made in the 1990s belong to the hybrid category. Earlier Shakespeare filmmakers were reluctant to embrace popular Hollywood codes and conventions for fear of soiling their elite Shakespearean material with film's populism. Such filmmakers, especially Olivier, were much more comfortable looking to the European art film for models rather than to Hollywood. Branagh's generation of Shakespeare filmmakers changed all that. Branagh and Baz Luhrmann are positively giddy to quote from a wide variety of popular movies, from John Sturges's *The Magnificent Seven* (1960) to John Woo's action films. Richard Loncraine links his 1930s setting for *Richard III* (1995) as much with the American gangster film genre that flourished in that decade as with the politics of some prominent members of England's royal family who flirted with Hitler and fascism—the screenplay's original concept for the film. Oliver Parker had erotic thrillers like *Fatal Attraction* (1987) in mind as a model when he came to make his 1995 film of *Othello*. It is no surprise that the hybrid Shakespeare film should suddenly appear in the age of postmodernism where pastiche and hybridity were aesthetically celebrated. The Shakespeare films in the era of Branagh and Baz were unembarrassed to poach ideas, images, and models from a variety of sources, including the commercial Hollywood film.

Conclusion

I hope this guide will prove useful to professors and students as they explore the rich relationship between Shakespeare's texts and their translation into film and television productions. It is meant to provide historical information, critical context, detailed examples, and helpful resource material for students working this territory for the first time. This guide moves from the long shot (the history of Shakespeare on film and television, the work of major directors) to the close-up (Macbeth's bloody hands, Claudius's wine goblet) and is meant to be used in whatever way best suits the interests of individual professors and students. Some may wish to skip the historical sections to plunge into the conventions and details of specific films, returning to gain a broader perspective only after close examination of a specific production or director. Shape this guide to meet your needs as you begin to explore the world of Shakespeare on screen.

When we read, we imagine. When we read a novel, for instance, we are almost always simultaneously constructing a movie of it in our imagination as we absorb and transform the words on the page into vital images of actors and action. Shakespeare productions are a director's vision and version of that process. A Shakespeare film enacts a paradox. It is tethered to the originating text at the same moment it exists as an independent work of art. Laurence Olivier, Franco Zeffirelli, Kenneth Branagh, and Michael Almereyda all create *Hamlet* movies indebted to the same source, but they fashion very different works of filmic art based upon their individual approach to their Shakespearean material. The student of Shakespeare on film needs to be attentive to both Shakespeare and film, understanding that each has an independent existence while engaging in a lively intertextual conversation. This book seeks to enhance your participation in that conversation.

A Brief Guide to Film Grammar and Rhetoric

At its most basic the narrative film consists of shots, scenes, and sequences. A shot consists of what is captured in the frame between the moment the camera starts running and when it stops, between the time the director calls for "action" and when he signals "cut." In the finished film, a single shot can last from several seconds to many minutes. Shots not only come in a variety of lengths but also in a variety of sizes (long shot, medium shot, close-up), angles (low angle, wide angle, overhead), and movements (pan shot, tracking shot, crane shot). Shots are then linked together into scenes. A scene is a shot or, more commonly, a series of shots depicting an action taking place at a single time and place. Scenes are then linked together into sequences that depict larger arcs of the film's narrative development. The opening shot of Branagh's *Much Ado about Nothing* (1993) focuses on white words popping up on a black screen as we hear a voice (soon to be discovered as Emma Thompson's, the actress playing Beatrice) reciting the words of Balthazar's song. That shot is followed by a series of shots capturing the scene of members of Leonato's household picnicking on a Tuscan hillside awaiting the arrival of men home from war. As the soldiers suddenly approach on horseback in the valley below, that scene becomes part of a larger sequence that visually creates a robust romantic energy as the men and women dash to bathe and dress to prepare for the celebration signaling the war's end.

The shot, the scene, and the sequence are film's building blocks. Generally, the movement in film is from long shot to close-up. Most scenes begin with an establishing shot that tells us where we are: in the mountains or a city or a courtroom. As the viewer becomes acclimated to landscape and setting, the camera then moves in to concentrate on the human action unfolding in the scene. Of course, some films intentionally reverse this process, disorienting us with the establishing shot so that we have to work to understand the context for the action.

Directors and their cinematographers (the professional camera operators who actually shoot the film) are especially concerned about the composition of the frame. In the theater our eyes take in the complete field of vision of the stage space. We see everything in long shot. The director (and actors) can of course direct our eyes to one part of the stage or another depending on the action, but they do not completely control the frame of our vision. The actor's body is always fully available to us unless intentionally hidden by a prop or a piece of furniture. If we decide, at one moment, to look only at the actor's hands, it is because we have made that decision (though often prompted to do so by the actor—Lady Macbeth's hand actions in the famed "Out, out damned spot" speech, for instance). In film, we see only what the director chooses for us to see. We are likely to be conscious of Lady Macbeth's hands because we are given a close-up of them as the only image in the frame. The director can then cut to a close-up of Lady Macbeth's face as her troubled speech continues, then pull the camera back to reveal the Doctor and Lady Macbeth's Gentlewoman observing her actions. And then a quick cut can take us back to Lady Macbeth's face or her hands. In each instance the director is tightly controlling our field of vision; in each close-up our attention is directed at a single isolated image impossible to achieve in the theater.

If the shot, scene, and sequence are the basic elements of film grammar, film rhetoric becomes the individual director's personal use of that language. Rhetoric is the particular style the director uses in constructing her film. How does she mix the series of shots that compose a scene? How does she employ the movement of the camera in tracking or crane shots? Does she prefer high or low angle shots? How does she establish rhythm and pace? How does she use music? These are some of the ingredients of film rhetoric that you should become familiar with as you think about how the director of a Shakespeare film employs them to realize her vision. Students of Shakespeare on film need to develop some knowledge of the vocabulary of film grammar and rhetoric. This guide contains a glossary of film terms in the appendix. The first time a film term is used in a chapter it is printed in **boldface** to signal that this is a glossary term, and it will come in handy in describing how a director has attempted to capture Shakespeare in the language of film. Chapters 6–10 provide detailed attention to these issues as they are revealed in a variety of Shakespeare films.

Hamlet (Laurence Olivier) with Yorick's skull in Laurence Olivier's *Hamlet* (1948, Two Cities Film).

PART I

A Brief History of Shakespeare on Film

Part I begins with an overview of Shakespeare on film from the silent era to the present in Chapter 1. Chapters 2 and 3 offer detailed looks at six major directors: Laurence Olivier, Orson Welles, Kenneth Branagh, Akira Kurosawa, Grigori Kozintsev, and Franco Zeffirelli. Chapter 4 examines the evolution of Shakespeare on television, and Chapter 5 looks at the remarkable revival of Shakespeare on film in the 1990s.

1

ESTABLISHING SHOT

History

The history of Shakespeare on screen reaches from the earliest silent films made in the late nineteenth century to the DVD of the most recent Shakespeare film loaded with a package of extras: **outtakes**, interviews with the director and cast members, and critical commentary. The relationship between the world's most famous dramatic poet and the twentieth century's most popular art form creates an appealing landscape where high art mingles with low, Renaissance drama meets *Lethal Weapon*, lyric poetry competes with **jump cuts** and **slam zooms**, epic energies are contained by postmodern pastiche, three-dimensional theatrical immediacy jostles with a magical flat surface, singular experience becomes infinitely repeatable, word and image and action collide, crumble, and recombine—all at twenty-four frames per second.

Film was attracted to Shakespeare from its invention. In 1899, just three years after the Lumière brothers shot and projected the first brief film in Paris, William Kennedy-Laurie Dickson (an associate of Thomas Edison) shot, in London, a four-minute scene from Shakespeare's *King John* featuring the noted classical actor Sir Herbert Beerbohm Tree. *King John* was never to visit the big screen again but Shakespeare was there to stay.[1]

Over the next hundred years Shakespeare on film and television progressed through five stages of development: the silent era, Hollywood and London's first experiments with sound, a great international phase following the end of World War II initiated by the films of Laurence

---

1. According to Kenneth Rothwell's definitive history of Shakespeare on film, *A History of Shakespeare on Screen*, 2nd ed. (Cambridge: Cambridge University Press, 2004) *King John* was not revisited on screen until 1985 when it appeared as part of the BBC's television productions of all of Shakespeare's plays.

Olivier and Orson Welles, the age of Shakespeare on television, and finally the recent commercial revival of Shakespeare on film in the last decade of the twentieth century.

Silent Shakespeare

The silent phase covered the first three decades of the twentieth century from Dickson's *King John* (1899) to Sam Taylor's *Taming of the Shrew* (1929), the first Shakespeare "talking picture" featuring two of Hollywood's most attractive stars, Mary Pickford and Douglas Fairbanks. Robert Hamilton Ball reports that in those thirty years, over four hundred silent films were made based on Shakespearean material.[2] Most were just ten or twenty minutes long (one or two **reelers** in film parlance), but Shakespeare provided early filmmakers with several useful elements: familiar stories, magical and supernatural elements that were inviting to film technology, stage antecedents, and cultural capital.[3]

Movies, like Shakespeare's Globe Theater, exist in the cultural tension between low and high, popular and elite forms of artistic entertainment. Shakespeare's company produced plays for a polyglot London audience who flowed, via bridge and via boat, across the Thames to the South Bank "liberties" where early modern drama competed with the bull- and bear-baiting pits for customers. By the time movies were born, Shakespeare had been refashioned, over the centuries, from his origins in the Elizabethan popular theater into an icon of cultural and class sophistication. Early filmmakers quickly learned that joining film and Shakespeare offered a cultural passport for the new art form into more traditional and elitist enclaves of the dramatic arts.

Many of the early American silent Shakespeare films were made by J. Stuart Blackton's American Vitagraph Company for showing in the nickelodeons (early movie theaters) springing up all over the country.

---

2. See Robert Hamilton Ball's *Shakespeare on Silent Film: A Strange Eventful History* (New York: Theatre Art Books, 1968) for the most complete treatment of the silent films based on Shakespeare's plays.
3. Rothwell, *History*, p. 12.

Film found in Shakespeare a kindred spirit and an opportunity for cultural as well as artistic appropriation. From its inception, the Shakespeare film has been grounded in the cultural and historical moment of its production. It has always been a product of the tension between popular and elite dramatic expression, a reality as true for very recent Shakespeare films such as Kenneth Branagh's *Much Ado about Nothing* (1993) and Baz Luhrmann's *William Shakespeare's Romeo + Juliet* (1996) as for Blackton's Vitagraph short silent films in the first decade of the twentieth century. By the end of that decade films were already outgrowing the nickelodeons as they expanded in size from one or two reels to five, six, or more. By a fine twist of historical accident, a silent Shakespeare film can claim to be the oldest surviving feature-length American movie: M. B. Dudley's *Richard III* (1912) starring Frederick Warde.[4] The only surviving copy of the movie was owned by an amateur film buff in Oregon, who donated the film to the American Film Institute in 1996 without knowing he had been preserving a national treasure.

Shakespeare's plays have global reach, and Shakespeare films build on this phenomenon. European filmmakers quickly became involved in the world of silent Shakespeare, with early films emerging from France, Germany, Italy, and Scandinavia. This international interest by filmmakers in Shakespeare is a feature of the genre that has been sustained throughout its long history. An interesting example of this international flavor is a German film of *Hamlet* (1920), directed by Svend Gade and starring the noted Danish film actress Asta Nielsen as Hamlet. Gade's film is silent Shakespeare at its best—as daring in its technique as in its casting and approach to Shakespeare's play. Nielsen is a great film actress. She has a mask-like face dominated by huge, expressive eyes that seem made for film's ability to shoot the human figure in close-up. Nielsen's eyes perfectly express Hamlet's ability to register and absorb the corrupt world he uncovers in Claudius's Denmark. Hamlet is also a great keeper of secrets, and Nielsen's Hamlet has to keep the biggest secret of all: that the prince is really a woman. Actresses before (Sarah Bernhardt) and after (Diane Venora) Nielsen have played Hamlet, but they were playing a male role, not a woman trapped in doublet and hose. Gade found the Hamlet-as-woman idea

---

4. "Full length" is considered to be forty minutes or longer.

in a book by an eccentric nineteenth-century American academic, Edward Vining. Vining's theory was that Hamlet was born a girl. As the birth came on the day (as reported by the Grave-digger) Hamlet's father was fighting the battle with Old Norway over the disputed lands between the two countries, Gertrude concealed the child's true identity as self-protection in case her husband was killed in the battle. When Old Hamlet survives, he agrees to continue the deceit to protect his queen. Shakespeare's Hamlet is an undercover spy working to confirm and expose Claudius's treachery; Nielsen and Gade make the character a deep double agent, protecting one lie (the character's true gender) while trying to expose another (Claudius's illegitimacy), all the while suppressing her passion for Horatio.

The film's technique takes as many chances as its revision of Shakespeare's text. It deftly employs the full range of film's early vocabulary and grammar largely developed by D. W. Griffith: a nicely paced mix of **long shots**, **two shots**, **close-ups**, and **iris shots** and a willingness to let visual details tell the story. For example, Gade allows the camera to follow Claudius down into the bowels of Elsinore to a viper pit writhing with snakes, where Claudius selects the instrument with which to dispatch his brother. The film makes literal Claudius's fiction that Old Hamlet was stung by a serpent while sleeping in his orchard.

Gade's *Hamlet* is an early example of the way the Shakespeare film reaches out to combine and synthesize a wide variety of creative elements and energies. Here we have a film made in Germany, starring a Dane, and using the ideas of an American academic for its narrative drive and surprise. This early transnational and cross-cultural pooling of talent became an eventual fixture of the Hollywood film industry, but it was at work in the Shakespeare film from its inception.

Talking Shakespeare

Silent film was a particularly congenial form for Shakespeare as the medium did not have to find ways to integrate his dense and dazzling language. Film images told the story without having to compete with Shakespeare's own rich rhetoric. But once the movies began to talk (and sing) with Al Jolson's *The Jazz Singer* (1927), it was inevitable that they would turn to Shakespeare and to trouble.

Shakespeare was easily absorbed into silent film because his plots were familiar and their basic outlines translated smoothly into images. But when film began to speak, it was suddenly confronted with Shakespeare's massive text. Shakespeare was a great theater-poet who managed to get everything—plot, landscape, psychology—into the words his characters spoke. As American method-trained actors like Marlon Brando, Dustin Hoffman, and Al Pacino came to discover, there is no subtext in Shakespeare—only text.

Hollywood struggled in the 1930s to harness Shakespeare's text to an art form that spoke in images and the conversational tones of its huge melting pot audiences. The first Shakespearean talking picture, Sam Taylor's *The Taming of the Shrew* (1929), relied on established film star power by linking two of Hollywood's most famous commodities: the husband and wife team of Douglas Fairbanks and Mary Pickford. The second paired the noted German stage director Max Reinhardt with his fellow German refugee film director, William Dieterle, to produce a star-studded and inventive version of *A Midsummer Night's Dream* for Warner Bros. in 1935. The Reinhardt/Dieterle *Dream* is an eclectic mixture of style, spectacle, cast, and technique that exudes a zany energy.

The film begins as a musical comedy extravaganza with the four lovers (led by Dick Powell and Olivia de Havilland) crooning to one another during Theseus's triumphal procession into Athens. It then swerves into a very different register for the "rude mechanicals" comedy dominated by Jimmy Cagney's cocky, beady-eyed Bottom and distinguished by Joe E. Brown's delicious Flute. The film takes another turn when it enters the woods, where we find Mickey Rooney's wild-child Puck, Victor Jory's black-clad, sexually threatening Oberon, and Anita Louise's chaste Titania, all surrounded by a train of balletic fairies streaming down from the night sky on a trail of moonbeams. The film's wonderful mix of styles mirrors Shakespeare's own play; his *Dream* mingles disparate elements from Ovid (Theseus and Hippolyta), his own Warwickshire countryside (Puck and Bottom), and conventional romantic comedy (the four lovers) to create a magical meditation on the confusions of love and transformation. What gets lost in the film's many wonders is the power of Shakespeare's language itself, which emerges best only in parody in Cagney and Company's performance of "Pyramus and Thisby."

Though loaded with popular film stars and inventive cinematic technique, the Warner Bros. *Dream* failed to find an audience. Shakespeare's early fate in Hollywood was sealed when Metro-Goldwyn-Mayer's (MGM) similarly extravagant *Romeo and Juliet* (1936) also proved to be poison at the box office. The film was produced by Hollywood legend Irving Thalberg and directed by the highly regarded George Cukor, but it was ultimately doomed by its reverential treatment of its source and by the advanced ages of its Romeo and Juliet (the forty-three-year-old Leslie Howard and thirty-five-year-old Norma Shearer).[5] Reinhardt and Dieterle's rough magic aggressively tried to reimagine Shakespeare in the language of film and was eventually to prove the better model for filmed Shakespeare than the literal, heavy-handed Thalberg-Cukor collaboration, but its promise would not come to fruition for another two decades. MGM's *Romeo and Juliet* effectively killed Shakespeare in Hollywood for twenty years.

Across the Atlantic the news was equally pessimistic. Elizabeth Bergner, a famous Polish actress, and her husband, German director Paul Czinner, fled Nazi Germany in the early 1930s for London. There Bergner starred in several stage plays, and she and her husband, in collaboration with the famed dramatist and creator of *Peter Pan*, J. M. Barrie, collaborated on a film of *As You Like It* (1936). The film is interesting not because of Bergner, whose attempt at gamin charm is weighed down by her heavy European accent, but because of her co-star: Laurence Olivier. Olivier's Orlando has that curious and sexy mixture of masculine and feminine qualities that are rightly Rosalind's in Shakespeare's play, and he steals the picture. He lets the camera come to him rather than coyly flirting with it as Bergner does. Olivier's work is a brief intimation of the way an actor can respect Shakespeare's language and make it work on film, but he thought the finished film a failure (as did the public) and determined that Shakespeare and film did not mix.[6]

5. The film was expensive ($2 million) and the pet project of respected producer Irving Thalberg. Thalberg was Shearer's husband; she was a major film star but he wanted to provide her with a vehicle that would enhance her status as an actress.
6. See John Cottrell's *Laurence Olivier* (Englewood Cliffs, N.J.: Prentice-Hall, 1975), pp. 101–103.

The Age of International Shakespeare

Olivier's skepticism proved to be powerfully ill-founded. His next Shakespeare film, *Henry V* (1944), secured the genre and began the great international phase of Shakespeare on film. With *Henry V* Olivier was in charge of the entire project: he directed, played the leading role, and co-authored the **screenplay**. He shot his film in 1943–44, just as the Allies were gathering in England to plan and launch the massive invasion of France to reclaim Europe from Hitler in World War II. Shakespeare's play concerns a much smaller but equally famous invasion of France, led in 1415 by a young English king eager to consolidate his rule and cement his legitimacy by following his father's deathbed advice "to busy giddy minds with foreign quarrels." Though Shakespeare's play, particularly for a modern audience, presents an ambiguous portrait of Henry V and the justification for attacking France, Olivier instinctively saw that the text, properly pruned, could bring Shakespeare's soaring poetry to the service of the war effort and in the process he created perhaps the most glorious propaganda film ever made.

Though he substantially trimmed the text (as do most screenplays of Shakespeare films), Olivier still found a way to foreground Shakespeare's language.[7] He opens the film with a **pan shot** of a model of Elizabethan London, with the camera eventually taking us down the Thames (its surprisingly blue water created by the motor oil Olivier's designer used to achieve the effect) into a replica of Shakespeare's Globe, creating a natural context for the nature of Henry V's elevated poetic rhetoric. After the opening scenes, shot as though at a performance of the play in the Globe, the film **cuts** back in time to France in the late Middle Ages depicted by painted sets and landscapes constructed on a film studio **soundstage**. Finally Olivier moves his film out of theater and soundstage into location shooting in Ireland where he films the Battle of Agincourt. Olivier deftly juggles three distinct historical moments in his handling of film time and space. He begins in Shakespeare's London, then moves us back in time to Henry's own

---

7. Only two Shakespeare films provide us with the full text of the plays they are based on: Peter Hall's *A Midsummer Night's Dream* (1968) and Kenneth Branagh's *Hamlet* (1996).

Laurence Olivier, as Henry V, commands the Globe stage in his *Henry V* (1944, Rank Films).

moment in the early fifteenth century, before returning us to the Globe in the final scene. Olivier accomplishes these moves by making us aware that they are achieved through twentieth-century film technology. Thus he manages to interweave his World War II present with Shakespeare's Elizabethan and Henry's medieval past.

Shot in bright, bold Technicolor, in intentional contrast with gloomy war-ravaged London, Olivier's film of *Henry V* was just what the country needed to lift its sagging spirits. It embraced England's storied cultural history at a moment of political crisis, and England rapturously received it on its release in 1944. America followed suit the following year, and *Henry V* became the first commercially successful Shakespeare film. To celebrate the end of the war and the victory of the Allied Forces, theatrical festivals began popping up all over England, Europe, and America with performances of Shakespeare's plays often at their core. A similar phenomenon took place in the world of film, and the three decades between the release of Olivier's *Henry V* in 1944 and Roman Polanski's *Macbeth* in 1971 became the richest in the history of the genre. The interest in Shakespeare as material for film was once again, as in the silent era, international. Film directors in Germany, Italy, Russia, Poland, and Japan as well as in England and America turned to Shakespeare as a source for their art. During the postwar period new Shakespeare films appeared on average once a year.

The genre became defined by the work of Olivier and his American rival and counterpart, Orson Welles. Both were men of the theater and came to filmed Shakespeare from the experience of having played and directed his works on stage. But even with that common theatrical background, their film styles radically diverged. Welles fell in love with film when he went to Hollywood to make his first picture, *Citizen Kane* (1941). Film became the medium that stimulated his creativity and shaped his genius. Olivier, though an experienced film actor, was first and foremost a man of the theater. The stage was the space where his imagination flourished. Olivier was hailed as the leading actor of his generation in a tradition stretching back four hundred years to Richard Burbage (the leading actor in Shakespeare's company); Welles helped establish film as the twentieth century's most popular and powerful art form. Olivier brilliantly extended on old tradition; Welles legendarily created a new one.

Olivier's three Shakespeare films, *Henry V* (1944), *Hamlet* (1948), and *Richard III* (1955), all honor their theatrical roots and search for different solutions to their translation into film. Welles's trio, *Macbeth* (1948), *Othello* (1952), and *Chimes at Midnight* (1966), all seek to leave their theatrical roots behind and become fully absorbed into the language of film. Olivier's films appealed more to the general audience, Welles's to the **cinèaste**. Neither produced a film that was a huge success at the box office, but Olivier's *Hamlet* did win the Academy Award for Best Picture in 1948, the only Shakespeare film ever to be so honored.[8]

The creative spark released by Olivier's and Welles's Shakespeare films quickly spread around the world, most prominently to Japan and Russia. In Japan, Akira Kurosawa established himself as the country's

---

8. While *Shakespeare in Love* did win the Academy Award for Best Picture in 1998, it is one of the many fine films that is based on Shakespearean material rather than an attempt to reproduce a Shakespearean text on film.

preeminent filmmaker in the postwar era. Kurosawa is unique among Shakespearean film directors in this period in seeking to completely reimagine his Shakespearean material not only in the language of film but also within his own cultural traditions, codes, and conventions. His three Shakespeare films, *Throne of Blood* (1957), *The Bad Sleep Well* (1960), and *Ran* (1985)—versions of *Macbeth*, *Hamlet*, and *King Lear*—move his source material either into his own postwar capitalist Tokyo (*The Bad Sleep Well*) or into Japan's Samurai past (*Throne of Blood* and *Ran*).

Russian directors were also at work in this period adapting Shakespeare to the screen in versions of *Twelfth Night* (1955), *Othello* (1955), *Hamlet* (1964), and *King Lear* (1971). The latter two films were directed by Grigori Kozintsev and, like Kurosawa's films, they reflect important elements of Russian life and culture. Kozintsev's *Hamlet*, for example, is one of the most politically charged versions of the play on film, rivaled only by Kenneth Branagh's massive four-hour version released in 1996. Kozintsev makes visually vivid Hamlet's sense that "Denmark is a prison" while also infusing his film with a particularly Russian sense of melancholy. Kurosawa's Shakespeare films, like Welles's, are great cinema poems where image and action trump text; Kozintsev's films follow Olivier's in merging the cinematic with the theatrical.

The other international figure who made a significant contribution to the development of Shakespeare on film is the Italian Franco Zeffirelli. Like Olivier, Welles, and Kurosawa, Zeffirelli has made three Shakespeare films: *The Taming of the Shrew* (1966), *Romeo and Juliet* (1968), and *Hamlet* (1990). His Shakespeare films all reflect his particularly Italian neo-romantic style derived from his work as an opera director. They are bold and vivid and conceived for a mass rather than coterie audience. Olivier and Welles cast their films with actors familiar with working with Shakespeare on the stage. Zeffirelli, followed later by Kenneth Branagh, broke with this tradition by brazenly casting Hollywood movie stars like Elizabeth Taylor, Mel Gibson, and Glenn Close in his Shakespeare films. Zeffirelli's *Romeo and Juliet* was the first Shakespeare film to find a large, mostly teenage, film audience, and it became the most commercially successful Shakespeare film in history until it was surpassed by Baz Luhrmann's *William Shakespeare's Romeo + Juliet* in 1996. Zeffirelli's *Romeo and Juliet* is as important in the history of Shakespeare on film as Olivier's *Henry V* because it brought the Shakespeare film, for the first time, out of the art house and into wide circulation.

The film appeared at the climax of the 1960s, a decade dominated by the young. Students marched for civil rights in Selma, Alabama; took to the streets in Paris and Prague in opposition to rigid or repressive governments; died in the jungles of Vietnam; challenged Mayor Daley and the Democrats in the streets and parks of Chicago; and championed rock music and free love at Woodstock. *Romeo and Juliet* was their Shakespeare movie, fueled by the ardent passion of Olivia Hussey's Juliet and Leonard Whiting's Romeo and Nino Rota's lyrical score. Zeffirelli's film continues to have a potent afterlife as the youth movement of the 1960s swept *Romeo and Juliet* into the American high school English curriculum, displacing *Julius Caesar* and *Macbeth* as the most commonly taught Shakespeare plays. With the advent of videotape, Zeffirelli's film quickly followed Shakespeare's text into the classroom.

The postwar boom in Shakespeare films came to an end in 1971 with the release of Peter Brook's *King Lear* and Roman Polanski's *Macbeth*. Brook's bleak and savage film was shot in a grainy black and white in Jutland and featured a variety of Brechtian alienation devices adapted for film: title cards, minimalist lighting, off-center camera angles, black screen moments between scenes, and the frequent use of a jumpy **handheld camera**. Brook's screenplay strips Shakespeare's text of much of its brilliant poetry to concentrate instead on the Samuel Beckett–like exchanges between Lear and his fool and Lear and Gloucester in their great mad scene on the beach at Dover. The film is a brave experiment but easier to admire than defend. It did not find favor with the critics or attract an audience, the first signal that perhaps the postwar boom in Shakespeare films was approaching a period of decline.

That decline was assured when Polanski's big-budget *Macbeth*, released in the following year, failed to find the young audience that had flocked to see Zeffirelli's *Romeo and Juliet*. Polanski is a well-regarded Polish filmmaker who had scored a significant critical and popular success with his first Hollywood film, *Rosemary's Baby* (1968). *Macbeth* was the first film he made after his actress-wife Sharon Tate was brutally murdered by Charles Manson's "family"—a fringe group of

1960s dropouts who mixed drugs with madness and murder. Polanski's movie is a skilled piece of filmmaking but it repeatedly emphasizes the bloody nature of Shakespeare's play by having the camera capture Macbeth's murder of Duncan, his henchmen's brutal slaughter of Lady Macduff and her children, and Macduff's eventual beheading of Macbeth. Critics speculated that Polanski was using Shakespeare to exorcise his own violent demons in response to his wife's murder, and the mass commercial audience for whom the film was intended never materialized. Brook's *Lear* failed to galvanize the art house audience for Shakespeare and Polanski's *Macbeth* had a similar fate with mainstream moviegoers. Together the two films brought to an end the steady stream of Shakespeare films that had been released since Olivier's *Henry V*. Once again, Shakespeare was box-office poison.

The Age of Television

In the period from 1944 to 1971 a new Shakespeare film was released almost every year; between 1971 and 1989 just four were made, and only one, Kurosawa's *Ran* (1985), was a critical success. The genre had seemingly exhausted itself. Television stepped into the vacuum.

Motion pictures developed from photography; television grew out of radio. Film belongs to the director; television to the writer. The smaller scope and intimacy of television suggested that it might prove to be an even better medium than film for presenting Shakespeare, and allowing his language its full expression. The evidence, however, is mixed. While there are fine television productions of Shakespeare, most of them began as highly successful stage performances—several directed by Trevor Nunn, a former head of England's Royal Shakespeare Company and National Theatre—which were then moved into a studio and reimagined for television.

The first experiments with Shakespeare on television began in London in 1937 with the BBC's (British Broadcasting Corporation) fledgling attempts to transmit brief scenes from several Shakespeare plays, including *As You Like It*. Those efforts ended with the beginning of the war but started up again as soon as the war ended, and the BBC broadcast sixty Shakespeare productions, either in whole or in part, from 1948 to 1975. In America, the early efforts at televising Shakespeare

were sponsored by the Hallmark Greeting Card Company. The director George Schaefer and the English actor Maurice Evans collaborated
on nine Shakespeare productions for the Hallmark Hall of Fame program in the 1950s and 1960s. But the most significant work on televised Shakespeare began in the mid-1970s.

Beginning in late 1975, the BBC began planning an ambitious project to create television productions of all thirty-seven of Shakespeare's
plays and to broadcast them, at the rate of five or six per year, from
1978 to 1985. Although critics panned the first few productions, citing
unimaginative sets, clumsy camera work, and performances better
suited to theater than television, several of the subsequent productions, especially of the less-often staged plays, demonstrated that under the right directorial guidance, Shakespeare could be successfully
translated into television.

Part of the early poor reception of the BBC series can be attributed
to its literalist production practices. Cedric Messina, the initial producer of the series, dictated that the plays were to be presented uncut
and in period costumes, running counter to contemporary theatrical
practice in England and America and distancing the productions from
the younger, school-age audience for which they were primarily intended. Artistic leadership of the series eventually passed to Jonathan
Miller, who introduced a less literal approach to the interpretation of
Shakespeare. However, some of the productions Miller himself directed, especially *The Taming of the Shrew* and *Antony and Cleopatra*,
now sank under the weight of their over-ingenious ideas. Certain productions did succeed: Desmond Davis's *Measure for Measure* (1979),
Elijah Moshinsky's *Coriolanus* (1983), and Jane Howell's *1, 2,* and *3
Henry VI* (1984) were all alive to television's potential for Shakespeare
and cast actors with experience on television and film as well as on
stage, and all found imaginative ways to stylize action and movement
in a rigidly realistic medium (for instance, in Howell's use of a unified
set for the *Henry VI* plays and Moshinsky's handling of the battle
scenes in *Coriolanus*).

The 1970s and 80s saw several television versions of the plays that
had life and energy. Most of these productions began as heralded theatrical performances and then were successfully reimagined in the
confines of the television studio. This practice has proven over time to
produce the most successful television Shakespeare. Two of these,

Antony and Cleopatra (1974) and *Macbeth* (1980), were Royal Shakespeare Company (RSC) productions directed by Trevor Nunn. Nunn's *Macbeth* began at the RSC's small black-box theater, The Other Place; perhaps its intimate setting there, in a minimalist production shorn of elaborate sets, costumes, and props, was what made its transition to the small screen so effective.

Two other productions, both from this side of the Atlantic, also fared well on television. Each originated in Joseph Papp's free summer Shakespeare in Central Park program under the auspices of his New York Shakespeare Festival Theater. The first was a lively version of *Much Ado about Nothing* (1973) set in turn-of-the-century America, with Don Pedro, Benedick, and Claudio returning from the Spanish-American War. This production was so successful that it transferred to Broadway after its summer run in the Park and was subsequently moved into a television studio and taped for broadcast. The second, *King Lear* (1974), starring the great African-American actor James Earl Jones, was televised live during a performance in the Delacourt Theater in Central Park. The production used eight cameras to capture the performance from a variety of perspectives and repeatedly included the audience in the background of many shots, providing some of the immediacy of live theater. The Nunn and Papp television productions started from performances that had already proved their merit with theater audiences. None of the BBC productions had the opportunity to be tested (and proven) before live audiences. They all began and ended their lives in a television studio, a space that has not proved, over the past fifty years, to be ideal for Shakespeare.

Despite these successes, when the BBC series concluded in 1985, no other television productions of Shakespeare rose to take its place. Shakespeare on film and television had reached a dead end. Miraculously, its rescue, from an unexpected source, was just around the corner.

Branagh and Baz

In 1989, Kenneth Branagh directed and starred in a film of *Henry V* that was to prove to be as important and influential to the genre as Olivier's film of the play forty-five years before. Olivier, in 1944, was something of a national hero. He was the most celebrated English classical actor of his generation. Branagh, in 1989, was a relatively un-known young upstart who, after one season (1984–85) of playing Henry V for the Royal Shakespeare Company, bolted to found his own small Renaissance Theatre Company. The company toured three Shakespearean productions around England in 1988 before eventually landing in London, where they concluded the season with a successful run. Based on this limited success, Branagh plunged forward with plans to make a film of *Henry V*. Turned down for financing by all the established British film producers, his chief backer, Stephen Evans, managed to secure the film's funding ($6 million) from the City, the London equivalent of Wall Street.

Though an unknown as a film commodity, Branagh had the advantage of youthful intelligence and ambition and was surrounded by an array of British actors experienced with Shakespeare on stage and in film. Branagh had the passion and pluck to attract established stage and screen actors—Paul Scofield, Judi Dench, Ian Holm, and Robert Stephens—to join with members of his own Renaissance Company— Emma Thompson, Michael Maloney, Richard Easton, and Richard Briers—to create a cast of British classical actors too long absent from the world of Shakespeare on film. Branagh created his *Henry V* in stunning contrast to Olivier's: dark, gritty, and conspiratorial rather than bright, bold, and heroic. Branagh's approach fit his skeptical post-Vietnam and Falklands War historical moment as appropriately as Olivier's had fit the heroism of the World War II era. The film was an immediate critical success in England and America and received several Academy Award nominations, including a prized double recognition for Branagh as Best Actor and Best Director. The critical success of the film led to box-office success and international attention.

What Branagh could not have anticipated, in a film conceived in 1987, shot in 1988, and released in 1989, was that its appearance would come at a moment of dramatic geopolitical changes in the world as the Soviet Union collapsed, the Berlin Wall fell, and the Cold War ended. In the decade of reduced world tensions between the fall of the Berlin Wall in 1989 and the terrorist attack on the World Trade Center in 2001, Hollywood suddenly found room, among its usual diet of international thrillers, horror flicks, romantic comedies, and Armageddon block-busters, to finance a remarkable range of films based on the works of

Henry V (Kenneth Branagh) as "Dirty Harry" at the end of the Battle of Agincourt in Branagh's *Henry V* (1989, the Samuel Goldwyn Company).

canonical authors ranging from Shakespeare and Jane Austen to Henry James and Edith Wharton. Branagh's film helped to initiate this trend and made Shakespeare suddenly respectable among Hollywood producers; as Al Pacino remarked, "Branagh opened it all up with *Henry V*. Now you say Shakespeare on film in Hollywood and people listen."[9]

People listened even more intently after the commercial success of Branagh's second Shakespeare film, *Much Ado about Nothing*, released in 1993. Three years later Baz Luhrmann's *William Shakespeare's Romeo + Juliet* hugely expanded on the teenage and college audience that Branagh's *Much Ado* had cultivated and went on to become an international commercial blockbuster, surpassing Zeffirelli's *Romeo and Juliet* as the highest-grossing Shakespeare film in history. Branagh and Luhrmann made possible the most prolific single decade in the history of Shakespeare on film. Between 1989 and 2001, over twenty major feature films of Shakespeare's plays were made and another twenty films employed Shakespeare as an essential component of the narrative, ranging from wild parody (*Tromeo and Juliet*) to Shakespeare in high

9. Quoted in David Rosenthal, *Shakespeare on the Screen* (London: Hamlyn, 2000), p. 215.

school (*10 Things I Hate about You* and *O*) to Academy Award–winning romantic comedy (*Shakespeare in Love*).

The 1990s produced a wide range of Shakespeare films, from Christine Edzard's quirky low-budget *As You Like It* (1992), set in London's Rotherhithe area during the Thatcher years, to Julie Taymor's powerful, inventive *Titus* (1999), which had a substantial $20 million budget (large for a Shakespeare film) and star-studded cast, including Anthony Hopkins and Jessica Lange. They bracketed films as varied as Branagh's quartet (*Henry V* [1989], *Much Ado about Nothing* [1993], *Hamlet* [1996], and *Love's Labour's Lost* [2000]), Zeffirelli's *Hamlet* (1990), Peter Greenaway's *Prospero's Books* (1991), Luhrmann's *Romeo + Juliet* (1996), Richard Loncraine's *Richard III* (1995), Adrian Noble's *A Midsummer Night's Dream* (1996), Oliver Parker's *Othello* (1995), Michael Hoffman's *A Midsummer Night's Dream* (1999), Trevor Nunn's *Twelfth Night* (1995), and Michael Almereyda's *Hamlet* (2000). Yet all of these films, except Edzard's *As You Like It* and Greenaway's highly stylized and idiosyncratic *Prospero's Books* (an adaptation of *The Tempest*), were distinguished by their willingness to link the Shakespeare film to the codes and conventions of the commercial Hollywood film.

Though Olivier and Welles both incorporated elements of **film noir** in their films of *Hamlet* and *Othello*, in general the Shakespeare films of their era were primarily focused on the elite art house film audience. Following Franco Zeffirelli's lead, Branagh and his contemporaries took steady aim at the much larger cineplex audience. Though only Branagh, Zeffirelli, Luhrmann, and Hoffman succeeded in getting their Shakespeare films released "wide" on multiple screens across America, most of the films of the 1990s were loaded with Hollywood stars and conventional film genre strategies. Branagh borrowed visual ideas from a wide range of popular films, including *Platoon* (1986), *The Magnificent Seven* (1960), *Doctor Zhivago* (1965), and *Swing Time* (1936). Oliver Parker attempted to remake *Othello* as an erotic thriller; Richard Loncraine raided the 1930s gangster movie as a structural subtext for his 1995 film of *Richard III*; and Baz Luhrmann confessed that he set his *Romeo + Juliet* in "the world of the movies."[10]

10. Quoted in James Loehlin, "'These Violent Delights Have Violent Ends': Baz Lurhrmann's Millennial Shakespeare," in Mark Thornton Burnett and Ramona Wray, *Shakespeare, Film, Fin de Siècle* (New York: St. Martin's Press, 2000), p. 134.

Though the steady flow of Shakespeare films began to slow after 2001, two films that have been released in the last five years, Michael Radford's *The Merchant of Venice* (2004) and Kenneth Branagh's *As You Like It* (2007), have sustained the pattern established in the 1990s. Radford's film is distinguished by Al Pacino's Shylock. Pacino's performance is enriched by our awareness of his many memorable screen roles, including fierce outsiders like Sonny Wortzik (in *Dog Day Afternoon*) and Frank Serpico (in *Serpico*) and cold revengers like Michael Corleone (in the *Godfather* films). Branagh's *As You Like It* follows his practice of setting his Shakespeare films in exotic locales (this time in late-nineteenth-century Japan) and mixing and mingling members of his Renaissance Company—in this case Brian Blessed, Richard Briers, and Richard Clifford—with American and British stage and film actors like Kevin Kline, Bryce Dallas Howard, and Alfred Molina.

Shakespeare has become firmly established in the world of film. No other canonical author rivals his attractiveness to the medium, and the long love affair between Shakespeare and the movies seems certain to continue even as it takes on new developments and novel directions.

Film history and criticism have taught us that the director is the true star of most films. This is particularly apparent in the world of Shakespeare films where the director, rather than a studio executive, screenwriter, or individual star, is most often the originating source of the project—and sometimes the producer, screenwriter, and star as well. The mature, successful Shakespeare film has been created mainly by six directors (Olivier, Welles, Branagh, Kurosawa, Kozintsev, and Zeffirelli) who have repeatedly returned to Shakespeare as a source for their films. The next two chapters will explore the work of those directors and their contributions to the development of the Shakespeare film.

2

CLOSE-UP: MAJOR DIRECTORS I

Laurence Olivier, Orson Welles, and Kenneth Branagh

Hollywood's hegemony in the world of film was challenged in the 1950s by the emergence of the European art house cinema dominated by strong and original film directors like Ingmar Bergman in Sweden; Federico Fellini, Michelangelo Antonioni, and Luchino Visconti in Italy; Akira Kurosawa in Japan; Luis Buñuel in Spain; and Alain Resnais, Jean-Luc Godard, and François Truffaut in France. These directors made highly personal, often autobiographical, films. Truffaut—who was an astute film critic before he became a filmmaker—developed the idea of the film director being the **auteur**, or author, of the film. Truffaut's idea became a powerful analytical tool for unlocking the director's signal importance in a world previously dominated by film stars and studio producers. Film critics, particularly in America, were quick to see that the auteur idea was not limited to avant-garde European film directors but also could be effectively applied to conventional Hollywood directors of commercial films like Billy Wilder, Howard Hawks, and Alfred Hitchcock.

Rather than treating the films of John Ford, for example, in isolation, film scholars began to study Ford's style as it matured over a series of pictures and to elucidate the major thematic ideas that linked one Ford picture to another. This practice had long been used to discuss the work of literary figures like Austen, Dickens, Hardy, James, Hemingway, and Faulkner, and now it was directed to the world of film, where the director was no longer seen as a hired hack, a tool of the producer and star, but as the crucial artistic intelligence pulling all of the creative and technical energies involved in filmmaking into an aesthetic whole.

The auteur idea emerged just as Laurence Olivier and Orson Welles were creating the first successful Shakespeare films in the late 40s and early 50s. Like most directors repeatedly attracted to translating

Shakespeare into film, Olivier, Welles, and (several decades later) Kenneth Branagh had already worked with Shakespeare in the theater, as actor or director before making their first Shakespeare films.[1] Their Shakespeare films were highly personal projects—they each wrote their own screenplays (Olivier in collaboration with Alan Dent)—and because of their experience as established Shakespeareans, they all had an authority over their Shakespeare films that was rarely granted to commercial directors in Hollywood or England. Each developed different strategies to release Shakespeare's power on film, but they all began from a common base: an experienced understanding of Shakespeare's inherent theatricality and the rich power of his language. Olivier and Welles were friends (and rivals) and were intimately aware of each other's work. Branagh, born when Olivier and Welles were in mid-career, was acutely conscious of their Shakespeare films when he came to direct his own. The alert viewer will trace a rich **intertextual** dialogue among the films of these three directors who have most shaped the Anglo-American version of the Shakespeare film.

Laurence Olivier (1907–1989)

Olivier's *Henry V* (1944) provided the seed that created the first flowering of great Shakespeare films. Olivier went on to make two more Shakespeare films, *Hamlet* (1948) and *Richard III* (1955), and to star in a fourth, *Othello* (1964).[2] In all four instances, Olivier had played the title role in lauded stage productions of the plays. Bringing Shakespeare to the service of England in World War II by introducing him to a wider public via film fired Olivier's imagination. The man, the moment, and the right Shakespearean material all coalesced to make, in *Henry V*,

---

1. Key exceptions to this practice are Joseph Mankiewicz, Roman Polanski, Michael Hoffman, and Michael Radford. These noted filmmakers each directed only a single Shakespeare film.
2. Olivier starred in a production of *Othello* at Britain's National Theatre directed by John Dexter. Olivier's performance was so electrifying that the production was moved into a studio and made into a film directed by Stuart Burge. The film is a curious hybrid of stage and screen and fails to capture the dynamism and danger of Olivier's stage performance at the Old Vic.

what Olivier proudly called "the first Shakespeare film."[3] He went on to celebrate the social and creative energies that went into the making of the film by observing: "There we were, a band of artists and technicians, humble in our souls because Hitler was killing our countrymen, imbued with a sense of history, gallantly overcoming wartime shortages and problems. . . . I felt Shakespeare within me, I felt the cinema within him."[4]

In *Henry V*, Olivier fashioned a bright, bold celebration of Shakespeare and the living legacy of his Elizabethan theater. He solved the problem of creating a film environment appropriate for Shakespeare's language, proudly rhetorical and trumpet-like in *Henry V*, by beginning his film in a re-creation of the Globe Theater, then moving out of the Globe, for the scenes set in France, into a highly stylized landscape of painted sets based on an illuminated medieval storybook, *Les Très Riches Heures*, and ultimately ending up in a real landscape (Powerscourt in Ireland) for the Battle of Agincourt, where the language of film eclipses Shakespeare's. Olivier realized that such moments, simply noted as "A short alarum" or "They Fight" in the text, are examples of what he calls "frustrated cinema" in Shakespeare.[5]

Olivier also trims Shakespeare's text to suit his heroic approach to the play. Shakespeare's Henry is a complicated figure: cunning politician, persuasive leader, imperial crusader, angry warrior, and comic wooer. Olivier eliminates Henry's darker qualities and removes the ironies and ambiguities that Shakespeare builds into the character (and play) to shade his appeal. Olivier is trying to rally a nation at a moment of crisis in 1944, and Henry's anger and Machiavellian skills are understandably jettisoned in such a project. Interestingly, because of Olivier's obvious charm and star qualities as an actor and director, the film never seems blatantly jingoistic.

Olivier turned a darker eye on his next Shakespeare project: *Hamlet*. Olivier was by nature a theatrical animal. His performances were noted for their physical energy and power. When he first played Hamlet on the stage, one critic dismissively commented that it was the finest performance of Hotspur he had ever seen. The remark stung,

3. Laurence Olivier, *On Acting* (New York: Simon & Schuster, 1986), p. 268.
4. Ibid., pp. 274–75.
5. Ibid., p. 269.

and Olivier undoubtedly overreacted when he came to imagine his Hamlet on film. His approach was heavily influenced by Freud's Oedipal theory that Hamlet is blocked in his ability to kill the king because Claudius has enacted Hamlet's own repressed desire to kill his father and marry his mother. The two men are intricately linked, and Hamlet subconsciously understands that to murder Claudius is to commit suicide.

As with his treatment of *Henry V*, Olivier boldly follows the suggestive visual logic of his interpretive approach. He abandons the brilliant Technicolor of *Henry V* to explore the mysterious **chiaroscuro** play of light and shadow afforded by filming in black and white. His film of *Hamlet* is as gloomy and deeply psychological as his *Henry V* was bright and brilliantly patriotic. In each instance his performance of the central character perfectly mirrors the world he created to contain him. Olivier, as actor and director, was delighted to give us Henry V's exterior charm and dazzle; with Hamlet he instead tries to take us inside the character's mind—literally. In one famous shot, influenced by a similar camera movement in Alfred Hitchcock's *Rebecca* (1940), the camera finds Hamlet on a high platform looking down at the waves crashing on the rocky shore below as Olivier begins to speak the "To be or not to be" soliloquy in **voice-over**. The camera slowly pans up Hamlet's back until it shares his perspective of the sea's turmoil. Then the camera bores into the back of Hamlet's head and finds a similar pattern of disturbance at work there as shapeless images pulse in Hamlet's brain.[6] Olivier finds his visual images in Shakespeare's verbal ones, especially "to take arms against a sea of troubles,/And by opposing end them" (3.1.61–62), but he is also visually insisting on Hamlet's internal struggle, a struggle that not only divides but incapacitates him.[7] Before the soliloquy ends we find the character prone on the platform, where his dagger (that "bare bodkin") slips from his grasp and tumbles down into the sea, and his will is drained of its passion and potential.

6. This shot is also admired by Kenneth Rothwell (see *A History of Shakespeare on Screen* [Cambridge: Cambridge University Press, 1999], p. 59). Hitchcock shot Olivier (playing Maxim de Winter) in a similar fashion looking down at the sea crashing below where his wife, Rebecca, had died.
7. All quotations are from *The Norton Shakespeare* (New York: W. W. Norton, 1997).

The film's most interesting element is Olivier's deliberately obtrusive camera technique as an overt visual accomplice to Hamlet's probing, covert intelligence. The camera prowls Elsinore, climbs its twisting staircases, and pries into its nooks and crannies, including an obsessive curiosity with Gertrude's bedroom. Olivier conjures the camera as another character in the drama: Hamlet's alter ego. In contrast, his performance of the prince, with one or two crucial exceptions, is remarkably passive. He is repeatedly floored by the appearance of the Ghost, conceived in the film as a giant shadowy figure who speaks with a disembodied voice, actually Olivier's recorded and replayed at a slower speed. Olivier rarely lets rip in his delivery of Hamlet's passionate and often self-destructive soliloquies, preferring to strike passive postures—leaning against a column, resting in a chair, sprawling on the floor—while often utilizing the film convention of voice-over to flatten Hamlet's heated rhetoric.

Olivier was influenced by Orson Welles's *Citizen Kane* and sought to adopt and adapt Welles's revolutionary use of **deep focus** photography, in which the image in both the front and back of the frame is held in clear focus. This allowed him to create the illusion of a **depth of field** on the screen's flat surface and thereby to stress visually Hamlet's isolation and alienation from a world where he was once at the social and political center. Most famously he used such shots to capture Hamlet's estrangement from Ophelia. In one heralded example, the camera is placed behind the seated Hamlet and stares out over his shoulder at Jean Simmons's Ophelia, who is standing several hundred feet away down a long corridor, framed in an arched Renaissance doorway. Hamlet is trapped in his chair within the castle while she is associated with the natural landscape we see behind her. Both images are vivid to the viewer but they are connected only by Hamlet's passive, melancholy gaze.

In trying to understand why George Cukor's *Romeo and Juliet* was a failure, Olivier made an interesting discovery. The natural movement of film grammar is from **long shot** to **close-up**. As the drama of the scene intensifies, the camera tends to move closer to the actor's face. Olivier thought this ran counter to Shakespeare's theatrical rhetoric, where his big explosive speeches needed space for the actor to give full vocal and physical expression to their emotional climaxes. In *Henry V*, rather than having the camera move in as the actor reached an emotional pitch,

Hamlet (Laurence Olivier) is overwhelmed by his father's ghost, in Olivier's *Hamlet* (1948, Two Cities Film).

Olivier slowly pulled the camera *back* as the speech developed, allowing the actor the maximum amount of film space to register emotion. He followed the same practice in *Hamlet*, most notably in the conclusion of the "O what a rogue and peasant slave" soliloquy: "The play's the thing/Wherein I'll catch the conscience of the king" (2.2.581–82).

Olivier—though an icon of the British classical theater and institutional Shakespeare—instinctively understood the difference between a **playscript** and a screenplay, and he was ruthless in refashioning Shakespeare's text for the screen. He believed it was better to eliminate entire characters and plot strands than to simply make across-the-board cuts when reducing Shakespeare's text to meet the time demands of the conventional film. His screenplay for *Hamlet* cuts more deeply into the fabric of Shakespeare's play than any other major film version of the play we have, including Michael Almereyda's. Olivier not only eliminates Fortinbras, Francisco,

Reynaldo, and the second grave-digger, but also Rosencrantz and Guildenstern.[8]

Henry V and *Hamlet* are two of Shakespeare's most **metatheatrical** plays. They repeatedly call attention to themselves as dramas: *Henry V* through the character of the Chorus who conjures the audience's imagination to fill in the limitations of "this wooden O"—the Globe Theater itself; *Hamlet* through Hamlet's own fascination with acting and actors and the central position given to the "The Mousetrap" in the development of the play's personal and political themes. Olivier's inherent theatricality naturally attracted him to such works, and that theatricality was very much at the heart of his directorial approach to his third Shakespeare film, *Richard III*.

Richard III was the first great Shakespearean role Olivier conceived after his film of *Henry V* had been released and the war in Europe had ended. He played the role in several productions from 1944 to 1949 and then reprised it one final time for film in 1955. His Richard combined elements of Hitler, Jed Harris—a Broadway producer Olivier thought had a touch of evil in his countenance—and Walt Disney's version of the Big Bad Wolf. As a stage actor, Olivier mesmerized audiences. He was both beguiling and dangerous and had a physical vitality that matched his remarkable vocal rhythms. Richard III was the perfect vehicle for his bravura talent. The character is one of Shakespeare's consummate roles, always "changing colors like the chameleon." He woos the audience with the same deft ironic ardor he uses to such advantage within the play in his relentless rise to power. Richard is a monster but he ends up manipulating the audience as skillfully as he does his rivals for the crown.

Olivier sought some cinematic device that would capture the power Richard's soliloquies have on the stage and found it by having Richard directly address the camera. The characters in most films ignore the camera to maintain the convention that we are observing reality rather than artifice. It is the rare film that risks acknowledging that it is a film, while Shakespeare is pleased to remind us often that

8. Olivier's removal of Rosencrantz and Guildenstern may have contributed to Tom Stoppard's decision to restore them to central prominence in his *Rosencrantz & Guildenstern Are Dead*, which had its first production at Olivier's National Theatre in 1967.

his plays are plays. Olivier's Richard, though dressed in black, frequently displays the peacock feathers of his craft before the camera. He struts, flirts, preens, confides, and threatens directly into the camera's lens. At one point, in the lengthy soliloquy sequence following the silent pageant that opens the film, Olivier's Richard looks as though he's actually going to lean his arm up against the camera to be able to confide in us even more intimately. The direct address of the camera is a stunning move, and it became so associated with Olivier and his film that it has been sparingly used in subsequent Shakespeare films (though the device does make a brief reappearance in Richard Loncraine's film of *Richard III* [1995] with Ian McKellen).

The Shakespeare films directed by Olivier, though quite varied in tone and atmosphere, all reveal the qualities of a Shakespearean film auteur. Their title figures, distinct as they are in context and character, are all remarkable actors thus releasing Olivier's physical and vocal power as an actor. Olivier constructs individual worlds for Henry, Hamlet, and Richard, but provides each an appropriate space for the actor to maneuver in: the Globe for Henry; Elsinore's gloomy gothic castle for Hamlet; an expansive set of several large medieval rooms and courtyards for Richard. Olivier's camera work is boldly theatrical, repeatedly calling attention to itself, rather than unobtrusive. Like Olivier the actor, his camera prefers power and surprise over patience and subtlety. Olivier's Shakespeare films are boldly cinematic but they are so in theatrical terms. Olivier never tries to film a successful stage production, as Stuart Burge did with John Dexter's National Theatre production of *Othello* starring Olivier. He always reimagines his Shakespearean material in cinematic terms, though he searches for film equivalents to theatrical conventions (such as Richard's direct address to the camera in his soliloquies or the use of voice-overs for many of Hamlet's soliloquies). Olivier's stature and success as the finest English actor of his generation and his daring ambition to bring Shakespeare to a wider audience through film, both contributed to making the Shakespeare film a vital genre rather than a failed experiment in stage to screen translation.

Orson Welles (1915–1985)

Olivier was aided in his effort to make Shakespeare film a vital genre by the man who became the most legendary American filmmaker and famous Hollywood outcast in movie history: Orson Welles. Welles's lifelong preoccupation with Shakespeare was as typically American as Olivier's was English. Olivier was the embodiment of a four-hundred-year-old English acting tradition reaching back to Richard Burbage and the Globe Theater. Olivier, and his nation, saw himself as the inheritor of a theatrical tradition that extended from Richard Burbage (c. 1567–1619) to Thomas Betterton (c. 1635–1710) to David Garrick (1717–1779) to Edmund Kean (1787–1833) to Henry Irving (1838–1905). Olivier was the first English actor to be elevated to the peerage, becoming Lord Olivier of Brighton. His funeral was a state occasion held in Westminster Abbey and was worthy of a great national hero like Wellington or Churchill or even, as some have suggested, Shakespeare himself.

Welles, on the other hand, had no Shakespearean or theatrical tradition to sustain him other than that of the itinerant actor. The most famous family of Shakespearean actors to work in America, the Booths, were stained by their connection to John Wilkes Booth and his assassination of Abraham Lincoln, and no other actors filled their place in American Shakespearean theater. Welles did much to create an American tradition of performing Shakespeare that was less reverential and more radical than approaches taken in England, at least until the last decades of the twentieth century.

Welles was eight years younger than Olivier. By the late 1930s he had established himself in New York as the young wunderkind of the American classical theater, a reputation that was largely based on an all-black production of *Macbeth* (produced in Harlem in 1936 under the auspices of the Federal Theater Project) and a fascist version of *Julius Caesar* (produced in 1937 for his own Mercury Theater Company). But even then Welles had a cultural reach far beyond the New York theatrical scene through a weekly CBS radio program that began as "Orson Welles and the Mercury Theater on Air," which aired the most famous broadcast in American radio history: Welles's version of H. G. Wells's *The War of the Worlds*. That program, broadcast on October 30, 1938, as something of a Halloween prank, terrified the nation into believing the United States had been invaded by Martians. Almost overnight Welles found himself a national figure and on the cover of *Time* magazine (with the title "Marvelous Boy"). He was all of twenty-three. Hollywood quickly beckoned, and in 1941 Welles released his first film: *Citizen Kane*, destined to be recognized as the greatest of all American films and to secure Welles's legacy as a cinematic wizard. *Citizen Kane* made Welles an international legend, but it also gave him a vigorous enemy in William Randolph Hearst, the newspaper baron who was the model for the film's John Foster Kane. As was to prove true with other Welles projects, the film created more controversy than box office.

Welles's next film, *The Magnificent Ambersons* (1946), was also a commercial failure. As he had in his past and would do repeatedly in his career, Welles turned to Shakespeare for creative nourishment. He convinced Herbert Yates, the head of Republic Pictures who was noted for making B Westerns, to back an experiment in bringing Shakespeare to a wider public through film.[9] The idea was to shoot fast and cheap to see if there was an audience for what we might call B Shakespeares. The result was Welles's *Macbeth* (1948), shot in twenty-three days (as opposed to the three to four months required for most films) on a budget of $750,000 (about a fifth of the budget for Olivier's *Hamlet*).

Welles's *Macbeth* is a ragged, jagged film with a troubled production history (a feature of all of Welles's Shakespeare films), a crazy assortment of costumes (including the often-mocked hats Welles wears as Macbeth), several versions of the soundtrack, and an interpretive concept that sees the play dramatizing the conflict between pagan and Christian ideas, allowing Welles to add the character of an old priest not present in Shakespeare's text. (Olivier did some brutal trimming in his screenplay for *Hamlet*; Welles demonstrated his American chutzpah and topped Olivier by *adding* characters to his adaptation of *Macbeth*.) What the film does have, to more than compensate for its obvious flaws, is cinematic life and imagination. Welles found the true expression of his artistic genius in film. He is particularly adept at creating a radically new cinematic landscape that perfectly mirrors the internal consciousness of the Shakespearean figure at the center of the frame (whether Macbeth, Lady

---

9. Films used to be informally graded depending on their budgets and target audiences. John Ford (with John Wayne as his star) made A Westerns; B Westerns often starred lesser-known actors like Joel McCrea and Randolph Scott and were often the second feature on a double bill.

Macbeth, Othello, Iago, Falstaff, Hal, or Henry IV). A classic example is his handling of Macbeth's reception of the news of Banquo's murder and Fleance's escape. The scene is set in an abandoned salt mine, long used in Republic Westerns, transformed by Welles's camera into an apt visual metaphor for Macbeth's mental state. "I am cabined, cribbed, confined, bound in/To saucy doubts and fears" (3.4.23–24) his deep baritone voice rumbles at the news of Fleance's escape. Welles shoots Macbeth from a low angle so we see the way he is physically trapped in the mine's shaft. When he staggers away from the murderers, a long **tracking shot** captures his anguished progress along the tunnel as water seeps down the rock and Banquo's voice ("Thou hast it now: King, Cawdor, Glamis, all....") echoes in Macbeth's mind. A close-up, with Macbeth's face caught against the stone and framed in the chiaroscuro patterns of light and shadow, reveals beads of sweat on his forehead. Macbeth's guilt and tortured imagination are as inexorably evident as that water wearing away at the subterranean walls of the mine. This is a stunning example of translating Shakespeare into film: language, action, camera, landscape, and acting all combine to create a new synthesis that produces the unique power of Shakespeare realized not just *on* but *through* film.

Macbeth, largely shot on a Hollywood soundstage in less than a month, stands in stunning contrast to Welles's next Shakespeare film, *Othello* (1952), shot almost entirely on location at multiple sites in Italy and Morocco with shooting, often interrupted for extended periods, stretched out between 1949 and 1951. Though the film was plagued with the financial problems that beset Welles's career once he abandoned Hollywood for Europe and the mercurial life of the independent film director and producer, what he managed to patch together from fragments shot on both sides of the Mediterranean won the top prize at the Cannes Film Festival in 1952 and ranks as one of the most visually baroque and audacious of all Shakespeare films. Once again Welles used black and white photography to stunning effect, this time as a visual emblem for the racial issues at work in the play. Welles brilliantly moves Iago and Othello in and out of sunlight and shadow until they merge, as Welles intended, "in one murderous image like a pattern of loving shadows welded."[10]

10. Quoted in Michael MacLiammoir's *Put Money in Thy Purse*, 2nd ed. (London: Eyre Methuen, 1976), p. 28.

The film is packed with interesting devices, images, and landscapes, from the opening overhead **iris** shot of Othello's face on his funeral bier, to Iago suspended from his cage on Mogador's battlements, to the famed murder of Roderigo in the Turkish bath with mandolins racing under the action on the **soundtrack,** to Iago's pursuit of Cassio in Cyprus's sewers, to the vaulted chapel in Viterburo, Italy, where Welles shot Othello's murder of Desdemona.[11] The film is a rich treat for the experienced **cinèaste** but demanding for the novice Shakespearean.

In *Othello*, Welles uses the black and white of his medium to create a vivid chiaroscuro "pattern of living shadows welded." After the shadows have merged and melded so murderously that they "put out the light," Welles returns to the sequence featuring Othello and Desdemona's funeral procession that frames the film. Their progress toward the harbor is shot in silhouette against the horizon—our first readjustment to a light/dark contrast since the beginning of the murder scene. We are given an interesting shot of the Cyprus battlements and Iago's cage swinging from the top of the tower's wall reflected on the harbor's surface. The shot is meant to call attention, yet again, to the nature of Welles's medium. Film is a reflection, a series of shadows projected on a wall, and Welles employs the very essence of film as the key metaphor for translating Shakespeare's play from stage to screen.

Welles's final Shakespeare film, *Chimes at Midnight* (1966), is considered by many to be the finest treatment of Shakespearean material on film.[12] Because Welles was dealing with his own amalgamation of elements drawn from several Shakespeare plays (primarily *1* and *2 Henry IV* with snatches of dialogue from *Richard II*, *Henry V*, and *The*

---

11. The Turkish bath sequence is one of the most famous in all of Welles's films. Welles and his cast and crew had arrived in Morocco ready to shoot the Cyprus scenes. Financial difficulties prevented the costumes, being made in Rome, from arriving as scheduled. The resourceful Welles, finding necessity ever the mother of invention, decided to begin by shooting the scene where Iago stabs Roderigo in a local Turkish bath as the actors had only to wear large white terry cloth towels.

12. From respected film reviewers like Vincent Canby of the *New York Times* to traditional Shakespeare scholars like Robert Hapgood to specialists on Shakespeare and film like Michael Anderegg. See Vincent Canby, *New York Times*, Sunday, March 2, 1975, p. 17; Robert Hapgood, "*Chimes at Midnight* from Stage to Screen: The Art of Adaptation," *Shakespeare Survey*, no. 39 (1987); and Michael Anderegg, "Every Third Word a Lie: Rhetoric and History in Orson Welles's *Chimes at Midnight*," *Film Quarterly* 40 (Spring 1987).

Merry Wives of Windsor) he was free to reshape and retell Falstaff's story without being bound by the expectations confronting a film-maker dealing with a single Shakespearean text. In addition, because Welles's own career came increasingly to parallel Falstaff's (a great artist forced to badger or amuse the rich and powerful for the means to sustain his life and art), the film added a layer of biographical resonance for Shakespeareans who were beginning to understand the nature of film and Welles's pivotal role in its development. Man, material, and moment all coalesced to make a film that wonderfully mirrors the vitality and melancholy of Shakespeare's conception of Falstaff and his world.

Welles's screenplay, as its title suggests, is centered on Falstaff and particularly the Falstaff of *2 Henry IV*. The film consists of Welles's long, loving good-bye to a figure he regards as a literary giant. The film begins with two solitary figures slowly making their way through a wintry landscape and finally coming in from the cold to sit before a roaring fire as one rasps to the other, "Jesus, the days that we have seen." "We have heard the chimes at midnight, Master Shallow," Welles's Falstaff replies. Welles begins with Falstaff, not with Henry IV or his son Hal, because this is to be Falstaff's story: we are to witness the glory of his days and lament their passing. The winter landscape, the two elderly figures seeking the warmth of the fire, their slow uphill trudge through the snow ending in stasis, all speak profoundly to Welles's observation that by focusing on Falstaff his Shakespearean material leads him into a universe of melancholy shadows; it is Falstaff's winter of rejection that dominates the black and white texture of the film, not Hal's summer of self-realization.

As he demonstrated in *Macbeth* and *Othello*, Welles is brilliant at employing physical landscapes that suggest psychological states of mind. *Chimes at Midnight*, like Shakespeare's *Henry IV* plays, has two dominant landscapes: the court and the tavern. The first is dominated by the castle's cold stone; the second by the warmth of the tavern's timber. John Gielgud's austere king is frequently shot against the castle's rough stone, often seated on an elevated platform and shot from a **low-angle** perspective, further heightening his power and isolation. Welles's Falstaff is most often framed against the tavern's timbered beams and captured at the center of its bustling vitality. Keith Baxter's Hal migrates between the two environments, repeatedly signaling

Falstaff (Orson Welles), framed against the timbers of the tavern in the "play extempore," with Prince Hal (Keith Baxter) in Welles's *Chimes at Midnight* (1966, Internacional Films Espagnol).

farewell to Falstaff, as he moves from the Boar's Head to Westminster. The film has a number of visually powerful sequences, including the Gad's Hill robbery scene, the famed tavern encounter between Hal and Falstaff that follows, and the final rejection scene where Hal, now crowned Henry V, assumes his father's elevated position (and receives his low camera angle) as he coldly banishes his former friend now forced to his knees in the child's supplicant posture.

The most remarkable sequence in the film is Welles's treatment of the battle at Shrewsbury between the king's forces and the rebels led by Hotspur. It is the only battle scene in all of Welles's films, and film critic Pauline Kael is right to see it as belonging with such famous sequences from Eisenstein, D. W. Griffith, Kurosawa, and John Ford.[13] Welles was clearly creating the dynamics of his battle in response to Olivier's treatment of Agincourt in his film of *Henry V*. Olivier shoots his battle from the perspective of the idealistic young king; Welles shoots his through the eyes of the jaded old realist, Falstaff. Welles

13. Pauline Kael, *Kiss Kiss Bang Bang* (New York: Bantam Books, 1969), p. 247.

concentrates on capturing Falstaff's understanding that war's appetite is fed by "mortal men" and that it can quickly transform them into "food for powder." Welles captures what war is like for the men in the trenches rather than for those Olivier-like heroes, mounted on dashing chargers, gliding athletically toward their opponents with cinematic dash and brio. Welles's treatment of Shrewsbury is a slow, painful, exhausting depiction of mud-caked soldiers enacting some primal destructive rite. Welles gives full expression to the language of cinema here, and his Shrewsbury was surely one source for the devastating twenty-minute D-Day battle scene that opens Steven Spielberg's *Saving Private Ryan* (1998).

While Olivier's films reveal a theatrical master harnessing film technique in the service of expressing Shakespeare, Welles shatters Shakespeare's theatrical origins to fully reconstitute his powers in the language of film. Shakespeare scholar Kenneth Rothwell observes: "If Laurence Olivier's work is Appollonian, reasonable, comfortably mainstream, and commodified, Welles's is Dionysian and passionate, rough-hewn and unpredictable, and uncommodified. Put reductively, Olivier's work remains theatrical and English; Welles's, cinematic and American."[14]

Kenneth Branagh (b. 1960)

While Orson Welles's films helped to catapult the Shakespeare film into a position of status within the scholarly world of cinema history and criticism, they were also box-office poison and contributed to the collapse of Hollywood interest in the genre in the early 1970s. That interest was dramatically revived in 1989 by the unexpected critical and commercial success of Kenneth Branagh's independently financed, low-budget film of *Henry V*. Branagh's film made a lively and intelligent synthesis of elements from Olivier's *Henry V* and Welles's *Chimes at Midnight*. In tone, atmosphere, and cinematic approach Branagh's film was Wellesian; in casting, the flair for the theatrically dramatic, and attention to Shakespeare's language, Branagh revealed his debt to Olivier. When Clint Eastwood set out to make his great Western, *Unforgiven* (1992), the works of John Ford, Howard Hawks,

14. Rothwell, *A History of Shakespeare on Screen*, p. 72.

George Stevens, and Sergio Leone were in his cultural blood and personal experience. Branagh had a similar relationship to Shakespeare and to Shakespeare movies when he began to make his first films.

Directors of Shakespeare films, like the makers of Westerns and other genre pictures, tend to be intimately aware of each other's work, and healthy intertextual visual conversations can often be traced between prominent Shakespeare films. Branagh studied Olivier and Welles when preparing his *Henry V*—but to that Shakespearean mix he added a knowledge of and admiration for more contemporary Hollywood war films like *Platoon* (1986) and *Full Metal Jacket* (1987). Branagh is not shy about his respect for popular films and his desire to incorporate their conventions into his Shakespeare films. His route to Shakespeare on film takes him through innovators like Olivier and Welles and beyond, to contemporary American filmmakers like Stanley Kubrick, Francis Ford Coppola, Steven Spielberg, and Oliver Stone. Combining elements from films past and present, Branagh created a new dynamic and style in capturing Shakespeare on film. The opening moment of his *Henry V* provides a clear example.

Olivier's *Henry V* begins on a bright, sunny Elizabethan London day with the camera **panning** over a view of the Thames, London Bridge, Southwark Cathedral, and then on down the South Bank to swoop in on the Globe Theater as an audience gathers for a performance of *Henry V*. Shakespeare's world sparkles before our eyes. We know when and where we are as we enter the Globe and our expectations are high. The opening of Branagh's *Henry V* reverses all of this. We are in the dark. Percussive chords of Patrick Doyle's striking **film score** puncture the silence. Suddenly we hear a match strike and and see it spark, and the camera is in tight on Derek Jacobi's partially illuminated face. "O for a muse of fire" he confides to us and then begins to move as we hear his steps ringing on a steel surface. The camera slowly pulls back and we discover that we are not in a theater but a film studio—Jacobi passes by elements prominent to the production: props, stacks of spears, a giant wind fan, and a Panaflex 35 movie camera as he delivers the Chorus's insistence that we must "on our imaginary forces work" to flesh out Shakespeare's tale.

Olivier's opening establishes his personal and cultural moment. He is England's national hero and Shakespeare is the country's great poet coming to the service of the nation at a moment of peril. Olivier is confident that actor, director, playwright, and country are equal to the task. Branagh's opening similarly reflects his own and the historical moment's dynamic. He's an unknown quantity, the cheeky pretender with relatively little experience rather than the nation's quintessential heroic actor. The times are muddy and muddled. After Vietnam and the Falklands War, military action is suspect and attitudes about leadership are skeptical if not cynical. Branagh's Henry, like Branagh himself, is a mystery, and Branagh's film will explore the dark corners of the young king's development. Branagh films the battle at Agincourt following Welles's skeptical spirit (and using some of his film technique as well) rather than Olivier's vibrant charge. Olivier studied films like Eisenstein's *The Battleship Potemkin* (1925), Michael Curtiz's *The Charge of the Light Brigade* (1936), and *The Adventures of Robin Hood* (1938) as sources for his Agincourt; Branagh's inspiration was battle sequences in films by Welles, Oliver Stone, and Stanley Kubrick.

Branagh made his name in Hollywood with *Henry V*, but he found his audience and important elements of his film aesthetic with *Much Ado about Nothing* (1993). Branagh's film is fast-paced, energetic, and broadly comic. He again acknowledges Hollywood by emphasizing *Much Ado*'s similarity to the great screwball comedies of the 1930s, like those starring Katharine Hepburn and Cary Grant. He also, for the first time, raids Hollywood for young American film stars like Denzel Washington, Robert Sean Leonard, and Keanu Reeves and mixes them with more experienced British stage actors like Emma Thompson, Richard Briers, and Brian Blessed (all also veterans of his film of *Henry V*). Branagh continued to utilize this Anglo-American cast mix in his subsequent Shakespeare films—*Hamlet* (1996), *Love's Labour's Lost* (2000), and *As You Like It* (2006)—trying to make Shakespeare films with "different accents, different looks . . . that belonged to the world."[15] Branagh's Shakespeare films also became known for his controversial casting of American comic actors (Michael Keaton, Billy Crystal, Robin Williams, and Nathan Lane) to play Shakespeare's clowns, but he broke that pattern in *As You Like It* by casting as Touchstone the English actor Alfred Molina, known for his dramatic roles in *Chocolat* (2000), *Frida* (2002), *Luther* (2003), and *Spider-Man 2* (2004).

15. Kenneth Branagh, Much Ado about Nothing: *Screenplay, Introduction, and Notes on the Making of the Movie* (New York: W. W. Norton, 1993), p. x.

Branagh not only achieved a synthesis of the best qualities of Welles's and Olivier's Shakespeare films, but he also imaginatively attempted to link the Shakespeare film to popular Hollywood models: the war film in *Henry V*, screwball comedy in *Much Ado*, the intelligent epic in *Hamlet*, the American musical comedy in *Love's Labour's Lost*, and the oriental romance in *As You Like It*. He is the first major director of Shakespeare films to emerge as much from movie culture as from the classical stage. His movies are not embarrassed visually to quote films as wide-ranging as *Swing Time* (1936), in the "Dancing Cheek to Cheek" number in *Love's Labour's Lost*; *The Magnificent Seven* (1960), as the soldiers come pounding home on horseback with their right fists high in the giddy opening sequence in *Much Ado about Nothing*; and *Dr. Zhivago* (1965), in the David Lean–inspired Russian atmosphere that permeates his film of *Hamlet*, from the casting of Julie Christie (Lean's Lara) as Gertrude to the storming of the Winter Palace as echoed in Fortinbras's assault on Elsinore in the film's final frames.

Branagh's films are distinguished by their sustained momentum, their visual romanticism, the spoken quality of Shakespeare's verse and prose, the importance of Patrick Doyle's scores, and the core company of actors the director has managed to employ over his five Shakespeare films. Branagh not only has emerged as the most prolific director of Shakespeare films in the history of the genre but he also belies his reputation as a banal popularizer by relentlessly pushing the Shakespeare film in new directions. His four-hour *Hamlet*, the longest commercial film since Joseph Mankiewicz's *Cleopatra* (1963), was a daring attempt to shoot a full-text version of Shakespeare's longest tragedy, aimed in style and technique not at the elite art house audience but at the kids who pack the cineplexes every weekend. He failed commercially as the film failed to find an audience, but in a manner that still makes his *Hamlet* a film that demands our attention. Branagh was equally daring in his next Shakespeare film, *Love's Labour's Lost* (2000), this time moving in the opposite direction by radically trimming the text of Shakespeare's prolix early comedy to fit the format of the Hollywood musical comedy. In a mere ninety-five minutes, in a remarkable feat of synthesis, he manages to include most of the play's plot; about a quarter of its text; and ten song and dance routines that echo movie musicals as diverse as the Fred Astaire-Ginger Rogers classics, Esther Williams's water ballets, and Gene Kelly's *An American in Paris* (1951). In his *Love's Labour's Lost*, Branagh pushes the Shakespeare film in provocative new directions by combining a four-hundred-year-old comedy with a 1930s Hollywood movie genre.

Olivier's films participated in the crisis of World War II and the subsequent celebration of its victory by the Allied forces. Welles's films are great triumphs of the modernist aesthetic, and his battle scene in *Chimes at Midnight* anticipated the American quagmire in Vietnam. Branagh's films, too, shared in their cultural milieu, springing to life in the period between the fall of the Berlin Wall (1989) and the terrorist attack on the World Trade Center (2001). In that long decade of peace between the end of the Cold War and the beginning of the war in Iraq, filmmakers and producers in London and Hollywood found re- newed interest in making films based on the work of classic authors like Shakespeare, Jane Austen, Charles Dickens, Henry James, Edith Wharton, and E. M. Forster. Fascinating films were made of all six Austen novels, ranging from popular, Hollywood versions of *Sense and Sensibility* (1995) and *Emma* (1996) to low-budget English versions of *Persuasion* (1995) and *Mansfield Park* (1999). For a moment, *Terminator* (1984 and 1991) and *Batman* (1989) and the apocalyptic Armageddon films like *Independence Day* (1996) were occasionally squeezed aside by *The Wings of the Dove* (1997), *The Age of Innocence* (1993), and *The Re- mains of the Day* (1993). Branagh's early Shakespeare films helped cre- ate the audience for this commercial revival of intelligent films based on canonical literary material, and his later ones undoubtedly found financing because of the success of the genre.

Olivier, Welles, and Branagh are all film auteurs. Each man devel- oped his own individual and unique style for translating Shakespeare into the language of film. Branagh was clearly influenced by both Olivier and Welles, but what he took from them he reshaped to his own artistic purposes. Olivier and Welles were contemporaries and intensely aware of each other's work. Olivier lifted Welles's pioneer- ing use of deep focus photography in *Citizen Kane* to help create the alienated, isolated world of his *Hamlet*. Welles's films of *Macbeth* and *Othello* were clearly reactions to Olivier's more mainstream *Henry V* and *Hamlet*, brazenly offering another way to imagine Shakespeare on film. Branagh linked Olivier's theatricality and Welles's cinematic bravado with his own ripe romanticism to lead the revival of the

Shakespeare film in the 1990s. The lively Shakespeare on film conversation we see at play in their work is one productive avenue of exploration in tracing the development of the Shakespeare film, and that conversation continues and is enhanced in the Shakespeare films of international directors like Grigori Kozintsev, Akira Kurosawa, and Franco Zeffirelli.

3

CLOSE-UP: MAJOR DIRECTORS II

Akira Kurosawa, Grigori Kozintsev, and Franco Zeffirelli

Beginning with the early silents, Shakespeare on film has had a strong international component and global reach. The three international filmmakers who have most shaped Shakespeare to the traditions of their own cultures are Akira Kurosawa (Japan), Grigori Kozintsev (Russia), and Franco Zeffirelli (Italy). The first two directors adapted Shakespeare into their own language, while Zeffirelli worked with Shakespeare's English text but from a perspective dominated by his experience as one of the world's foremost directors of Italian opera. Besides the differences inherent in their cultural backgrounds, each director brought to his films differences from his creative background: Kurosawa was purely a man of the cinema; Kozintsev spent the majority of his creative life moving between theater and film; and Zeffirelli has moved back and forth between the worlds of opera, theater, and film.

This international trio offers some parallels with their Anglo-American counterparts discussed in chapter 2, Olivier, Welles, and Branagh, in that their individual signatures as **auteurs** track the evolution of cinematic Shakespeare itself. Olivier and Kozintsev seek to combine theatrical and film devices and conventions; Welles and Kurosawa are great cinema poets; Branagh and Zeffirelli are bold populists who attempt to transfer the Shakespeare film from the art house to the cineplex.

Akira Kurosawa (1910–1998)

Akira Kurosawa was a leading figure in the revival of Japanese cinema after World War II and was the first Asian filmmaker to find large American and European audiences for his films. He joined the French New Wave and Italian neo-realist directors in making a significant impact in America in the 1950s and 60s.

Kurosawa was a remarkably eclectic filmmaker. His films were set both in modern Japan and in the country's Samurai past. He borrowed elements from Japanese Noh drama and Buddhist traditions as well as from Western writers as varied as Shakespeare and Dostoyevsky. In turn, Hollywood directors saw obvious parallels between Kurosawa's Samurai pictures and the American Western, and they raided Kurosawa's *Rashômon* (1950) and *Seven Samurai* (1954) as sources for *The Outrage* (1964) and *The Magnificent Seven* (1960).

Kurosawa's films are distinguished by their energy and action; at the same time, he creates vivid film images that expose the bleak corruption or bitter melancholy at the heart of human experience. Stephen Prince rightly insists that "Kurosawa's film style stresses the excessive, the transgressive, the flamboyant."[1] These qualities are shared by Shakespeare, and it should come as no surprise that Kurosawa turned to *Macbeth*, *Hamlet*, and *King Lear* as the sources for his three films based on Shakespearean material: *Throne of Blood* (1957), *The Bad Sleep Well* (1960), and *Ran* (1985). As Robert Hapgood has observed, "Kurosawa plainly sees Shakespeare as a source of themes on which he can play variations."[2]

Shakespeare imagines his Macbeth as a representative of medieval Scotland's warrior culture. He is "Bellona's Bridegroom" who, with a single ripping blow, can unseam his opponent "from the nave to th' chops." Shakespeare places his warrior-hero in a world where "fair is foul, and foul is fair," as the witches chant. This condition is reflected in Macbeth's own ambiguous and tormented imagination as he contemplates, executes, and suffers the consequences of Duncan's murder. Kurosawa brilliantly captures this inner and outer landscape in the images he employs in *Throne of Blood*.

When we first encounter Washizu (Macbeth) and Miki (Banquo), they are lost in the labyrinthine woods near the Castle of the Spider's Web.[3] A fierce rain is falling and thunder rumbles and lightning crackles on

---

1. Stephen Prince, *The Warrior's Camera: The Cinema of Akira Kurosawa* (Princeton: Princeton University Press, 1991), p. 11.

2. Robert Hapgood, "Kurosawa's Shakespeare Films: *Throne of Blood, The Bad Sleep Well*, and *Ran*," in *Shakespeare and the Moving Image* (Cambridge: Cambridge University Press, 1994), ed. Anthony Davies and Stanley Wells, p. 240.

3. A more accurate translation of the film's Japanese title would be *The Castle of the Spider's Web*.

the soundtrack. The two soldiers spur their horses back and forth through the woods trying to find the way out. In several remarkable **tracking shots**, Kurosawa's camera shoots them through the tangled lower branches of the forest's towering trees as they race their horses first in one direction, then turn and speed back. Washizu and Miki are trapped. They counter confusion with energy. They race their horses, shoot arrows up into the trees, and laugh wildly at their predicament. Suddenly their frenetic activity ceases as they encounter a strange, androgynous forest figure dressed all in white, sitting in a bamboo hut, spinning silk. The film's rapid pace stops, the rain and thunder cease, and the two warriors stare in wide-eyed amazement at the mystical figure slowly spinning thread from one spool to another. We first observed Washizu and Miki through the forest's undergrowth; now they gaze at the forest figure through the bamboo slats of his cage.

This scene is Kurosawa's reimagining of Macbeth and Banquo's encounter with the witches. He has found a series of powerful visual images to capture the play's fractured, ambiguous landscape where fair is foul and foul is fair. The rain, fog, tangled forest, and spinning wheel all speak to the myriad ways Macbeth becomes "cabined, cribbed, confined" by his "horrible imaginings" as, provoked by his wife and his own ambition, he seeks "to catch the nearest way" to ultimate power. Macbeth is a curious combination of energy and stasis, a conflicted character expressed cinematically here by Washizu's confused response to the forest and its strange prophetic figure. Kurosawa even **metacinematically** associates the forest spirit with the film director and his art, as the spinning wheel bears a striking resemblance to a movie projector.[4]

Kurosawa blends elements from both Eastern and Western traditions in his adaptation of *Macbeth*. He incorporates a variety of elements out of Noh drama, where stasis and vehemence co-exist.[5] Noh is a highly stylized form of Japanese theater in which the main actors wear masks that depict stereotyped emotions and character types (witch, old woman, de-

4. See Peter S. Donaldson's *Shakespearean Films/Shakespearean Directors* (Boston: Unwin Hyman, 1990), pp. 76–77, for a brilliant reading of the meta-cinematic issues at work in this sequence.
5. See Prince, *The Warrior's Camera*, pp. 146–48 for a discussion of the Noh influences on Kurosawa's film.

mon). Kurosawa showed pictures of Noh masks representing the warrior and a beautiful woman no longer young to the actors playing the Macbeth (Toshiro Mifune) and Lady Macbeth (Isuzu Yamada) characters, and asked them to capture the essence of the masks' expression in their performances. Washizu also wears a traditional Samurai warrior's banner on the back of his armor, and its emblem is a scorpion suggested by Macbeth's self-description: "O, full of scorpions is my mind" (3.2.36). Shakespeare is famous for his eclecticism, raiding sources from ancient Roman history to Elizabethan prose romances for the plots for his plays. In *A Midsummer Night's Dream*, for instance, he mixes pagan gods and goddesses (Oberon and Titania), taken from the works of the Roman poet Ovid, with figures from his local Warwickshire countryside (Puck and Bottom). Kurosawa mirrors Shakespeare's genius for appropriation by borrowing plots, themes, narrative devices, and symbolic landscapes from multiple sources.

Kurosawa's next film based on a Shakespearean source, *The Bad Sleep Well* (1960), is a veiled retelling of the Hamlet story set not in Japan's warrior past but in its modern corporate present. Kurosawa's film seeks to expose the corruption at the core of Japan's giant corporations, employing a suicidal Hamlet-figure (Wada) to destabilize a rigidly hierarchal world. *The Bad Sleep Well* does not reimagine *Hamlet* in the Japanese context as powerfully as *Throne of Blood* does *Macbeth*, but Kurosawa's source allows him to develop his own variations on themes prominent in *Hamlet*, including spying, concealment, corruption, power, psychological instability, isolation, deception, and betrayal.

In his final Shakespearean adaptation, *Ran* (1985), Kurosawa returns to a late medieval Samurai setting. Here he reshapes *King Lear* so that the king (Hidetora) seeks to divide his kingdom between his three sons (rather than three daughters) and suffers the consequences, as civil strife rather than family harmony results. Kurosawa's early films, including *Throne of Blood* and *The Bad Sleep Well*, were all in black and white, but in his later years he worked in Technicolor, and *Ran* is visually stunning in its use of a full color palette.

The landscape in *Throne of Blood*, like that of Shakespeare's play of *Macbeth*, was intense and constricted. Nature was defined by rain, fog, and forest. The built environment featured a massive squat fort whose inner rooms were defined by low ceilings and strict geometrical patterns—all reflecting the way both Macbeth and Lady Macbeth become trapped and ultimately destroyed by a claustrophobic world projected by their own guilty consciences after the exercise of their murderous ambition.[6] In contrast, the destructive powers of *Ran*, like those of *King Lear*, can't be contained within a single room or consciousness but reach out to embrace an apocalyptic vision of the entire universe. *Ran* means "chaos" in Japanese, and Kurosawa's film creates a huge canvas on which chaos reigns.

Ran's opening landscape is immense. Hidetora (Lear) and his hunting party are encamped on a high plateau with magnificent vistas of Japan's green and sacred mountains. Kurosawa reverses the gender of Lear's daughters by giving Hidetora three sons, each identified with a primary color: yellow for Taro the eldest, red for Jiro the second son, and blue for Saburo, the youngest and the Cordelia figure. He makes sons of Shakespeare's daughters partly in response to Japan's Samurai tradition, but also to make an even more daring gender reversal, collapsing Cornwall and Edmund into a single female character, Lady Kaede, the wife of Hidetora's eldest son. She burns with revenge for being born a woman and made a victim of patriarchal power. Kaede embodies the consequences of Hidetora's past bloody military triumphs. Taro's castle was once her father's, and she means to make it hers by the same bold means Edmund employs to move himself from the margins to the center of power in Shakespeare's play: brazen sexuality, ironic self-assurance, and amoral drive.

Edmund and Kaede feel themselves constrained by the conventional social order. Kurosawa plays against culture and convention—much in the same manner as Shakespeare allows Edmund to exploit the soliloquy for his own radical purposes in *King Lear*—in capturing Kaede's lethal appeal. Kaede's great scene, and the stunning culmination of Kurosawa's twist on the character of Edmund in Shakespeare's play, comes halfway through the film. Hidetora has relinquished his power to his sons, inspiring aggression rather than agreement. Saburo is exiled for opposing his father's decision, and Jiro (the second son) attacks his older brother, Taro, so that he can have supreme power. His

---

6. In a wonderful example of colonial power serving native art, the United States Marines were instrumental in helping Kurosawa build his massive fort.

forces succeed (one of them shoots Taro in the back) and Jiro comes to claim Taro's wife, Kaede, as his prize.

In a brilliant scene, filled with Shakespearean reversals and tiny telling details, Kaede adopts the conquered woman's conventional position as supplicant. Jiro boldly presents her with Taro's helmet, the symbol of his victory. She seductively pushes the helmet back toward Jiro while sinuously crawling toward him, appearing to acknowledge his triumph. As Jiro eyes his sexual prize, she hurls herself upon him, unsheathing his dagger in the process. With her legs astride his body she presses the dagger to his throat and demands to know the circumstances of Taro's death. Jiro is shocked and surprised by her sudden dominance. When he hesitates to answer, Kaede slices the side of his neck and draws blood. Jiro immediately confesses that his henchman did the killing. Kaede springs to her feet and the camera remains fixed on her as she laughs in his face, taunting his cowardice. As she laughs at her prey, she slides shut the doors of the chamber, tosses the dagger away, and catches Jiro in her arms as his feet become tangled in her kimono and they both tumble to the floor.

After their first hungry embrace, she caresses the blood on Jiro's neck and kicks Taro's helmet across the floor. The film then cuts to the postcoital moment when Kaede presses her advantage by feigning to weep over her status as a fallen woman, little better than Jiro's concubine. The camera captures her mock tears while revealing that they are having their intended effect on Jiro, who stands in the rear of the frame. As Kaede's seemingly abject performance reaches its climax, a moth hops onto her kimono and we see her hand, in **close-up**, quietly crush the insect between thumb and forefinger. She doesn't miss a false sob. This sequence rivals Edmund's cocky social Darwinism in its daring mixture of power, performance, and sexual charge. Kaede literally levels traditional male power as she straddles Jiro with his weapon in her control. The sexual politics at work here is as stunning as Edmund's manipulation of Goneril and Regan in Shakespeare's play. Edmund and Kaede become radical studies in what constitutes status and legitimacy and how it is created or subverted.

Further underscoring his resonance with his Shakespearean source, Kurosawa frames the Kaede-Jiro seduction with the scenes of Hidetora's move out into the storm, his rescue by Tango (Kent), his finding momentary shelter in the hovel, and his move back into the world of nature, where he accepts a straw helmet that has been worn by Kyoami (the Fool)—the equivalent of the crown of wild flowers Lear wears when he reappears in his brilliant lunacy at Dover after the storm.

Hidetora's rage in *Ran*'s storm scene is triggered by the battle between Taro and Jiro. He wanders through the carnage of the battle shouting, "I am a messenger from heaven. This is heaven's war. Smash the rebels . . . have no mercy. This is heaven's punishment. Come on, I will give you a taste of destruction."[7] This is Kurosawa's vision and version of Lear's call for the "all-shaking thunder" to "strike flat the thick rotundity of the world" (3.2.7–9). A triple leveling is at work here, three worlds are being turned upside down and into chaos: Hidetora's personal journey from the pinnacle of his society to its depths (represented literally in the film's landscape, from the mountain plateau of the opening sequence to the death valley littered with the slain warriors he now wanders through); his empire's collapse by internecine civil war; and his culture's radical turn with the emergence of a powerful female political figure. "Crack nature's molds, all germains spill at once" (3.4.8) has been brilliantly realized by Kurosawa in his film's movement through these three contiguous sequences.

Kurosawa was largely responsible for bringing the Japanese film into the international marketplace. He significantly expanded the reach of Shakespeare on film by deftly absorbing *Macbeth*, *Hamlet*, and *King Lear* into an Asian context. He also acknowledged his admiration for the films of the master of the American Western, John Ford. In fact, Kurosawa's relationship with the actor Toshiro Mifune paralleled Ford's movie partnership with John Wayne. Kurosawa acknowledged that "I am the kind of person who works violently, throwing himself into it. I like hot summers, cold winters, heavy rains and snows, and I think my pictures reflect this. I like extremes because I find them most alive."[8] Kurosawa's cinematic universe extends from Japan's Samurai past to John Ford's American West and gathers Shakespeare into its huge reach as well. Kurosawa was largely responsible for bringing

7. Quoted from the screenplay. Akira Kurosawa, *Ran* (London: Shambhala, 1986), p. 24.
8. Donald Richie, "Kurosawa on Kurosawa," *Sight and Sound* 33 (Summer 1964), p. 111.

Shakespeare to Asia, but equally important, he brought Japanese motion pictures to the attention of Western audiences. His Samurai films had a stunning impact in Hollywood, where they brought new energies to the genre of the American Western. Films speak a powerful international language, and Kurosawa brought a fresh perspective on Shakespeare to Europe and America by revealing how seeing something familiar through foreign eyes can make it seem as though we are experiencing it for the first time.

Grigori Kozintsev (1905–1973)

Akira Kurosawa's influence extended not only to Europe and America, but to Russia as well. The noted Russian stage and film director, Grigori Kozintsev, was stunned by Kurosawa's films. He realized that

> Kurosawa is perhaps one of the most daring innovators. . . . In *Throne of Blood* . . . he refused to have any close-ups. The most tragic scenes were taken in long shots; the actors sat for a long time in silence on mats. The decor was sometimes no more than a patch of mould on a paper wall. The Noh Theatre had migrated to the screen: Lady Macbeth was made up like a mask; the actor's walk made one think of the ritual step; the movement of fingers like a dance; the asymmetrical arrangement of figures on a bare stage— the style itself belonged to ancient times.
>
> But when the Samurai's horses burst out of the mist and one saw the ferocious eyes and black threatening weapons—the signs of death and the signs of greatness, and the fighters circled round the same place eight times, powerless to break out of the mist— one caught one's breath at the greatness of Shakespeare and at the same time the greatness of the cinema.[9]

Inspired by Kurosawa's example, Kozintsev also attempted to merge the greatness of Shakespeare with the greatness of the cinema in his films of *Hamlet* (1964) and *King Lear* (1971). Though Kozintsev

9. Grigori Kozintsev, King Lear: *The Space of Tragedy* (Berkeley: California University Press, 1977), p. 11.

had directed *Hamlet* in the theater in the 1940s, Soviet funding to create his film was made possible by the cultural and political thaw that followed Stalin's death in 1953. For a decade or so, during the rise of Nikita Khrushchev, Russian filmmakers were no longer tightly bound by the strictures of Soviet social realism, and Kozintsev's *Hamlet* is both a moving reaffirmation of Russian romanticism and a covert critique of Stalinist power politics.

Kozintsev used Boris Pasternak's Slavic-inflected prose translation of Shakespeare's play to shape his **screenplay**, and he found another noted Russian creator in Dmitri Shostakovich, who composed a powerful score for the film. Picking up on Kurosawa's use of a few essentials like fog, rain, and forest to create the visual landscape for his version of *Macbeth*, Kozintsev crafted his *Hamlet* out of images of sea, stone, iron, and fire. After the opening credits, rolled against images of the sea pounding against the rocky base of Elsinore and torches flickering against the castle's walls, the film cuts to Hamlet on horseback, his great gray cape flowing out behind him, racing home from Germany for his father's funeral. The camera follows his horse's clattering progress into the castle's courtyard and then catches the huge portcullis being lowered behind horse and rider as they enter Claudius's domain. The camera shoots through the iron bars of the portcullis as Innokenti Smoktunovski's handsome, blond Hamlet dismounts and dashes up Elsinore's stone steps to be greeted by his mother. The prison imagery is extended into the realm of human interaction as Kozintsev's camera catches, in medium close-up, Gertrude's black-gloved right hand reaching down Hamlet's back to pull him into her fatal embrace.

These vivid opening images, underlined by Shostakovich's staccato, percussive score, suggest the constricted and deadly world Hamlet confronts upon his return to Denmark. "Denmark's a prison" he declares to Rosencrantz and Guildenstern, and Kozintsev builds his film around a series of visual images of imprisonment, impasse, and implosion. Hamlet is trapped, literally and figuratively, within Elsinore's massive stone fortress: he delivers his first soliloquy in **voice-over** as he negotiates his way through the maze of Claudius's court packed with international courtiers and diplomats. Later Hamlet and Ophelia are shot framed against the balusters of a staircase in the nunnery scene, visually reinforcing the ways both are literally and psychologically imprisoned by uncle and father.

Ophelia (Anastasia Vertinskaya) being strapped into an iron corset in preparation for Polonius's funeral in Grigori Kozintsev's *Hamlet* (1964, Lenfilm).

Ophelia (Anastasia Vertinskaya) is a tall, willowy blond and a dutiful child, trained by her father to be a beautiful, graceful ornament and automaton. We see her being given formal dancing lessons while Kozintsev's camera revealingly captures her pet bird in its iron cage at the edge of the **frame**. (Ophelia later receives her own iron cage, when we see her being strapped into an iron corset as she is dressed for Polonius's funeral.) Her movements in her mad scene, as well as the theme music Shostakovich creates for her, becomes a touching parody ("sweet bells jangled, out of time and harsh") of her dancing lessons and its lute accompaniment. The only moments when Kozintsev's camera breaks from impasse into expanse in its treatment of Ophelia is in shots of the sea and sky at Ophelia's death. Her drowning is linked to Hamlet's return from his aborted sea-journey to England by the flight of a solitary seagull that crosses the sky at her death and that Hamlet sees as he steps back on Denmark's shore.

Olivier's Elsinore was a gloomy gothic space empty of life's quotidian details. His Hamlet was an isolated, haunted figure wandering a landscape more psychological than material, in keeping with Olivier's Freudian approach to the play. Kozintsev's film acknowledges Olivier's in its use of black and white photography, its Elizabethan setting, and its use of light and shadow to define Hamlet's world. But Kozintsev creates, as in the crowded court scene mentioned earlier, a much fuller and more detailed version of Elsinore, one in which the play's political themes are given equal weight with its psychological drama. Claudius (Michail Nazwanov) is a squat bull—a cross between Stalin and Henry VIII. He is a powerful adversary and a stunning physical contrast to Smoktunovski's lean and lithe Hamlet. After Hamlet is dispatched to England, Elsinore's halls and walls suddenly sprout with busts and pictures of Claudius. Hamlet has provoked the tyrant's insecurity, and now Claudius's image is everywhere. These details spring from Kozintsev's symbolist vision, and critic Jack Jorgens posits that the filmmaker is responding to a key element in Hamlet's mode of thought, for "Hamlet perceives life's meaning in terms of *things*: an unweeded garden, a prison, carrion, a recorder, a nutshell, a mildewed ear."[10]

Smoktunovski's Hamlet is ironic and witty. He embodies a strong sense of Russian melancholy and fatalism without ever becoming defeated by it. He prowls his prison, taking subversive delight in unsettling Claudius's regime. After the fatal duel with Laertes, he uses his last drop of energy to stagger from the court and find his way to Elsinore's outer walls, where he is, for the last time, exposed to sea and sky and freed from Elsinore's grasp. As he slumps against the stone, Smoktunovski and Kozintsev discover a wonderful pun in Hamlet's last words: "The rest is silence" (5.2.359). Hamlet is, at last, at rest, while the rest of his story remains, not for him, but for Horatio to recount.

Kozintsev's second Shakespeare film, *King Lear* (1970), is dark and barren, but it avoids the savage nihilism of Peter Brook's somewhat similar film treatment of the play released in 1971. Kozintsev's *Hamlet*, much more than Olivier's, is grounded in a specific social and political world. His approach to *Lear* follows a similar aesthetic. The film opens with the camera following first a few and then a growing crowd of peasants as they make their way along a rutted path in a rocky, empty

10. Jorgens, *Shakespeare on Film*, p. 253.

landscape. One is on crutches, another pushes his child in a wheelbarrow, another—without legs—pulls himself along on a makeshift cart. These are the "poor naked wretches" that Lear will eventually discover he "has taken too little care of," and they are headed, we discover, to the outskirts of Lear's castle, summoned by the news that the king is to announce his future plans. Kozintsev reminds us that Lear is not just a stubborn father but a powerful king. He's connected not just to his daughters and his political advisors but to the people of his country, particularly the lowest and most wretched.

When Lear travels he does so with a huge retinue. Film can impress upon us the size and logistics of the one hundred knights he has reserved as the last vestige of his power and authority (and the problems they create for Goneril and Regan), something that can only be suggested on stage. In Kozintsev's film, Lear's entourage is made up of primitive carriages and carts, caged hawks for hunting, a large pack of Russian wolfhounds and other hunting dogs, as well as his human followers. At the other end of the social spectrum, when Edgar escapes and is forced to re-create himself as Poor Tom, his disguise is prompted by the Bedlam Beggars he sees wandering the rocky landscape and whose progression he joins. Kozintsev grounds Lear and Edgar's parallel journeys in human communities, however radically opposed. The payoff comes when Lear and his fool stumble into the hovel in the storm where they discover not only Poor Tom but a host of other social misfits and outcasts as well.

Kozintsev's Lear, played by Yuri Jarvet, is not a big man, but his sad, penetrating eyes and wrinkle-lined face, topped by a shocking mane of white hair, create an indelible image of the old king. He doesn't dominate his world; he represents it. Kozintsev always frames him surrounded by others to locate his struggle and suffering in a social context. Even in his final moments, standing over the body of the dead Cordelia, Lear is not alone but surrounded by Kent, Albany, Edgar, and a group of soldiers. Kozintsev insists on placing Lear in a social and material context rather than in a mythic landscape. To underline this reality his screenplay does not, like Shakespeare's text, abandon the fool at the end of 3.6 but keeps him at Lear's side through his encounter with the blind Gloucester and reunion with Cordelia. In the last sequence of the film, the fool plays a melancholy note on his flute as he mourns Lear's death. In a final bitter irony, the soldiers carrying the dead Lear and Cordelia from the scene kick the fool aside as the power of bureaucratic routine cruelly reasserts itself.

Kozintsev's Shakespeare films are a unique mixture of Russian tough-mindedness and sentimentality, and in their rough beauty they never forget that Shakespeare's tragic narratives are palpable as well as symbolic, realistic as well as mythic.

Franco Zeffirelli (b. 1923)

Kurosawa and Kozintsev's Shakespeare films are tough and unsparing. They contain moments of cinematic grandeur (the opening scene and the later battles in *Ran*) and energy (Hamlet riding home to Elsinore in Kozintsev's film), but their primary focus is on exploring the dark underside of human experience exposed in Shakespeare's great tragedies within a Japanese or Russian cultural or political context. The third major international director of Shakespeare films, the Italian Franco Zeffirelli, brings other qualities to his realization of Shakespeare on screen.

As a young man during World War II, Zeffirelli participated in the Italian resistance and eventually became a translator for the British Army in its campaign against the Axis powers. He was dazzled by Olivier's film of *Henry V* in 1944, further reinforcing his romantic attachment to the English and his desire to become a director. He first worked in film for the great Italian director Luchino Visconti, then became a promising young opera director and finally made a name for himself as a theatrical director when his idol, Laurence Olivier, invited him to London in 1962 to direct a production of *Romeo and Juliet* for Britain's newly launched National Theatre at the Old Vic. That production, starring a very young Judi Dench as Juliet and John Stride as Romeo, was a sensation. It played to packed houses and brought a new, younger audience to Shakespeare. The production eventually toured Europe and the United States, again drawing young audiences with the passion and vigor of the performances.

Zeffirelli quickly became a lively fixture on the international artistic scene and developed a friendship with Richard Burton and Elizabeth Taylor, who were just beginning their tumultuous relationship. Zeffirelli, accustomed to working with great opera divas like Maria Callas and riding the wave of his British Shakespearean success, became the ideal director to realize Burton and Taylor's idea to star together in a film of *The Taming of the Shrew* (1966).

The film established the key elements in Zeffirelli's style that would flower and mature in his later films of *Romeo and Juliet* (1968) and *Hamlet* (1990): on-location settings, lush film scores, energetic camera movements, quick cuts, a packed frame, and a neo-romantic, almost operatic, approach to his Shakespearean material. Zeffirelli was the first Shakespearean filmmaker since Olivier (in his *Richard III*) to employ Technicolor and the first since Cukor (in the 1936 *Romeo and Juliet*) to cast established Hollywood stars with little or no Shakespearean experience. These moves were part of Zeffirelli's attempt to reclaim Shakespeare for the wide, popular-moviegoing audience from the art-film elite.

Zeffirelli announces his approach to filmed Shakespeare in the raucous opening sequence of *Taming*. He has Vincentio and Tranio arrive in Padua on the opening day of the new academic term. The city is swept up in festive revelry as the two travelers make their wide-eyed way through Padua's packed, narrow streets. Zeffirelli loves to crowd the frame and frame the crowd to provide a lively, energetic, robust context, mirroring the equally hyperbolic relationship between Katherine and Petruchio at the heart of Shakespeare's tale. The release of festive impulses in Zeffirelli's opening sequence, film critic Jack Jorgens argues, aligns Petruchio and Kate "with the saturnalian forces that stand the everyday on its head and turn reason inside out. As Zeffirelli sees it, the comedy is not primarily about a taming, but about the release of Dionysian energies."[11]

Elizabeth Taylor's Kate and Richard Burton's Petruchio are attracted to each other from their first encounter and recognize each other as kindred independent spirits in opposition to the conventional, materialistic types who surround them. Their famous fights are treated as farce but also as a healthy form of vigorous foreplay.

For instance, their first meeting and rapid-fire sparring match is reduced from one hundred twenty lines to sixty in the screenplay, but Zeffirelli visually expands this exchange into twelve minutes of **film**

11. Ibid., pp. 73–74.

time that tracks Petruchio chasing Kate from house to barn to rooftop as she hurls insults and objects at him. He keeps up his dogged pursuit and clownish antics by swinging across the barn on a rope and doing a tight-rope dance down the narrow peak of the barn's roof. Eventually they both crash through the roof to land on top of one another in a huge container of wool. The attractiveness of the two stars, the physical slapstick energy of the humor, and their fierce good spirits carry the scene far more than Shakespeare's witty repartee. Film values repeatedly trump text, another distinguishing feature of Zeffirelli's Shakespeare films. Ultimately, Zeffirelli's *Taming* becomes more about Burton and Taylor than Petruchio and Kate. Their obvious self-satisfaction with the enterprise is part of its charm but also its most damaging feature. With repetition, the broad humor loses its punch.

Zeffirelli avoided the potential distractions of star power in his next Shakespeare film. His *Romeo and Juliet* (1968) holds a place as important in Shakespeare on film history as Laurence Olivier's *Henry V* (1944) and Kenneth Branagh's *Henry V* (1989). Building on the success of his National Theatre stage production, Zeffirelli cast two young, unknown English actors as Romeo and Juliet: Leonard Whiting was sixteen and Olivia Hussey fifteen when shooting began. Zeffirelli surrounded them with several older, established British actors (Pat Heywood, Natasha Parry, Milo O'Shea, Robert Stephens) and a few other young actors just beginning their careers (Michael York and John McEnery), but none of them were familiar faces to the broad moviegoing audience. The star of this *Romeo and Juliet* is its director. Zeffirelli is in full command of his Shakespearean material from the film's opening shot of a misty Verona at dawn to the final funeral procession following the bodies of Romeo and Juliet into Verona's square and up the steps to the cathedral, as Laurence Olivier's off-screen voice recites the opening prologue and final couplet of the play.

Zeffirelli's *Romeo and Juliet* was the first widely popular and commercially successful screen Shakespeare. It became a cult hit among the young. Made for $2 million, it grossed more than $50 million in worldwide box office. With its emphasis on youth, energy, and passion being stifled and snuffed out by the ancient grudges of an older generation, Zeffirelli's film captured the spirit of the 60s. In 1968 the young had taken to the streets in Selma, Alabama, Chicago, Paris, and Prague to protest denied civil rights, meaningless wars, and repressive governments. The generational battle lines had been drawn. "Don't trust anyone over thirty" was the student mantra, and they saw that as part of Romeo and Juliet's fatal error—not only to become caught in a family feud but to trust older confidants (the nurse and Friar Laurence) as well.

Zeffirelli's film makes no direct nods to the 1960s. It is set in the Italian Renaissance with Botticelli-inspired costumes. Primary colors dominate, with reds and yellows distinguishing the Capulets and blues and greens the Montagues. The screenplay sacrifices over 50 percent of the text, but it compensates with a lightning-fast film style and a rich, haunting **film score** by Nino Rota. The film arranges its Shakespearean material around four primary spaces: the town square, Capulet's estate, the church, and the burial vault. The hot dusty square becomes the perfect landscape for the film's two great fight scenes: the opening quarrel between the Montagues and Capulets on market day and the fatal confrontation between Mercutio and Tybalt when the square is empty except for the prickly males on the prowl for provocation. The speed of Zeffirelli's camera work and cutting in these two extended sequences is a stylistic expression in film language of the quicksilver fire of Shakespeare's poetry.

Zeffirelli finds a similar cinematic equivalent for the dizzy rapture of Romeo and Juliet's initial encounter in the swirling movements of both dancers and camera during the ball scene. The only dialogue in ten minutes of film time is Tybalt's petulance at discovering Romeo's presence at the party, the interpolated song "What is a youth?" sung at a break in the dancing, and the sonnet Romeo and Juliet create together in their first exchange.

The same breathless pace and passion is given to the lovers' famed encounter in the orchard and on the balcony. Olivia Hussey's raven-haired, wide-eyed, eager Juliet, blessed with an unforgettable throaty giggle of delight at her awakening sexuality, and Leonard Whiting's eager Romeo with an angelic face and eyebrows to rival Brooke Shields's, bring a fresh spontaneity to their famous encounter. She dashes from one end of her long balcony to another, he clambers up a tree to reach her, they punctuate their lyrical exchange of devotion with several passionate embraces, and when she retreats at the nurse's call he hangs, like a giddy monkey, one-handed from the tree he has climbed to reach her. This sequence is one of the few moments in the film (Mercutio's Queen Mab speech is another) where Zeffirelli allows

Shakespeare's language equal billing with action, camera movement, and music. Zeffirelli found a film language and landscape that made Shakespeare's text fresh and available to a contemporary film audience, and in the process he produced a Shakespeare film that spoke as meaningfully to its turbulent era as Olivier's *Henry V* did on the eve of the Allied invasion of France in 1944.

Zeffirelli's final Shakespeare film, *Hamlet*, released in 1990, was an attempt to mingle and merge his reliance on Hollywood stars from *Taming*, his romantic approach to Shakespearean material, and his personal and cultural debt to Laurence Olivier. *Hamlet* is not a natural fit for Zeffirelli's romantic Italian style and his operatic aesthetic. In traditional readings, Hamlet is a melancholy Dane, an ironic intellectual rather than a passionate firebrand. The play, on stage and film, has most often been told in dark shades—whether in Olivier's or Kozintsev's black and white photography, both heavily dependent on chiaroscuro to establish landscape and atmosphere, or in Tony Richardson's and Michael Almereyda's Technicolor versions, the first dominated by muted amber and burgundy tones and the second by the cold blues and grays of Manhattan's glass and steel skyscrapers.

Zeffirelli takes another approach. He retains Olivier's cold dark stone castle (though he shot exteriors on location rather than in the studio), but he frequently lets the sun break through the Danish mist. He carries Olivier's Freudian subtext into the visual center of his film by making the relationship between Glenn Close's Gertrude and Mel Gibson's Hamlet (actors relatively close in age) the central story in his treatment of Shakespeare's play. By casting Close and Gibson, two of Hollywood's biggest stars, Zeffirelli was not only appropriating their box-office appeal but insisting, as Kenneth Branagh's films of the period also demonstrated, that American film actors were more than capable of handling Shakespeare's verse on screen. Zeffirelli was also aware that his approach to the Hamlet-Gertrude relationship, given his stars' most recent films, would lead witty viewers like Anthony Dawson to make the natural connections: "Lethal weapon meets fatal attraction in what turns out to be a dangerous liaison."[12]

12. Anthony Dawson, Hamlet *in Performance* (Manchester: Manchester University Press, 1996), p. 205.

Though Zeffirelli draws on Hollywood conventions in his film, his primary source for organizing his material is the world of opera. Glenn Close becomes the film's great diva. Her blond, blue-eyed, radiant Gertrude is at the center of the film. She mesmerizes all the men in her life with her beauty and vitality, including Ian Holm's pedantic Polonius. This version of *Hamlet* is not about fathers and sons, or sons and lovers, but about mothers and sons. Alan Bates's Claudius is not a powerful and cunning politician but a shifty-eyed satyr moved to murder less for the crown than for the queen. Paul Scofield's brilliant Ghost is shocking only in his naturalism; he is an exhausted, baggy-eyed old man drained not only of his life but also of his anger and command. Gibson's Hamlet is centrally concerned only with his mother, and their showdown comes in their famous encounter after the chaotic interruption of the performance of "The Mousetrap."

Zeffirelli bathes Gertrude's bedroom in a golden glow that emanates as much from Close's face and hair (down and fully displayed for the first time in the film) as from the fire that blazes in her immense fireplace. Passion and violence infuse the encounter between mother and son. Hamlet threatens Gertrude with his sword, rams it into Polonius through the arras, and later straddles his mother and thrusts away at her in a terrifying mock rape to the rhythm of the text's ugliest image: "Nay but to live / In the rank sweat of an enseamed bed / Stewed in corruption, honeying and making love / Over the nasty sty!" (3.4.82–84).

As Hamlet hammers away at Gertrude, Close finally pulls Gibson into a passionate kiss meant not only to silence his aggression but to express her own repressed longings as well. This embrace, not the intrusion of the ghostly authorial father, is the climax of the scene. In Zeffirelli's reading of the play, the murder of Polonius and the simulated rape of Gertrude have made Hamlet an errant knave and allowed him a perspective from which, finally, to understand, share, and forgive his mother's flawed humanity. By enacting the ugly image that has both disgusted and transfixed him, Hamlet has freed its powerful hold on his imagination. When he leaves, he gives Gertrude his chain with the locket of his father's picture in it, and she signals her acceptance of their new compact by tucking the locket away as Claudius enters the room.

Hamlet (Mel Gibson) and Gertrude (Glenn Close) in passionate conflict in Franco Zeffirelli's *Hamlet* (1990, Warner Bros.).

The climactic duel that ends the film is less about Hamlet and Laertes or Hamlet and Claudius than about Hamlet and Gertrude. She is the golden seraphic mother dressed in virgin blue, her hair now arranged in two long braids. Gibson plays the scene as the vigorous, clownish son, mocking, for his mother's delight, the machismo of the duel. There is no suspicious anxiety on either of their faces in the repeated **cross-cutting** Zeffirelli makes between Gibson and Close as the duel progresses. Hamlet even signals one of his physical jokes with a wink, directed not to us, but to his mother. Gertrude collapses from the poisoned wine at the moment Hamlet receives his fatal hit. She dies in an ugly parody of orgasm, her powerful sexuality having helped to lead her quartet of male admirers (Old Hamlet, Polonius, Claudius, and Hamlet) to dusty death.

Zeffirelli's three Shakespeare films span the transition in the genre from the age of Olivier and Welles to the age of Branagh. If Kurosawa and Kozintsev accomplished a brilliant translation of Shakespeare into cultural traditions at a vast remove from his Elizabethan roots, Zeffirelli helped to bring the Shakespeare film from the art house to the modern cineplex, where the genre discovered it could compete with conventional Hollywood films.

Kurosawa, Kozintsev, and Zeffirelli made six of their eight Shakespeare films in the great international flowering of the genre after World War II. They provided the Shakespeare film with new landscapes, new energies, and new audiences. Unfortunately, the commercial success of Zeffirelli's *Romeo and Juliet* was not sustained by the next two major Shakespeare films to appear, Peter Brook's bleak *King Lear* (1970) and Roman Polanski's bloody *Macbeth* (1971), and suddenly the genre was once again poison to film producers. In the two decades between Polanski's *Macbeth* and Branagh's *Henry V* (1989), only four Shakespeare films were released. However, television stepped into this vacuum in screen Shakespeare and provided the twentieth century's most comprehensive attempt to realize Shakespeare on the tube.

4

LONG SHOT

Shakespeare and Television

Though television and film appear to be similar media, in fact they are radically different art forms. Film grew out of still photography where the frame and the image are central; television developed from radio where the word predominates. The director is the key player in the world of film, while the writer (or, more accurately, writers) dominates in the world of the television series. Consequently, television Shakespeare has given greater emphasis to his words by rarely trimming his text in the radical manner of most screenplays; it has provided more opportunities for the actors to control the performance rather than the director; and it has brought Shakespeare into an arena of mass entertainment even more widespread and accessible than the world of film, at least before the advent of video and DVD. The pace of televised Shakespeare is more leisurely and static than that of film, where the camera is much more mobile, the editing process more complex and powerful, and the budgets more generous.

There have been three basic forms of televised Shakespeare. The first creates a production unique to television and is usually shot in a television studio; the second moves a highly successful stage production of a Shakespeare play into a television studio, where it is modified for the medium and then recorded for broadcast; the third records (or sometimes even simulcasts, as is frequent in the world of opera) a stage production before a live audience in the theater where it originated. The early attempts to perform Shakespeare on television in the 1950 and 60s as well as the British Broadcasting Company's effort to create television productions of Shakespeare's entire dramatic canon in the 1970s and 80s fell largely in the first category. The second category contains television versions of successful stage productions produced by England's Royal Shakespeare Company and the National Theater and America's New York Public Theater, which began its life as the New York Shakespeare Festival. The third category features prominent examples from Stratford, Canada's Shakespeare Festival Theatre, the New York Shakespeare Festival, and the English Shakespeare Company.

Though there are interesting examples of televised Shakespeare from all three categories, several of which I will explore in greater detail in later sections of this chapter, the most successful productions have most often come from the second category: successful stage productions that have been moved into a studio and recorded for broadcast. The reasons for this are multiple. Most significantly, these were productions that had already found an audience and attracted attention. By the time the productions were moved into a studio and recorded for television, they had had a long theatrical run and so were confident and polished in approach and execution. Most of these productions were conceived by veteran Shakespearean directors (Trevor Nunn, Michael Bogdanov, and Richard Eyre) who were working with experienced repertory company actors long familiar with Shakespeare. As an added bonus, several of these productions, most significantly Trevor Nunn's *Macbeth* (1979) and *Othello* (1991) and Richard Eyre's *King Lear* (1998), were initially performed in small playing spaces seating fewer than two hundred, so they already had been imagined on a small scale and had achieved an intimacy that nicely suited a transfer to television's small screen.

Early History of Shakespeare on Television

The history of Shakespeare on television begins, as does Shakespeare on film, in London. In early 1937, the British Broadcasting Corporation (BBC) transmitted the first televised Shakespeare. The excerpt was from *As You Like It,* and the segment lasted eleven minutes. The BBC made several other attempts to transmit bits of Shakespeare via television in the late 1930s before World War II intervened and closed down the experiments.[1]

1. See Kenneth Rothwell's chapter on "Electronic Shakespeare" in his *A History of Shakespeare on Screen* (Cambridge: Cambridge University Press, 1999), pp. 95–124, for a more detailed history of the early years of Shakespeare on television.

Not surprisingly, Shakespeare on television was back in business as soon as the war ended. The Allied triumph over Germany and Japan released a celebration of Anglo-American cultural values that was displayed in arts festivals springing up in England, America, and Europe. The proliferation of summer Shakespeare festivals across North America (the most famous being the Shakespeare Festival Theatre in Stratford, Canada) dates from this postwar period, as does the golden age of international Shakespeare on film, inspired by the work of Laurence Olivier and Orson Welles.

As Shakespeare was being claimed as prime cultural capital in postwar Britain and America, so too was he claimed by the newly emerging television industry. Like film, television appropriated Shakespeare as a means of elevating its cultural status. According to Kenneth Rothwell, from 1947 to 1978 the BBC telecast "over sixty performances of individual plays, in whole or in part, and a complete run of the English and Roman history plays as mini-series. Only such notoriously unpopular titles as *Henry VIII*, *Titus Andronicus*, and *Pericles* got neglected."[2]

In 1978, the BBC launched a massive project to produce and televise all of Shakespeare's plays. Unlike American networks, the BBC was largely free from corporate sponsorship at the time. Not only was it funded by an annual licensing fee assessed on all television set owners in England, but it had also held a monopoly for decades, giving it the freedom to produce programming without competition. (Once commercial channels were introduced in the 1980s, and then cable television in the 1990s, the BBC began to resemble an American network more than a completely independent enterprise.) But in planning its Shakespeare project, the BBC wanted also to air the series on America's Public Broadcasting System, so it sought corporate sponsorship from Exxon, the Morgan Guarantee Trust Company, and Metropolitan Life. The American rights to the series were eventually purchased by Time Life. The BBC produced and telecast five or six productions each year from 1978 to 1985.

American television was also eager to get into the Shakespeare business. In the early years of American television, programs like *Play-*

---

2. Ibid., p. 95.

house 90, Omnibus, Studio One, and the Hallmark Hall of Fame broadcast original or adapted dramas live on a weekly basis. Many film stars like Paul Newman, Ben Gazzara, Rip Torn, Rod Steiger, and Eva Marie Saint got their start acting in these televised dramas in the 1950s. American television's most ambitious extended attempt to tackle Shakespeare also came in this period.

Maurice Evans was a modestly successful British stage actor who immigrated to New York in the 1930s and found success playing Shakespeare, especially *Macbeth* and *Hamlet,* on Broadway. When World War II broke out Evans became an American citizen and joined the Army, where he worked in its entertainment unit performing for the troops. There he met and collaborated with the Broadway director, George Schaefer. After the war, the two men teamed up and between them produced nine Shakespeare plays for television (including Cole Porter's *Kiss Me, Kate,* an adaptation of *The Taming of the Shrew*) under the sponsorship of the Hallmark Greeting Card Company. All were telecast as part of the Hallmark Hall of Fame series and seven productions— *Hamlet, Macbeth* (twice), *Richard II, The Taming of the Shrew, Twelfth Night,* and *The Tempest*—were broadcast between 1953 and 1970.

All the productions were performed on studio sets and televised live (except the 1960 *Macbeth* and 1970 *Hamlet,* shot as films on location in Scotland and England). Because studio television has little **depth of field** and lacks film's ability to employ the resources of a fluid camera, television directors have to discover a meaningful way to capture the actor in space, and to create a setting that seems appropriate for the unfolding of the particular universe of any Shakespearean play. Schaefer's early efforts in *Hamlet, Macbeth,* and *Richard II* were stilted, as the plays were placed against quasi-realistic backgrounds that rather obviously revealed themselves as painted sets. As Michael Anderegg reports, the three comedies Schaefer produced were more successful, perhaps because Schaefer changed designers for those productions so that Richard Sylbert's "elaborate and crowded sets gave way to Rouben Ter-Arutunian's clean and minimalist designs."[3]

Schaefer also understood that television's three camera setup meant that most of the dialogue would be shot in medium **close-up**

---

3. Quoted in Michael Anderegg, *Cinematic Shakespeare* (Lanham, MD: Rowman and Littlefield, 2004), p. 152.

with sustained attention given to one or two actors captured in the frame. This places a premium on the actor's ability to command our attention with the camera in tight on his performance. Maurice Evans and his powerful co-star in the *Macbeth* productions, Judith Anderson, were trained as classical stage actors and were accustomed to projecting voice and gesture to the rear seats of the theater. Unfortunately, such rhetorical power and vocal intonation lose their impact when delivered in close-up. Evans and Anderson were lauded in the 1950s for bringing Shakespeare, their classical British training, and the legitimacy of the stage to television, but their performances often strike today's audiences as artificial and old-fashioned.

The Tempest was the most successful of the Schaefer-Evans collaborations. Prospero fit Evans's acting style and persona; playing master and magus came to him with greater ease than did lending his sonorities to the quicksilver passions of either Hamlet or Macbeth. Rouben Ter-Arutunian's open stylized set, distinguished by gauze-like silk curtains that could shimmer in the island's breezes, expressed the play's fairy-tale and romance qualities and provided the production with a symbolic landscape where one's imagination could be engaged, rather than constricted by papier-mâché realism. The production also featured Schaefer's best cast, with the young American actress Lee Remick playing a winsome Miranda, Roddy McDowall bringing some prickly bite to his Ariel, and Richard Burton portraying a growling Caliban, sporting a turtle's carapace and a false nose Laurence Olivier would have been proud to wear.[4]

Television Shakespeare in America: Joseph Papp

The other major American attempt to televise Shakespeare had a very different origin and agenda from the Schaefer-Evans Hallmark Hall of

---

4. *The Tempest* has inspired the most radical screen translations of all of Shakespeare's plays. We have wonderful spin-offs like Fred Wilcox's *Forbidden Planet* (1956) and Paul Mazursky's *Tempest* (1981) and brilliant personal versions of the text from Derek Jarman (1980) and Peter Greenaway (1990), but we have no single film or television adaptation of the play that is ideally suited for use in the traditional Shakespeare course.

Fame productions. In the early 1950s, producer Joseph Papp began a long labor of love to bring Shakespeare to the many cultures of New York City. Papp was born into a poor Jewish family in Brooklyn, and he came to believe that Shakespeare was a great popular playwright and that he could and did speak in many different accents to New York's huge multiracial population. Papp's initial dream, to bring the Bard from Broadway to the Boroughs, later expanded to invite all New Yorkers into Central Park each summer for free Shakespeare productions. Papp thus continued and enlarged the postwar emphasis on festival Shakespeare. Papp wanted Shakespeare to resemble New York's multiracial audiences, and he inaugurated, in the 50s and 60s, race-blind casting policies—several decades in advance of their adoption in the American and British theater. Papp cast actors like James Earl Jones, Gloria Foster, and Raul Julia in his Shakespeare productions, and they opened the doors for others who followed, like Denzel Washington and Morgan Freeman.

Papp was outraged at American corporate sponsorship for the BBC Shakespeare series, believing that that money should have been devoted to backing American productions of Shakespeare. As a result he arranged for CBS, and later PBS, to televise several of his New York Public Theater's Shakespeare productions: *Much Ado about Nothing* (1973), *King Lear* (1974), *A Midsummer Night's Dream* (1982), and *Hamlet* (1990). *Much Ado*, set at the turn of the nineteenth century with the soldiers returning from the Spanish-American War, was originally staged in Central Park; because of its popularity, it transferred to Broadway for a successful run, and then it moved into a studio to be reimagined for television. *Hamlet*, directed by and starring Kevin Kline, began as a stage production at Papp's indoor Public Theater at Astor Place and then was adapted to be shown on PBS's Great Performances Series. *Lear* and *Dream* were taped for television during live performances at Central Park's Delacourt Theater.

These productions reveal the vast range of choices available for producing Shakespeare, both in casting and in directorial interpretation, and also illustrate several of the standard options for presenting Shakespeare on television. A chief distinction between these productions and those of the Hallmark Hall of Fame and BBC series is that each of Papp's productions originated on stage and had already proved to be popular with audiences before it was adapted for television.

(They share this pre-tested quality with the English productions directed by Trevor Nunn and Richard Eyre that are discussed later in this chapter.) Papp's *Much Ado about Nothing*, directed on stage by A. J. Antoon, wraps itself up in a particularly American version of populism defined by patriotic pride celebrated by festive parades and picnics on the fourth of July.

The production set the play in the recognizable landscape of small-town America circa 1900, with the action moving in and around Victorian houses, bandstands, gazebos, fishing ponds, boathouses, and barber shops. Kathleen Widdoes's Beatrice, sneaking a cigarette on Antonio's porch, was conceived as an early American suffragette, and Sam Waterston's Benedick, with a wonderfully droopy mustache, had something of the swagger and dress of that most famous of American Rough Riders, Teddy Roosevelt. Dogberry and the Watch were translated into a version of Mack Sennett's Keystone Cops. The production's colors were bright and bold, featuring yellows, reds, and blues. Bunting hung from the village bandstand and balloons danced in the air. The music, following the period, was a mix of banjo and marching band, and giddy high spirits prevailed. Don John was a droll one-note villain who expressed his ferocious rigidity by pounding out chopsticks on the piano.

The camera gave us enough long shots to vividly establish time and place while still finding private nooks and crannies of the Victorian environment (Leonato's garden room for the baiting of Beatrice; a rowboat and upturned camp canoe for Benedick's similar entrapment; a barber's chair for Benedick's purging of mustache and pride as he prepares to woo Beatrice) to close in on Beatrice and Benedick's comic self-disclosures. The production moved at a swift pace—to the point of speeding up the action in fast-forward, as in early silent films, when the Watch goes into its Keystone Kops chase routine. While many found the production's obvious high spirits and comic inventiveness engaging, some resisted its charms, including the discerning performance critic H. R. Coursen, who dismissed the production by saying it "demolishes Shakespeare's play very effectively, but it leaves in its place a cultural disaster."[5]

5. "Anachronism and Papp's *Much Ado*," in *Shakespeare on Television* (Hanover: University Press of New England, 1988), ed. J. C. Bulman and H. R. Coursen, p. 151.

James Earl Jones as King Lear in the New York Shakespeare Theater's television production of *King Lear* recorded live in Central Park (1974, Thirteen/WNET New York,
Theater in America).

Papp's *King Lear*, directed by Edwin Sherin, revealed another approach to televised Shakespeare. In this instance, the production employed a number of television cameras to capture a live performance
of the play. Sherin was determined to make the audience an important
presence both on the screen and soundtrack. We hear its laughter at
Edmund's boasts and the fool's wit, and its shock when Lear's destructive energies are first released against his daughters. The camera
intentionally included some members of the audience in shots to give
us a feeling in our isolated living rooms of being part of a larger theatrical experience. One camera caught the action from the rear of the
thrust stage, so that from its perspective we shared the actor's point of
view. These shots also provided us with a sense of surrounding the action rather than being fixed to the single perspective of the stage audience. In Papp's *A Midsummer Night's Dream*, director Emile Ardolino
followed Sherin's pattern in *King Lear* by including the audience (and

in this case the New York City skyline looming beyond the Delacourt Theater as well) in its, as H. R. Coursen notes, "splendid establishing shot in which the camera roved down across the settling audience to the stage."[6]

Kevin Kline's *Hamlet*, played on a simple wooden platform surrounded by arched walls, concentrated on the **metatheatrical** elements in the play itself. The television production, directed by Kurt Browning, was shot in a studio in a minimalist style following the stage production's bare design, with many close-ups to focus as much on the text as on the action. The cast was strong and featured a canny Polonius from Joseph Sommers and Diane Venora's edgy Ophelia.[7] The Papp productions are an eclectic mix, but at their best they reveal the energy, imagination, and risk-taking that distinguish American television productions of Shakespeare.

Television Shakespeare in England: The BBC Series

The BBC Shakespeare Series was an ambitious project developed in the mid-1970s to create television productions of all thirty-seven of Shakespeare's plays and to broadcast them, at the rate of five or six a year, from 1978 to 1985. The series was conceived by Cedric Messina, a long-time producer of drama for the BBC, who supervised the initial productions. He was succeeded by Jonathan Miller, an experienced director of Shakespeare in the theater, and the series was concluded by Shawn Sutton, another veteran BBC producer. The series was an attempt to unite three British cultural powers: British classical actors, Shakespeare, and the BBC. As Susan Willis reports, the series aimed to be "gloriously British and gloriously BBC."[8] The series was a glorious commercial success: the rights were sold worldwide before the first productions were even shot. And the productions have had a powerful

---

6. Ibid., p. 284.
7. Venora has the distinction of being the first actress to play all three roles of Hamlet (for Papp's theater in 1982), Ophelia, and Gertrude (in Michael Almereyda's film of the play).
8. Quoted in Susan Willis, *The BBC Shakespeare Plays: Making the Televised Canon* (Chapel Hill: University of North Carolina Press, 1991), p. 5.

educational afterlife as they have been widely adopted by academic institutions across the world, allowing students to see Shakespeare in performance as they study the plays. But many of the productions did not meet with critical approval.

Why was the series so uneven in its achievements? One problem is that the producers were conservative in their interpretations, dictating that the productions must be set in a period that would be recognizable to Shakespeare, that the text could be trimmed only marginally, and that all the productions would be produced by the BBC rather than having some co-produced by the Royal Shakespeare Company, the National Theatre, or lively London fringe companies. Further, as Susan Willis points out in her comprehensive history of the series, no sustained, communal thought was given to what might be called "best practices" for creating effective Shakespeare on television. Deciding those strategies, within the general rules the BBC had established for setting and text, was left up to each individual director.

As a result, over the years, the productions tended to fall into three modes—the realistic, the pictorial, and the stylized—without ever discovering which one best suited the medium. Several of the realistic productions were shot on location (*As You Like It*, 1978, and *Henry VIII*, 1979) but most were performed in period sets created for the television studio. Tight budgets prevented those sets from being as expensive and elaborate as audiences were accustomed to from films, and so they had the effect of destroying the realistic illusion the sets were intended to convey. The pictorial mode took one step away from realism by locating the scenic inspiration for the production in a famous classical painting. Vermeer and Veronese, for instance, were the visual sources for Jonathan Miller's 1980 productions of *The Taming of the Shrew* and *Antony and Cleopatra*. The stylistic mode took an even further step away from representation into abstraction. Jane Howell's productions of *1, 2,* and *3 Henry VI* (1981, 1981, 1982) and *Richard III* (1982) were performed against a single unitary set resembling a thrust stage playing space rather than a realistic landscape.

Some individual productions sustained interest in approach, delivery, and performance—Derek Jacobi's performances in the title roles of *Hamlet* (1980) and *Richard II* (1978) were highly lauded, for example. But the most successful productions turned out to be of Shakespeare plays less well known to the general public: *Measure for Measure* (1979),

Henry VIII (1979), *The Winter's Tale* (1980), *1, 2,* and *3 Henry VI* (1983), and *Coriolanus* (1984). Desmond Davis's *Measure for Measure* was distinguished by Kate Nelligan's fine performance of Isabella. Nelligan is an accomplished actor on both stage and screen and she knew how to underplay for the tight focus of the television camera. She was well matched by Tim Pigott-Smith's Angelo, who caught the character's sharp mix of hypocrisy and emotional vulnerability. The two great scenes between Angelo and Isabella crackled with repressed energy and tension.

Henry VIII, directed by Kevin Billington, was shot on location in several castles (Hever, Penshurst, and Leeds) where the historical characters in Shakespeare's plays had either lived or visited. The particular use Billington made of these locations served Shakespeare's text well. As critic Peter Saccio observed:

> The televised *Henry VIII* is largely governed by a contract between public scenes with the king and private colloquies among two or three lords or the two gentlemen who serve as semi-narrators. These private scenes are usually shot in passageways, on staircases, in tunnel-like arcades . . . they are employed so consistently [as] to become metaphorical. These are the cunning corridors of history, to be punctuated occasionally by public display.[9]

The costumes were rich and the acting—especially by John Stride (Henry), Timothy West (Wolsey), Claire Bloom (Katherine), and Ronald Pickup (Granmer)—was solid. The only problem, according to critic Jack Jorgens, was Shakespeare himself, for his script had weaknesses that were "all too apparent to a public television audience which has seen other versions of the story of Henry and his wives, versions that take much better advantage of the historical material."[10]

Jane Howell was one of the most experienced television directors invited to work on the series, and she ended up directing six productions: *1, 2,* and *3 Henry VI, Richard III, Titus Andronicus,* and *The Winter's Tale.* Howell moved the design of the productions away from the

9. *Shakespeare on Television,* p. 211.
10. Ibid., p. 256.

realistic and representational and into the world of symbol and style. Her productions of the first tetralogy were played on a simple unitary set as far from the actual castles used in *Henry VIII* as imaginable. Her set for *The Winter's Tale* was appropriately white and cold, distinguished by a series of symbolic pyramids and cones, letting us know we were in the fairy-tale world of romance while the abstract design promised the unexpected in human behavior. Though television is noted for its lack of depth of field, Howell managed to place Leontes strategically close to the camera as he and we watch Hermione and Polixenes sharing a joke in the rear of the frame—so that we share Leontes's perspective as his wild jealousy puts him in the grip of "tremor cordis." Of the many directors in the BBC series, Howell was one of the most consistently successful at developing a style that best suited Shakespeare on television.

To examine some of the problems that beset other productions in the series, particularly those in the realistic and pictorial modes, let's look at *Julius Caesar* (1979) and *Antony and Cleopatra* (1980). Like *Romeo and Juliet*, *Julius Caesar* was a staple of the high school English curriculum; unfortunately, it offered little to command the attention of a young school-age audience. The production was musty, from the painted backdrops and Roman columns to the unimaginative and stilted camera work, where five or six actors suggested a crowd or a camera would linger on the back of an actor's head just so he could make an unnatural pivot to speak directly into the lens. The actors struggled to find an effective means of delivering public oratory in the smaller, more private medium of television. In the camera's eye, the sets became flattened and reduced to cardboard, so that the viewer's eye was distracted rather than engaged. Rome became a diminished rather than dynamic presence in the production.

Antony and Cleopatra debuted four years after *Julius Caesar*, when Jonathan Miller had taken over as producer of the series. Miller found his inspiration, and his answer to the BBC dictum that the plays should be set in an age recognizable to Shakespeare, at London's National Gallery of Art. Miller inaugurated what has come to be known as the pictorial or "painterly" style in televised Shakespeare as a substitute for realism as the guiding design aesthetic of the series.

Miller based his costumes and set designs for his production of *Antony and Cleopatra* (1980) on Veronese's Renaissance painting *The*

Family of Darius at the Feet of Alexander, which hangs prominently in the National Gallery. This decision led Miller to approach Shakespeare's explosive, subversive, adulterous love story with classical Roman restraint. Miller's version is formal, even chaste, as Antony and Cleopatra rarely touch and never kiss—even when the text tells them to—until Antony's dying moments. The production makes no distinction in landscape or atmosphere between Egypt and Rome (a contrast that Shakespeare builds, at every opportunity, into the fabric of the play's poetry). The same blue velvet drapes, similar Renaissance costumes, and typical Baroque music (chiefly violin and cello) are used to create both worlds. While this overturns production stereotypes and allows Miller to slip radical ideas about Shakespeare's play into its "safe" Renaissance setting, it also works unhappily against Shakespeare's contrasting textual images of Rome and Egypt, Caesar and Cleopatra, to have Antony and Enobarbus welcomed in Rome to a meal far more lavish than anything they encounter in Egypt.

The production's central performances, too, presented images counter to the text. Jane Lapotaire's Cleopatra is thin and angular with an ironic, mocking intelligence but little sex appeal. There's nothing exotic or "other" about her; with her hair up, a choker of pearls at her neck, and matching earrings, she bears little relationship to Shakespeare's Cleopatra, who is "with Phoebus' amorous pinches black / And wrinkled deep in time" (1.5.28–29). Lapotaire's Cleopatra is a Renaissance princess, not an Egyptian queen.

Miller's determination to reduce Cleopatra's hyperbolic appeal leads him to undercut the viewpoint of that keen Roman observer, Enobarbus (Emrys James), who refuses to follow Caesar in finding Cleopatra a strumpet and whore. James brilliantly resolves this by making his Enobarbus a garrulous old windbag who is always sticking his nose in other people's business—particularly in the confrontation between Antony and Caesar in Rome—where he repeatedly squeezes himself into the frame to give his unwelcome advice. James appropriates the camera, speaking directly to us like an old gossip rather than as Antony's trusted lieutenant and friend. This comic approach to the character is an inventive means of discounting Enobarbus's Egyptian enthusiasms and his intimate knowledge of Antony's fatal attraction to Cleopatra, but it is at odds with the tragic manner in which Shakespeare has this honest Roman earn a place in the story.

Miller's pictorial production of *Antony and Cleopatra* is emblematic of his work for the series: intellectually fascinating but dramatically perverse. Jane Howell's productions, as mentioned earlier, broke away from both the realistic and pictorial models by creating settings that were more abstract and symbolic, where the action could unfold, much as on an open **thrust stage** like the Globe's, driven by language rather than landscape. That said, there were successful productions in the BBC series in each style, perhaps indicating that outstanding productions are less the result of design than the imaginative collaboration between director and cast.

Televised Shakespeare Produced by Repertory Companies

As with the case of televised Shakespeare in America, some of the best English productions grew out of highly successful stage versions of the plays and were often, perhaps unsurprisingly, produced by three of England's major repertory acting companies: the National Theatre (NT), the Royal Shakespeare Company (RSC); and the English Shakespeare Company (ESC). These include Jonathan Miller's National Theatre (NT) production of *The Merchant of Venice* (1974) starring Laurence Olivier as Shylock; Trevor Nunn's Royal Shakespeare Company productions of *Antony and Cleopatra* (1975), *The Comedy of Errors* (1978), *Macbeth* (1979), and *Othello* (1990), and his NT production of *The Merchant of Venice* (2001); Richard Eyre's NT Production of *King Lear* (1998); and the English Shakespeare Company's cycle of Shakespeare's histories, known collectively as *The Wars of the Roses* (1989), directed by Michael Bogdanov.

Several of Trevor Nunn's productions illustrate the often happy relationship between successful stage versions of the plays moved into the television studio and imaginatively captured for the small screen—for instance, *Antony and Cleopatra*. The play is huge, with the action expanding from Rome to the eastern frontier of its empire. One might think that such expanse could not be realized within the small confines of the television screen. Nunn's production proved otherwise. Rather than using elaborate backdrops, which can fall flat on the small screen, he hints at locale, evoking a sense of place rather than defining it. He conceived of Egypt as golden and languorous, less a specific place than a state of mind. Cleopatra's palace could be either tent or barge, defined by oriental rugs, gigantic yellow and brown cushions, transparent curtains in yellow and white, and the loose, flowing caftans and burnooses worn by Cleopatra, Antony, and Enobarbus. Nunn's camera catches at Shakespeare's images of Egypt as fluid, melting, and discandying by often distorting the edges of the camera's lens so that only figures framed in the center of the shot are held in a clear focus. This creates a shimmering, hazy texture to the production's evocation of Egypt and perfectly captures Antony's inability to hold himself or Cleopatra in steady focus.

In contrast to the rich, shape-shifting textures associated with Egypt, Nunn's Rome is seen all in bright white with the camera preferring the static close-up, often framing a series of Roman faces in profile. Cleopatra's music is dominated by woodwinds and strings while Caesar's is all brass. The performances are commanding, having been polished over a season in the RSC's repertory. Janet Suzman's Cleopatra has the proper "tawny front" and is both playfully erotic and politically quixotic as she seeks to have her Antony and tilt at Roman windmills as well. Richard Johnson's Antony is a large, generous, bear-like man who is by turns delighted, perplexed, and ultimately baffled by Suzman's Cleopatra. Patrick Stewart's Enobarbus, quite unlike Emrys James's, is a stable, reliable Roman guide to Egypt and to Antony's tragic decline. Nunn's intelligent and imaginative production demonstrates television's ability, in the right hands and circumstances, to successfully translate one of Shakespeare's most difficult and demanding plays into its confines by the art of suggestion rather than realistic representation.

Macbeth seems more naturally suited to such translation because of its brevity, focus, and psychological realism. Nunn's stage production of the play was conceived in the RSC's small, black-box theater, The Other Place. From its inception, the production was minimalist in design and restrained in word and action, which certainly smoothed its translation into television. The playing space was a white circle inscribed on the floor. The actors sat on benches outside the circle when they were not immediately involved in the play's action. The costumes were generic and modern without trying to define a particular historical moment. All of the characters were dressed in black except Duncan, Malcolm, and Lady Macduff, who were in white. For instance, Duncan

Lady Macbeth (Judi Dench) tries to eradicate that "damned spot" in Trevor Nunn's television production of *Macbeth* (1979, Thames TV).

wore a white robe, making him seem more clergy than king. The lighting design was also stark, with actors emerging out of the shadows into the lit playing area and then exiting once again into the shadows—nicely capturing the murky, almost hallucinogenic, nature of Macbeth's Scotland.

Ian McKellen's sharp, tense, angular Macbeth was a brilliant study in paranoia, and he was well matched by Judi Dench's repressed Lady Macbeth. They constantly touched and caressed one another, seeking a solace neither could provide. Television rarely provides images as powerful as film's, but the close-up of Macbeth's bloody hands dancing before McKellen's face on "What hands are here? Ha! They pluck out mine eyes!" (2.2.57) rivets itself in the viewer's imagination, as does Dench's agonizing scream at the climax of Lady Macbeth's own attempt to cleanse hand and mind, discovering that "all the perfumes of Arabia will not sweeten this little hand" (5.1.53–55).

Nunn's *Othello*, a decade later, also originated in The Other Place, though in a production that was more minutely detailed in props and setting than his more abstract *Macbeth*. The setting suggested the Civil War period in America. We were in a decidedly military world—even in the first act's Senate scene, here imagined as a war room with the duke and senators (except for Brabantio) all dressed in military uniforms resembling those of Yankee soldiers. Nunn set the action around a series of small tables until the final catastrophe where the bed was the central focus of the action. In the Senate scene, the duke received dispatches about the Turks while seated at a round table covered in green felt and loaded with papers, maps, a brandy decanter, and a cigar box. This was a male, military world where Othello, in his magnificent blue uniform studded with silver buttons, was in command. Brabantio's paternal and racist hysteria about Othello's marriage to Desdemona was quickly routed.

Willard White, a great opera singer with little experience as a stage actor, was an imposing Othello, and one determined to constrain his rage once Iago's poison began to do its work. The small screen, like the claustrophobic space of The Other Place, did not allow him the distance to really let rip when his Othello finally exploded. White seemed like a caged bull driven to distraction by Iago's prods and pricks, but he never escaped his cage by a devastating rampage. Iago, in the sure hands of Ian McKellen, dominated the production on stage and screen. His Iago was a repressed psychopath whose envy of Othello was driven as much by class as by race. Iago was the stereotypical noncommissioned officer, always fixing things for others while lining his own pockets. The performance was a dazzling combination of tiny details: McKellen pinching cigars from the Duke's humidor in 1.2, returning half-smoked cigars to a tin he carried in his tunic's breast pocket, efficiently arranging (and stage managing) the drunken brawl in the barracks that brings Cassio down, and giving Emilia an ugly kiss as a reward for swiping Desdemona's handkerchief. McKellen builds his chilling portrait from these details and through his understated irony delivered directly to the camera.

The production creates a harrowing version of 5.2 where Othello first strangles and then smothers Desdemona. Othello enters dressed, for the first time, in a white burnoose trimmed in brown, suggesting a return, in his tragic dislocation as husband and general, to his proud

African roots. The camera repeatedly captures Othello through the steel bars of the bed he shares with Desdemona, indicating his imprisonment not only by his jealousy but his own deluded sense of himself as the defender of his adopted culture. Imogen Stubbs's Desdemona is passionate and playful, and her resistance to Othello's threats is heroic. She refuses to play the passive victim but exhibits the same independent spirit in physically opposing Othello's violence as she once demonstrated in loving him.

When Othello finally subdues and then smothers Desdemona, he does so in a frightening parody of sexual consummation. He straddles his wife on their bed as he kills her, and they enact Shakespeare's version of the ancient fellowship of sex and death so potent in the Western imagination. The last image we see is Othello and Desdemona alone together on their fatal wedding sheets with Iago standing at the foot of the bed, staring at his handiwork.

Trevor Nunn has commented that making a Shakespeare film requires "shooting the action," but translating Shakespeare from stage to television involves "shooting the text."[11] His television productions of Shakespeare demonstrate that "shooting the text" can work when the text is given a context appropriate for the medium and is performed by actors deeply familiar with the material through repeated performances.

There has been little interest in England in following Joseph Papp's example of recording a successful stage production for television before a live audience. A major exception is Michael Bogdanov's epic cycle of Shakespeare's English history plays produced under the title *The Wars of the Roses* (1989).

Bogdanov and the actor Michael Pennington created the English Shakespeare Company in 1986 with the intention of creating a touring company that would bring Shakespeare to Britain's second- and third-tier cities without theater companies of their own. They began with productions of 1 and 2 *Henry IV* and *Henry V* that proved to be hugely popular, especially with the young. In subsequent years (1987–89),

---

11. Nunn is quoted in an interview about his film of *Twelfth Night* in *cahiers elisabehains* 52 (October, 1997), p. 89. For more on the film/television contrast in producing Shakespeare see Michèle Willems, "Video and Its Paradoxes," in *The Cambridge Companion to Shakespeare on Film* (Cambridge: Cambridge University Press, 2000), ed. Russell Jackson, pp. 35–46.

buoyed by their initial success, they added *Richard II*, a two-play condensation of *1, 2,* and *3 Henry VI* (*The House of Lancaster* and *The House of York*), and *Richard III*, thus making a complete cycle of Shakespeare's plays covering the English civil wars from the fall of Richard II in 1399 to the rise of Richmond (Henry VII) in 1485.

Bogdanov is the great stage champion of Shakespeare scholar Jan Kott's mid-twentieth-century dictum that Shakespeare is our contemporary. He set the plays on a largely bare stage with a steel superstructure at the sides and rear, from which could be draped the red and white flag of St. George (for court scenes) or sheets and carpets (for the tavern scenes) to suggest landscape. The actors were costumed in twentieth-century garb, ranging from the Edwardian period (formal morning court and striped trousers for Henry IV) to the Thatcher present (pin-striped suits for Richard III and Buckingham) with a little Elvis (for Pistol) and a punk-rocker's Mohawk (for Gadshill) and American casual (blue jeans and denim jacket for Hal) added to the mix. The productions were irreverent and populist. They proved so popular that they toured not only England but the world, from Berlin to Tokyo to Brisbane. On the final weekend of the performance of the complete seven-play cycle, in the Grand Theatre in Swansea in Wales, they were taped for television.

Bogdanov employed seven cameras to provide a greater variety of perspectives on the action than is typical of studio television (which normally uses three or four). The productions can be taken as a challenge to the conservatism of the BBC Shakespeares in their sharp cynicism, mocking spirits, and relentless effort to make Shakespeare's history plays speak to a modern audience as much about the present as the past.

It is perhaps appropriate that Bogdanov's cheeky and radical productions should bring television's dominance in the realm of Shakespeare on screen to a close. Just as Bogdanov and his English Shakespeare Company were completing the long run of *The Wars of the Roses* in April of 1989 and taping their final performances for television, another upstart, Kenneth Branagh, was deep into postproduction work on his film of *Henry V*. Bogdanov's ambitious cycle capped the Age of Shakespeare on Television just as Branagh's film was about to spark a dazzling revival of Shakespeare on film.

5

WIDE ANGLE

The Films of the 1990s

The last decade of the twentieth century, from the fall of the Berlin
Wall to the terrorist attack on the World Trade Center, proved a rich revival for the Shakespeare film genre. Many artistic and cultural elements contributed to this renaissance, from the rise of the independent
film—spurred by the success of Steven Soderbergh's *sex, lies, and videotape* and Kenneth Branagh's *Henry V* (both released in 1989)—to a less
anxious political climate that welcomed a rash of films based on classic
literary material.

The critical success of Branagh's *Henry V*, followed quickly by the
box office success of Zeffirelli's *Hamlet* (1990) and Branagh's *Much Ado
about Nothing* (1993), challenged Hollywood's skepticism about the
commercial liabilities traditionally associated with the Shakespeare
film. Al Pacino remarked about pitching his *Looking for Richard* to potential distributors: "Branagh opened it all up with *Henry V*. Now you
say Shakespeare on film in Hollywood and people listen."[1]

Hollywood listened even more keenly after the sensational global
commercial success of Baz Luhrmann's *William Shakespeare's Romeo +
Juliet* (1996). With a budget of just $14.5 million, the film made over $46
million in the United States alone—over $147 million worldwide.
Those numbers point at one reason for the proliferation of Shakespeare films in the 1990s. In an era when the average cost of a typical
Hollywood film reached $60 million, Shakespeare films were generally
shot on budgets of $5 million to $15 million. When several garnered
box office returns three or four times larger than their costs, they became financial risks worth taking.

1. Quoted in David Rosenthal, *Shakespeare on Screen* (London: Hamlyn, 2000),
p. 215.

The Shakespeare films released in the 1990s ranged from the highly personal and idiosyncratic work of Christine Edzard (*As You Like It*, 1992, and *The Children's Midsummer Night's Dream*, 2001), made on shoestring budgets of less than $1 million, to more high-powered films such as Zeffirelli's *Hamlet* (1990), Luhrmann's *William Shakespeare's Romeo+Juliet* (1996), and Michael Hoffman's *A Midsummer Night's Dream* (1999), made with budgets approaching $20 million and loaded with Hollywood stars such as Mel Gibson, Glenn Close, Leonardo Di-Caprio, Claire Danes, Michelle Pfeiffer, and Kevin Kline.

A second reason for the proliferation of Shakespeare films in the 1990s stems from the end of the Cold War. Hollywood, momentarily released from fashioning films based on the anxieties arising from Cold War tensions, turned its attention to more subtle material based on classic British and American novels by authors as varied as Jane Austen, James Fenimore Cooper, and Henry James. Even noted directors Martin Scorsese and Francis Ford Coppola, famous for exploring the violent underside of American life, made films based on Edith Wharton's *The Age of Innocence* and Bram Stoker's *Dracula*. The 1990s brought us at least twenty major films based on Shakespeare's plays, while the seven-year period since the terrorist attacks of September 11, 2001, has seen the release of two Shakespeare films—and one of them, Kenneth Branagh's *As You Like It* (2007), was shown in America on HBO television.

Shakespeare, Hollywood, and the Cineplex

The collaboration between Shakespeare and Hollywood became a distinguishing feature of the Shakespeare films of the 1990s. Directors were no longer leery about mixing American film stars with established English stage actors in a Shakespeare project. Olivier's Shakespeare films were made with all-English casts. Welles was more adventurous in his casting (particularly in *Chimes at Midnight*) but he never used Hollywood stars. Joseph Mankiewicz was criticized for using actors from traditions as disparate as those represented by John Gielgud and Marlon Brando in his *Julius Caesar* (1953). It wasn't until 1990 that Zeffirelli made the first successful cross-Atlantic casting breakthrough in his film of *Hamlet*, where Hollywood stars like Mel

Gibson and Glenn Close more than held their own with Royal Shakespeare Company veterans such as Paul Scofield and Ian Holm. Branagh followed Zeffirelli's lead in his *Much Ado about Nothing* by casting mostly younger Hollywood stars—Michael Keaton, Denzel Washington, and Keanu Reeves—along with members of his Renaissance Theatre Company—Emma Thompson, Richard Briers, and himself. Branagh placed this American and British casting mix at the heart of his Shakespeare on film aesthetic:

> [I wanted] to find experienced Shakespearean actors who were unpracticed on screen and team them with highly experienced film actors who were much less familiar with Shakespeare. Different accents, different looks. An excitement borne out of complementary styles and approaches would produce a Shakespeare film that belonged to the world.[2]

The Shakespeare films of the 90s not only had a strong touch of Hollywood in their casting practices, but they raided the codes and conventions of popular film as well. Directors like Richard Loncraine (*Richard III*, 1995), Michael Hoffman (*A Midsummer Night's Dream*, 1999), Oliver Parker (*Othello*, 1995), and Adrian Noble (*A Midsummer Night's Dream*, 1996), along with Branagh and Baz Luhrmann, were all unapologetic about linking the Shakespeare film with such established Hollywood genres as the gangster film, the war film, film noir, the erotic thriller, screwball comedy, and the movie musical. These bold new connections gave the Shakespeare film fresh energy and made it available to a much wider audience. Luhrmann, Branagh, and Hoffman in particular captured the major fifteen- to twenty-five-year-old movie audience that had been wooed and won by only one previous Shakespeare film: Zeffirelli's *Romeo and Juliet* (1968). In the 1990s the Shakespeare film suddenly broke free from the art house audience and found itself competing with more traditional commercial movies at the cineplex.

It was a heady change and something of an ironic reversal of what had attracted film to Shakespeare a hundred years before. Then, film

---

2. Kenneth Branagh, Much Ado about Nothing: *Screenplay, Introduction, and Notes on the Making of the Movie* (New York: W. W. Norton, 1993), p. x.

producers sought to elevate film's low cultural standing by exploiting Shakespeare's high art status. In the 1990s film rescued Shakespeare from the art house and restored his plays to the great polyglot popular audience who had originally been drawn to them at the Globe Theater.

Branagh's films, in particular, borrowed from popular film genres: the war film in *Henry V*, screwball comedy in *Much Ado about Nothing*, the intelligent epic—epitomized by films like *Lawrence of Arabia, Doctor Zhivago*, and *A Passage to India*—in *Hamlet*, and the 1930s American movie musical in *Love's Labour's Lost*. Branagh's formative encounters with Shakespeare came when he was a student at London's foremost drama school, the Royal Academy of Dramatic Art (RADA), and as a young actor at the Royal Shakespeare Company (RSC). In both cases he was working in two of England's most prestigious institutions for classical actors. When he began filming *Henry V* at the age of twenty-eight, he had no formal training as a film director, nor did he have any formal experience with film tradition. He was a novice basing his work on instinct, a firm grounding in Shakespeare, and a love of the Hollywood popular films he had watched as a kid growing up in Belfast and Reading.

Henry V reveals the influence of the Vietnam War film, including Oliver Stone's *Platoon* (1984) and Stanley Kubrick's *Full Metal Jacket* (1987). Branagh himself has confessed that when "making both *Much Ado* and *Henry V*, I've been influenced by a number of movies. I know a lot of war movies, a lot of battle movies. I remember bits of Orson Welles's *Chimes at Midnight* and Kurosawa's *Ran* as also being very influential. Everything, from *The Great Escape* through *The Longest Day*, *The Magnificent Seven* . . . you name it. A whole pile of stuff I can't coherently reference. Ideas stolen from everywhere."[3] Even here Branagh is making a synthesis between past Shakespeare films, *Chimes at Midnight* and *Ran*, both featuring great battle sequences, and Hollywood war films like *The Great Escape* (1963) and *The Longest Day* (1962). In *Henry V* Branagh married the Shakespeare tradition he had absorbed at RADA and the RSC with his own instinctive understanding of the power of popular films. The marriage would go on to produce many

3. Quoted in Jon Naughton, "The Return of the Magnificent Eight," *Premiere* (September 1993), p. 48.

more offspring, making Branagh the most prolific director in the history of Shakespeare on film. Branagh continued to develop and refine his film style in subsequent Shakespearean and non-Shakespearean films, though he has not yet managed to repeat the critical and commercial success he had with his first two Shakespeare films: *Henry V* and *Much Ado about Nothing*.

Oliver Parker's *Othello* (1995) is another film that tries to make a synthesis between Hollywood and Shakespeare. Parker wants to reimagine Shakespeare's great tragedy about gender, race, and class as an erotic thriller in the mode of *Fatal Attraction* (1987). He casts two young sexy international film stars, the American Laurence Fishburne and the Swiss-French Irene Jacob, as Othello and Desdemona. Shakespeare's Othello is middle-aged, having, he confesses, "declined / Into the vale of years" (3.3 269–70), but Fishburne's Othello is young and sleek and powerful. His romance with Desdemona is sexually heightened by the film's use of **flashbacks** to their lovemaking as they celebrate Othello's arrival in Cyprus and the dispersal of the Turkish threat. The film returns to those images when Othello, prompted by Iago's suggestions, obsesses about Desdemona making love with Cassio. Parker's film visualizes this fantasy by having Cassio replace Othello in Desdemona's embrace.

Parker, like Branagh in his *Much Ado*, wanted to bring Shakespeare to a new, younger audience more attuned to the conventions of film than classical tragedy. In an interesting cultural twist, his film was made (in London and Italy) at a time when the murder trial of O. J. Simpson dominated American media. At its release in the United States, the film was quickly swallowed up in the racial, social, and sexual issues generated by Simpson's sensational trial. Some Shakespeare films, Oliver's *Henry V* and Zeffirelli's *Romeo and Juliet*, for example, emerged at just the right cultural and historic moment; others, like Mankiewicz's *Julius Caesar* and Parker's *Othello*, could not compete with, even as they commented on, the headlines of their day.

If Oliver Parker wished to link *Othello* with the Hollywood erotic thriller, Richard Loncraine found the inspiration for his film of *Richard III* in such 1930s gangster films as *Public Enemy* (1931), *Scarface* (1932), and *White Heat* (1948). Loncraine's film grew out of a noted stage production of *Richard III* at London's National Theatre (NT) directed by Richard Eyre and starring Ian McKellen. That production set the play in 1930s England, when several prominent members of the Royal Family had fascist leanings and expressed an admiration for Hitler. McKellen played Richard III and was the driving force behind wanting to make a film based on the production, but he was relatively inexperienced as a film actor (this was a decade before his Gandalf) and, unlike Branagh, he lacked the ambition or confidence to direct. Loncraine, a journeyman director more recognized for making effective television commercials than films, was recruited to direct McKellen's screenplay.

Loncraine quickly put his visual mark on the film. For Loncraine, Richard III's story was even more powerfully linked with the classic American gangster film than with 1930s fascism, yet conveniently they both were associated with the same decade. Critic James Loehlin cleverly sees that *Richard III* is an archetype of the gangster movie where the hero

> is an ambitious man who feels unfairly excluded from society . . . [and] . . . is often haunted by bitterness, shame, or some unfulfilled psychological need, usually related to his family. . . . [T]he hero has difficulties with other women; he often wins, and then neglects a beautiful wife. . . . The hero's daring and ruthlessness win him the admiration of the audience . . . [but] . . . when the hero reaches the top he begins to forfeit audience sympathy; he becomes paranoid, violent and increasingly isolated as outside forces rise against him.[4]

Loehlin's summary captures almost everything about Richard III except his savage irony and brilliant wit. The American gangster film paradigm doesn't always rest comfortably on top of the very British 1930s fascist political parallels the film also wishes to exploit, but Loncraine's *Richard III* is another provocative example of the ways in which the Shakespeare films of the 1990s were brazen in raiding Hollywood conventions and genres for inspiration.

---

4. James Loehlin, " 'Top of the World, Ma': *Richard III* and Cinematic Convention," in *Shakespeare, the Movie* (London: Routledge, 1997), ed. Lynda E. Boose and Richard Burt, pp. 73–74.

The most media-saturated film of the period, and the greatest commercial success, was Baz Luhrmann's *William Shakespeare's Romeo+Juliet*. Luhrmann's film takes Shakespeare deeper into contemporary teen culture than any other Shakespeare film. It might be the greatest teen flick ever made: a cross between *Rebel without a Cause* (1955) and *Fast Times at Ridgemont High* (1982). Luhrmann's film is loaded with the **zooms**, **slams**, and **jump cuts** that mark its opening sequence and become its cinematic signature. The film is like "watching *Romeo and Juliet* under strobe lights," as Kenneth Rothwell wryly observed.[5] Luhrmann, through the magic of film technology, creates a virtual Verona that is a dazzling mix of Miami Beach, Los Angeles, and Mexico City. The culture Luhrmann creates to contain his young lovers is not only saturated by the media but by references to Shakespeare as well. The pool hall where the Montagues hang out is called the Globe; the nearby ruined beach resort is the Sycamore Grove; the Montagues and Capulets exchange snatches of lines lifted from various Shakespeare plays in the film's opening shoot-out at the Phoenix gas station ("Double, double, toil and trouble," "pretty piece of flesh," "more fuel to the fire"); advertising billboards proclaim: The Merchant of Verona Beach, Such Stuff as Dreams Are Made On, and Shoot Forth Thunder.

Though Luhrmann is determined to translate Shakespeare so successfully into the 1990s that the historical gap separating our age from his is erased, he is also clever enough to repeatedly take his visual inspiration from elements and images in Shakespeare's text. Shakespeare opens his tale with a sonnet spoken by a choric figure and closes it with the prince's famous couplet "For never was a story of more woe / Than this of Juliet and her Romeo" (5.3.308–309). Luhrmann neatly translates Shakespeare's framing device to the present by opening and closing his film with a television newscaster reading these lines, thus absorbing Shakespeare's language (and its images) into a familiar media setting and simultaneously making Shakespeare fresh and "news."

Here Luhrmann is working with one of Shakespeare's structural devices; elsewhere he is equally alert to making good use of Shakespeare's rich verbal images. *Romeo and Juliet* is filled with water imagery, espe-

---

5. Kenneth Rothwell, *A History of Shakespeare on Screen*, 2nd ed. (Cambridge: Cambridge University Press, 2004), p. 229.

Juliet (Claire Danes) and Romeo (Leonardo DiCaprio) first spy one another through an aquarium at the Capulet's ball in Baz Luhrmann's *William Shakespeare's Romeo+Juliet* (1996, Twentieth Century Fox).

cially associated with the young lovers. Juliet declares that "My bounty is as boundless as the sea, / My love as deep" (2.1.175–76) and Romeo responds "call me but love and I'll be new baptized" (2.1.91). Luhrmann picks up on these images by introducing us to Juliet when she is submerged in her bathtub, by having Romeo first spy Juliet at the ball through the glass of a huge fish tank, and eventually playing the famous balcony scene in the Capulets' swimming pool. Water becomes an element where the lovers are able to explore their emotions and awakening passion free from the invasive tumult of the world dominated by the fatal enmity between Montague and Capulet. In fact, the encounter between Romeo and Juliet in the swimming pool is the one moment where Luhrmann slows his film's relentless pace, turns down the volume on the driving **soundtrack**, and lets his young Hollywood stars actually try to communicate *through* Shakespeare's language rather than racing away from it into action.

By contrast, Michael Hoffman's *A Midsummer Night's Dream* seeks other Hollywood models to emulate. Hoffman's film is lush, "a visual masterpiece."[6] He follows Branagh's path to Tuscany, setting Shakespeare's mix of Ovid and Warwickshire in the late nineteenth century in and around the fictional Italian hill town of Monte Athena. But Hoffman's film is influenced far more by the 1935 Warner Brothers *Dream* than by Branagh's *Much Ado*. Like Reinhardt and Dieterle, Hoffman loads his film with visual details, from the opening montage, where his camera lingers over piles of fruits, vegetables, roasting birds and boars being prepared for Theseus's wedding feast, to the final images of a Tinkerbell-esque pixie reminding Bottom of his magical experience in the woods. Hoffman, like Reinhardt and Dieterle, wants to use film's full resources to capture the imaginative dazzle of Shakespeare's incandescent poetic evocation of the woods near Athens, where fairies "seek some dewdrops here" to "hang a pearl in every cowslip's ear" (2.1.14–15).

Interestingly, while Hoffman shoots the opening scenes on location, introducing us first to Theseus and then to Bottom in natural surroundings, he then moves onto a **soundstage** at Rome's famous Cinecittá movie studio for the forest scenes. He wants to challenge Shakespeare's poetic pastiche with his own cinematic imagination, but the experiment is only partially successful. Hoffman loads his woods with an overdose of competing cinematic references. Puck (Stanley Tucci) hangs out in a fairy bar all too reminiscent of Jabba the Hutt's joint in *Return of the Jedi*; Rupert Everett's Oberon is often shot against the backdrop of huge carved Etruscan stone faces overgrown with vines and vegetation; and the bower Hoffman creates for Michelle Pfeiffer's Titania is a neo-classical gazebo that might have adorned a Hollywood starlet's swimming pool. Hoffman is right to see that

6. Ibid., p. 254.

Shakespeare, in his *Dream*, is making a poetic synthesis of widely divergent literary and theatrical traditions as he daringly deposits Ovidian gods, English folk sprites, classical heroes, bourgeois lovers, and Warwickshire workmen into the same landscape and space—but he can't quite achieve the same effect in his film. Hoffman's teeming cinematic inventiveness just doesn't know when to stop. He becomes so stimulated by Shakespeare's fine frenzy that he can't bring his own under control. Hoffman is a bit like Bottom: he wants to be the lunatic and the lover and the poet.

Two areas where his film succeeds wonderfully are in Kevin Kline's performance as Bottom and in its soundtrack. Kline joins Marlon Brando, Laurence Fishburne, and Al Pacino as Hollywood stars who have given great Shakespearean performances on film, putting to rest the common cultural assumption that only classically trained British actors can master Shakespeare. Hoffman makes good use of his late nineteenth-century Tuscan setting by incorporating Italian opera into his film score. Bottom and Company arrive in the woods to rehearse to the rousing strains of the festive "Libiamo" ("Let's Drink") from Verdi's *La Traviata*, and later Kline's Bottom will unlock the magic of the phonograph in Titania's bower by playing a recording of Bellini's "Casta Diva" ("Chaste Goddess") from *Norma*. The bel canto aria perfectly registers both Bottom's worship of this sylvan goddess and Titania's romantic rapture at his mastery of the new technology, helping to bring opera to a wider audience in late-nineteenth-century Italy just as Hoffman's film seeks a broader audience for Shakespeare a hundred years later.

Branagh, Parker, Loncraine, Luhrmann, and Hoffman all infuse their 1990s Shakespeare films with elements we associate with popular movies. Each director is drawn to different technical and narrative dimensions of the Hollywood film, but each does so in an effort to bring his Shakespearean material to the vast, global, moviegoing audience. The Luhrmann and Hoffman films opened wide, which means that they were released on multiple screens across the country on their opening weekend. Branagh, Parker, and Loncraine's films opened more selectively in a few major cities like New York, Los Angeles, and Chicago and expanded to secondary markets based on reviews and initial box office returns. Of those films, only Branagh's *Henry V* (after its Academy Award nominations) and *Much Ado about Nothing* eventually made it to the local cineplex—but all of these films aspired to that destination. Other films made in the decade had different audiences in mind.

Another film from this period, Trevor Nunn's *Twelfth Night* (1995), also has its roots in popular culture. Nunn succeeded Peter Hall in 1968 as the second director of the Royal Shakespeare Company, which he then headed for almost twenty years. When he left the company he didn't abandon Shakespeare for Hollywood, but for musical comedy. Nunn became famous for his direction of a series of Andrew Lloyd Webber musical blockbusters, including *Cats, Starlight Express,* and *Sunset Boulevard.* Even more important, he directed the most powerful new musical of the 1980s, *Les Misèrables.* His film of *Twelfth Night* became his path back to Shakespeare and the classical theater when he assumed the directorship of England's National Theatre in 1996. He directed several important Shakespeare productions there but also stunning revivals of classical musical comedies such as Rodgers and Hammerstein's *Oklahoma* and *South Pacific,* Lerner and Loewe's *My Fair Lady,* and Cole Porter's *Anything Goes.* When he did turn to Shakespeare, Nunn was more interested in linking Shakespeare with the energies and conventions of the popular stage musical comedy than with genre elements of the commercial Hollywood film.

Nunn's cast in *Twelfth Night* was all British and ignored established film actors with the exception of Helena Bonham Carter.[7] The film's principal actors—Imogen Stubbs, Nigel Hawthorne, Ben Kingsley, Imelda Staunton—were all veterans of the Royal Shakespeare Company. The film's exteriors were shot on location in Cornwall, a landscape familiar to the English but certainly not to the global film audience. Nunn clearly intended to make a film that would speak more to those already familiar with Shakespeare than to the mass cineplex audience courted by Branagh and Luhrmann.

Nunn hits on the felicitous device of making the play's wry clown, Feste, the film's narrator. He is an omniscient witness to the unfolding of the plot and to Viola's disguise, which provides the humor and confusions of the play's romantic entanglements. Feste's complex

7. Helena Bonham Carter's film career began when Trevor Nunn cast her as the title character in his first feature film, *Lady Jane* (1985).

sensibility is expressed as much through his songs as through his wit, and Nunn uses them not only to establish atmosphere but to solidify relationships. In particular, he uses Feste's singing of "O Mistress Mine" to weave together through a series of **cross-cuts** the romantic longings of Toby and Maria, Malvolio and Olivia, and Orsino and Viola/Cesario. Song is a primary vehicle for conveying meaning and providing pleasure in the film, and in Nunn's skillful hands it shows how Shakespeare's comic art anticipates Mozart's comic operas and the great mid-century American musical comedies. If most of the Shakespeare films of the 90s found their inspiration in Hollywood, Nunn's *Twelfth Night* parted company and found it on Broadway.

Shakespeare, the Avant-garde, and the Art House

The Shakespeare film has traditionally been aimed at the art house rather than the cineplex audience. Even filmmakers as culturally savvy as Laurence Olivier and Orson Welles realized that the audience for their Shakespeare films, though gigantic compared to the audience for stage Shakespeare, was a specialized segment of regular filmgoers, an elite group already familiar with Shakespeare and the avant-garde film tradition. This more specialized audience was the target for Shakespeare films made in the 1990s by such directors as Michael Almereyda, Christine Edzard, Michael Radford, and Julie Taymor.

Edzard is the most unique of this quartet because she is the farthest removed from traditional Shakespearean culture on stage or film. She is an independent filmmaker working out of her tiny Sands Film Studio, refashioned from several abandoned nineteenth-century warehouses along the Thames in Rotherhithe—once Fagin and Bill Sikes territory for those familiar with Dickens's *Oliver Twist*. Edzard is perhaps best-known for making a brilliant two-part, four-hour film version of Dickens's *Little Dorrit* (1987).

Edzard has made two Shakespeare films, *As You Like It* (1992) and *The Children's Midsummer Night's Dream* (2001), and both reveal her attachment to Dickens. Her *As You Like It*, though set in 1990s London, shapes the play as a Dickensian social critique of Margaret Thatcher's free market, entrepreneurial economics that overturned decades of

England's political commitment to democratic socialism. The film re-fashions Shakespeare's Arden as an abandoned construction site where the impoverished homeless and aristocratic exiles gather to establish a community based on shared values and resources. An-drew Tiernan's scruffy Orlando colorfully spraypaints his love po-ems for Rosalind on the makeshift walls of the construction site. He and Emma Croft's tomboy Ganymede trade their comic barbs about love as they skip about like two teenagers playing hooky from school. Russell Jackson rightly notes that Edzard places an impossi-ble interpretive burden on Shakespeare's pastoral romance, but the film has a resilience and staying power derived from its radical credentials.[8]

The Children's Midsummer Night's Dream is Dickensian in the imagi-native and nostalgic power it assigns to children, especially children from deprived, urban neighborhoods. Edzard made her *Dream* utiliz-ing schoolchildren between the ages of eight and twelve from her local Southwark Education Authority. She was determined to demonstrate that kids from a variety of backgrounds could inhabit and express Shakespeare's *Dream* world and in the process claim it for themselves. The film is another experiment in putting Shakespeare in the service of community-making, and it is the most personal of the films made dur-ing this period of revival.

Across the Atlantic, Michael Almereyda's *Hamlet* (2000) took its in-spiration from Orson Welles's idiosyncratic approach to translating Shakespeare into the language of film. Almereyda radically cut and re-arranged the text to fashion a truncated version of the play to appeal to college students and **cinèastes**. His only nod to Hollywood was the film's star, Ethan Hawke. Though he relied on other actors with estab-lished film and television reputations, like Bill Murray and Kyle MacLachlan, he cast them in surprising roles: Polonius and Claudius. With equal daring he cast the great American playwright, Sam Shep-ard, as the ghost of Hamlet's father, and Shepard's encounter with Hawke is harrowing. Almereyda traps Hawke's Hamlet in the prison of Manhattan's glass and steel skyscrapers and the city's ubiquitous

8. See Russell Jackson, "Shakespeare's Comedies on Film," in *Shakespeare and the Moving Image* (Cambridge: Cambridge University Press, 1994), ed. Anthony Davies and Stanley Wells, p. 101.

neon jungle. Almereyda's Manhattan is soundless and sinister. It is a looming presence, from the film's opening frames shot through the sun roof of Claudius's limousine as it prowls Times Square to the final duel sequence filmed on the balcony of Claudius's penthouse. Almereyda's camera catches the cold blues and grays of those glass towers and transforms them into one vast glittering mirror, refracting light and reflecting images.

Though Almereyda's setting is contemporary Manhattan, the inspiration for the film's Hamlet seems to emanate from the 1950s. Hawke is sad and morose, hiding his pain beneath a Peruvian knit cap and behind an ever-present pair of sunglasses. He's filled with angst and alienation: a soulmate of such 1950s icons as James Dean and Holden Caulfield.

Almereyda shot the film "fast and cheap" in Manhattan in Super 16mm (later blown up to 35mm format for theatrical distribution) "to make everything as urgent and immediate as possible."[9] Super 16mm is a cheaper film stock often used by amateurs before the advent of video recorders. *Hamlet* has Orson Welles's remarkable quality of the spontaneously discovered landscape, shot from odd camera angles, providing an imaginative resonance with the odd twists and turns of Hamlet's mind and the verse that captures them. Almereyda's film intentionally sets out to be "alternative Shakespeare"—especially to the accessible model established by directors like Zeffirelli and Branagh—and it succeeds. It's the *Hamlet* many students of Shakespeare on film wish they had made: jagged, daring, American, and brief.

Two other films of the period also explore alternative modes in translating Shakespeare into film: Julie Taymor's *Titus* (1999) and Michael Radford's *Merchant of Venice* (2004). Both films were made on budgets at the high end ($15–20 million) of the Shakespeare film range; both feature casts that include a mixture of Hollywood film stars (Anthony Hopkins, Jessica Lange, Al Pacino, and Jeremy Irons) with American and British stage actors (Harry Lennix, Geraldine McEwan, Ron Cook, David Harewood, and Alan Gorduner); both combine location shooting (in Rome and Venice) with studio scenes; and both mix elements of the cineplex with the art house.

9. Michael Almereyda, *William Shakespeare's* Hamlet: *A Screenplay Adaptation* (London: Faber and Faber, 2000), p. ix.

Radford's film is the more conventional. It precisely locates the action of *Merchant* in the Venice of 1596 and provides an opening montage and scripted scroll that establishes the laws and customs governing Venice's Jewish population. Radford, an experienced filmmaker, smoothly handles the unfolding of the narrative, cutting skillfully back and forth between the Venetian scenes that focus on Shylock's relationship with Antonio and the Belmont scenes that dramatize the wooing of Portia. The strength of Radford's film is Al Pacino's powerful and central performance of Shylock. Pacino joins Marlon Brando, Laurence Fishburne, and Kevin Kline as experienced American film actors who have demonstrated that they are as adept as their British counterparts in inhabiting great Shakespearean characters on film.

There are touches of some of Pacino's famed portrayals—including Serpico, Sonny Wortzick, and Roy Cohn—in his Shylock, especially after his discovery of Jessica's elopement, when there are strong traces of Michael Corleone's bitter revenger buried deep behind his eyes. Yet physically, Pacino disappears into the role: his face is covered with a beard; his shoulders are stooped; he walks with a slight shuffle; and he needs spectacles (perhaps more for effect than necessity) when checking the interest rates early on and when rereading the bond in the trial scene. Shylock is one of Shakespeare's most ambiguous characters: is he a comic villain, revenge figure, or tragic hero? Pacino's performance manages to embody many of the character's contradictory elements even as Radford's film wants us to see Shylock almost exclusively as a victim of Christian hypocrisy.

If Radford reaches across the Atlantic from London to cast his central character, the American stage director Julie Taymor looks to Britain for her star: Anthony Hopkins. Taymor's *Titus* is a more daring and complicated film than Radford's. Radford is working with one of Shakespeare's best-known, however controversial, works while Taymor chooses to adapt Shakespeare's earliest and bloodiest revenge tragedy. Taymor is not, however, interested in using Shakespeare's play to make a contemporary horror film.[10] She takes

---

10. Seeing *Titus Andronicus* as the archetypal slasher film is the focus of three low-budget movie versions of the play made at the end of the decade: Lorne Richey's *Titus Andronicus: The Movie* (1997), Christopher Dunne's *Titus Andronicus* (1999), and Richard Griffin's *William Shakespeare's* Titus Andronicus (2000).

Titus Andronicus seriously and sees in it a parable about family, state, and power that speaks about the link between empire and violence from classical Rome to contemporary America (note that she made her film before the attack on the World Trade Center and America's war with Iraq).

Taymor uses a variety of devices to jolt the viewer into considering how the film insists on simultaneously inhabiting several spatial and temporal landscapes. The first is to use young Lucius (Osheen Jones) as a framing device and as an innocent witness to the family horrors that multiply as the play's narrative unfolds. In Titus's triumphal military entry into the Colosseum at the beginning of the film, Taymor intentionally includes military hardware that reaches from Titus's age to the present. Her film continues to mix and mingle past and present, most notably in setting scenes against Roman architectural sites both ancient (the Colosseum, Hadrian's Villa, a Roman aqueduct) and modern (Mussolini's EUR building). She also periodically interrupts the narrative flow of the action by inserting a series of silent dream image sequences that she calls "Penny Arcade Nightmares," taking us back to film's origins in England's penny gaffs and America's nickelodeons. These sequences capture Taymor's understanding that the violence of Shakespeare's play leaps beyond realism into the surreal and symbolic.

What anchors Taymor's production in the narrative tradition of Shakespeare on film are the two performances at its center: Harry Lennix's Aaron and Anthony Hopkins's Titus. Taymor's visual imagination is sparked by Aaron and Titus: Titus, the patriarchal insider pushed from the center to the margins of his world, and Aaron, the proud outsider who prowls his way to the center by devouring everything in his path, only to discover that his rough nihilism melts in the face of paternity. Taymor, and her film, understands that "Titus and Aaron are mirrors, absolute mirrors of each other. As you watch Titus become a monster, you watch Aaron become a father."[11] That understanding pushes Taymor to revise the end of Shakespeare's play, which is dominated by the bleak reality of Titus's savage revenge. She returns to her framing device and has young Lucius—a largely silent

11. Miranda Johnson-Haddad, "A Time for *Titus*: An Interview with Julie Taymor," *Shakespeare Bulletin* 18, no. 4 (2000), p. 36.

Titus Andronicus (Anthony Hopkins) discovers that Rome is a "wilderness of tigers" in Julie Taymor's *Titus* (1999, Fox Searchlight Pictures).

witness to the play's horrors—pick up Aaron's tiny son and cradle him in his arms as they exit the Colosseum together into the dawn of a new day.

The Shakespeare films at the end of the century revitalized the genre and brought it to new heights of artistic and commercial success. Never in its one hundred years of history had the Shakespeare film played such an active role in the ever-expanding global film culture. By linking Shakespeare's culturally iconic and elite texts to the conventions and genres of the popular Hollywood film, many of the directors of the period managed to tap into, for the first time since Zeffirelli's *Romeo and Juliet*, the mass international moviegoing audience. Shakespeare on film, at least for the moment, was liberated from the art house and found itself competing with more conventional films at the cineplex.

The golden period of revival in the 1990s flourished between the two most significant events in recent history: the fall of the Berlin Wall on November 9, 1989, and the terrorist attacks on the World Trade

Center and the Pentagon on September 11, 2001.[12] In those twelve years of geopolitical peace, Hollywood was free to turn from spy films and nuclear war blockbusters that reflected national anxieties to more culturally nuanced material. With the collapse of the Twin Towers, the launch of the war on terrorism, and the war in Iraq, that period has ended and with it the Shakespeare-on-film renaissance. Undoubtedly Shakespeare films will continue to be made, as witness Michael Radford's *Merchant of Venice* (2004) and Branagh's *As You Like It* (2007), but not at the remarkable pace of release maintained during the last decade of the twentieth century.

12. See my *Shakespeare at the Cineplex: The Kenneth Branagh Era* (Athens: Ohio University Press, 2003), pp. 1–24.

Beatrice (Emma Thompson) caught in "a happy hour" in Kenneth Branagh's *Much Ado about Nothing* (1993, the Samuel Goldwyn Company).

Analyzing Shakespeare on Film

While Part I focused on the history of Shakespeare on film, including influential filmmakers, the impact of television, and the revival of Shakespeare in the 1990s, Part II focuses on the films themselves and issues associated with translating Shakespeare into film. Chapter 6 looks at four technical elements of film—camera work, editing, music, and acting—and examines how each can influence a filmmaker's interpretation of Shakespeare's words. Chapters 7–10 all investigate various problems that haunt the process of translating Shakespeare into film and then provide some examples of how directors have attempted to solve them. Each chapter considers how astute filmmakers link the cultural or critical environment of their age and the technical resources of film with ideas, issues, and images of Shakespeare's text to create independent works of art inspired rather than driven by their source.

6

AUTEURS AND ACTORS

Camera, Editing, Music, and Acting

Four elements are at the heart of the filmmaker's art and craft: camera work, editing, music, and acting. Understanding the importance and function of each of these aspects of movie-making should prepare the student of Shakespeare on film to write with confidence about the larger issues addressed in later chapters (cultural and historical contexts, verbal and visual images, beginnings, soliloquies, signature shots, and extended sequences).

Students exposed to the study of Shakespeare on film for the first time often understandably rush to judgment. Their first reaction is to make a sweeping general claim for the film's merits (or demerits) as an interpretation of Shakespeare's text. Such judgments are perhaps inevitable, but they are convincing only when they come as the result of careful exploration and analysis of the film's unique combination of directorial approach, camera work, editing, music, and acting rather than as a simple statement of opinion. The alert student of Shakespeare on film needs to appreciate the differing ways filmmakers combine the technical elements of camera work and editing with the craft of the actors and the power of the film score to successfully translate Shakespeare into the language of film. This chapter will explore examples of how these crucial elements of film are employed in a wide variety of Shakespeare films and will also consider the contrasting ways they are used in creating television productions of Shakespeare.

Camera Work

The camera is the film director's single most important tool in constructing his art: the camera tells the story. The film camera's remarkable mobility allows it to **track**, to **pan**, to fly above and swoop down (via a **crane** shot), to weave in and around the action on a **dolly** or the shoulders of the **steadicam** operator, or close in on the actor's face at a moment of emotional crisis. How a director employs the camera in a Shakespeare film is especially revealing—and also problematic, because the camera has such complicated verbal material to master. How does the camera capture the soliloquy or the long set speech (Titania's "forgeries of jealousy" speech or Polonius's advice to Laertes, for example), or enhance the humor of the rapid-fire exchanges between characters like Beatrice and Benedick? How do some directors employ the camera not simply to tell the story but to become a part of the story (as told on film) itself?

The Camera as Character

As both director and star, Laurence Olivier often makes the camera an extension of his power as an actor. In his film of *Hamlet*, Olivier endows the camera with some aspects of Hamlet's restless, probing intelligence. The camera is an extension of Hamlet's prying eyes as he becomes an undercover operative in Claudius's corrupt dispensation, and it becomes an agent of Hamlet's determination to seek out the difference between "seems" and "is." It prowls Elsinore's staircases and long corridors, poking into Gertrude's bedroom, Ophelia's sewing room, and Claudius's dark corners in an effort to discover how "a king may go a progress through the guts of a beggar" (4.3.31).

Olivier is particularly clever in the way he uses the camera in the shooting of the "Mousetrap" scene. The court is seated in a semicircle around the playing space. Olivier's screenplay retains only the Dumb Show, so there is no spoken dialogue for five minutes between Hamlet's crude remark to Ophelia that "It would cost you a groaning to take off mine edge" (3.2.228) and Claudius's cry "Give me some light!" (3.2.247) that ends the play and scatters the spectators. Hamlet and Ophelia are seated on the left of the action, Claudius and Gertrude in the center, and Horatio stands on the right. The camera begins shooting the play-within over Horatio's shoulder and slowly circles behind the audience so that we view the Dumb Show from the perspective of the key members of the audience. We understand that the camera represents a third pair of eyes closely associated with those other two keen watchers of both action and audience: Hamlet and Horatio. The camera makes three slow circuits behind the audience, as the action of the Dumb Show unfolds, each time pausing when it reaches either Hamlet or Horatio to reinforce its identification with their perspective. The tension builds, aided by William Walton's music scored for oboe, recorder, and lute, and we see that Claudius has become distracted and agitated by what he has seen. Suddenly we realize that the court spectators, led by Hamlet and Horatio, have turned their gaze from the player-king to the real one. He rises from his seat, rubs his fists into his eyes, and in a tight **close-up** bellows out "Give me some light!" We hear Hamlet's mad laugh as the camera focuses on the flaming torch Hamlet swirls in front of Claudius and which the king snatches out of his hand as he bolts from the room. The camera, here, has been a player in the action. Its scrutiny (as a second for Hamlet's and Horatio's eyes) plays as large a part in forcing Claudius to rise and exit as does the action of the "The Mousetrap."

The Camera as Omniscient Narrator

If Olivier's camera is repeatedly linked with the drama's central character, Kenneth Branagh's camera, in his film of *Hamlet*, fulfills a different function. By shooting the full text of Shakespeare's play and by setting his film in the late nineteenth century, Branagh presents us with an expansive view of *Hamlet*, something in the manner of an epic nineteenth-century European or Russian novel. Branagh's camera functions much like the **omniscient narrator** common to that genre, constantly providing us with information that is not precisely the province of any individual character in the play.

This device is used most prominently in the film's presentation of Fortinbras. Branagh wants to emphasize the political context of Shakespeare's play, and to do so he needs to expand Fortinbras's role as witness in the unfolding of the drama, for in Shakespeare's text he appears in only two scenes. In the first scene of the play, Horatio has a long speech in which he fills in Barnardo and Marcellus on the recent history between Denmark and Norway as a means of explaining why Denmark is on a military alert with guards on the ready and the munitions factories working overtime. When he reaches the lines about Fortinbras's attempt to reclaim lands his father lost to Hamlet's father thirty years ago, Branagh's camera cuts to a depiction of Rufus Sewell's hooded-eyed Fortinbras making his military preparations to invade

Denmark. Horatio has no direct knowledge of Fortinbras. Nothing in the text indicates that they have ever met. These images, then, are not those of the **first-person narrator** (Horatio) of this information but of the omniscient camera. This pattern is repeated when Fortinbras is next evoked in the text. Claudius dispatches his ambassadors to Norway to tell the king to put an end to his nephew's military adventurism. When they return, the camera provides us with a **flash-cut** that shows Old Norway remonstrating with Fortinbras and Fortinbras angrily ripping the map of his invasion plans off the wall of the war room. Later, Branagh includes a completely extratextual moment when the camera discovers Horatio reading a newspaper whose headline announces the news of Fortinbras's planned invasion of Poland, and again the camera flash-cuts to the mounted Fortinbras leading his troops on his new military mission. At the climax of the film, during the fencing match between Hamlet and Laertes, the camera repeatedly cuts away from their robust and deadly duel to shots of Fortinbras and his army charging through the snow as they storm the Danish Palace. Again, this information is available only to the camera's omniscient eye.

Branagh's camera also provides us with **flashbacks** to Hamlet and Ophelia's love-making; Gertrude, Claudius, and the king playing a game of curls; Claudius poisoning Hamlet's father; the death of Priam; and a short sequence of the young Hamlet getting a piggy-back ride from Yorick as the jester entertains the royal family. The camera is privy to this visual information because of its omniscient role in Branagh's cinematic conception of the play as both vast historical epic and intense family drama. Olivier's camera concentrates on the personal and psychological while Branagh's wants to capture the political and historical dimensions of the text.

The Contested Camera

An innovative example of the use of the camera in a *Hamlet* film comes from the most recent film of the play—the Derry *Hamlet* (2005). The film is a product of the Derry Film Initiative in Northern Ireland and was directed by Stephen Cavanagh, who also plays the prince. The film is groundbreaking on many levels: it is the first Shakespeare film to be shot in Northern Ireland, self-consciously using important landmarks in the troubled history of that region for location shooting; it uses both Shakespeare's language and Gaelic, with the "To be or not to be" soliloquy delivered entirely in Gaelic; and it goes beyond even Michael Almereyda's *Hamlet* (2000) in its radical use of the camera.

Cavanagh's Hamlet, like Ethan Hawke's in Almereyda's film, is a filmmaker, but unlike Hawke he does not possess sole control over the camera. The camera **handheld** is contested in the film following the premise that he who controls the camera controls the narrative. The camera begins by reflecting Hamlet's perspective. As he becomes more absorbed by his involvement in Claudius's world, he passes the camera on to Horatio, who tries to maintain Hamlet's subversive angle on the action. As their efforts become a threat to Claudius's dispensation, the camera is wrested away from Horatio by Polonius and is controlled for much of the middle of the film by a key representative of the established power. Only with Ophelia's aggressive embrace of her madness, here seen as a powerful political act meant to destabilize Claudius's regime and her father's control of the narrative, does Horatio regain control of the camera and with it the responsibility to tell Hamlet's "story."

Olivier, Branagh, and Cavanagh all bring fresh ideas to the use of the camera as a key ingredient in the filmmaker's approach to his Shakespearean material. Charting the course of the camera and the perspective it provides us on the action is a productive avenue of exploration in understanding film's power to capture and present the particular universe and narrative flow of any given Shakespearean text.

Editing

Editing is the final process in completing the finished film. The editing room is crucial because that is where the final print of the film is constructed and all its constituent parts brought together and woven into an aesthetic whole. Editing establishes the film's pace and rhythm; it can also subtly add nuances to the film's narrative. The way a film is edited often reveals the stamp of a filmmaker, as a closer look at the editing of Orson Welles and Baz Luhrmann shows.

Editing as Storytelling

Orson Welles shot all of his Shakespeare films on shoestring budgets. He did not have the financial luxury to re-shoot scenes that did not work out as planned. As a result, he became a master film editor, weaving together the final version of the film using the resources of his imagination to link shots together in clever ways that would mask gaps in the film's continuity. He had to construct his *Othello* from fragments shot over a period of almost two years (most films are shot in three to six months) spanning location landscapes from Venice to Rome to Morocco. The great French film critic Andrè Bazin admiringly described Welles's *Othello* as "profoundly faithful to Shakespeare's dramatic poetry. I can think of no other director in the world who could cut so much out of the original written text and replace it with visual spectacle without inviting ridicule."[1]

Nowhere is Welles's talent as an editor more brilliantly revealed than in his film of the Hal-Falstaff story, *Chimes at Midnight*—in particular, in the segues between scenes, which creatively unite text, image, and editing. A few examples will demonstrate. After the king's angry confrontation with the fiery Hotspur early in the film, Hotspur dismisses Hal, the king's son and his rival, by commenting that he could have him "poisoned with a pot of ale." Welles then cuts to a **close-up** of the bottom of a tankard tipped to Hal's lips as he enjoys a life of cakes and ale at the Boar's Head Tavern. The transition effectively moves us from Westminster and the corridors of power and politics to the tavern and the world of pleasure and play, and simultaneously links the two young rivals who will eventually confront one another at the Battle of Shrewsbury. At the end of this first extended sequence in the tavern, culminating in Hal's famous "I know you all" soliloquy, Welles plucks an exchange between Hal and Falstaff from earlier in the scene about the "hanging of thieves" and on the word "thieves" cuts to Hotspur in his tub reading (and arguing with) the letter from an unnamed conspirator who is urging caution in the rebel plan to overthrow the king. Welles's cut reminds us that while Hal and Fal-

1. André Bazin, "*Othello*," reprinted in *Film Theory and Criticism* (New York: Oxford University Press, 1974), ed. Gerald Mast and Marshall Cohen, p. 337.

Prince Hal (Keith Baxter) tipping a tankard to his lips as the film cuts from Hotspur (Norman Rodway) saying about the Prince that he could "poison him with a pint of ale" in Orson Welles's *Chimes at Midnight* (1966, Internacional Films Espagnol).

staff set out to take purses at Gadshill, the Percies are the more dangerous thieves in their desire to steal a crown from Henry IV.

At the conclusion of the Gadshill robbery scene, in which Hal and Poins turn the tables on Falstaff and his gang by robbing the robbers, Hal says of Falstaff, "Were it not for laughing I should pity him." Welles then cuts to Westminster where King Henry is lamenting, "Can no man tell me of my unthrifty son . . ." Again, these lines are rearranged from their position in Shakespeare's text to create a visual transition between Hal's life of sport and laughter to the king's world of care and concern. The troubled father is certain that his son's behavior is God's punishment for Henry's overthrow of Richard II.

Another example of Welles's intelligent editing underlines the way Shakespeare's two plays repeatedly suggest the links between the king, Hal, and Falstaff. The mood of *Henry IV, Part Two* is far more melancholy than the robust energy that distinguishes *Part One*. With the death of Hotspur at Shrewsbury, the rebels have lost their military leader and animating spirit, the king is emotionally and physically spent and consumed by guilt, Hal is caught in the limbo between his reformation and his father's decline, and Falstaff, sent to the countryside on a recruiting mission, no longer has the spark of Hal's intelligence to engage his own quick wit. Once again, Welles skillfully rearranges Shakespeare's text so that he can visually capture these psychological states. He cuts from the king's long speech about the cares of leadership, ending with "Uneasy lies the head that wears the crown," to Hal's confession to Poins that he is "exceeding weary." The king is tired of governing and Hal of playing the truant, but both are trapped in these roles until the king finally releases his grip on life and Hal inherits the crown as Henry V. Welles then cuts from Hal's weariness to Falstaff's melancholy as we discover the fat knight in the tavern, Doll Tearsheet perched on his ample lap, as he mumbles "I am as melancholy as a lugged bear," a line Welles lifts from *Part One*. Each of these edits, as Welles makes the transition from scene to scene in *Chimes at Midnight*, demonstrate his visual understanding of the Shakespearean material he is adapting to film and the clever way he repeatedly links text and image to capture the interlocking plot lines and resonances involving Hotspur, Hal, the king, and Falstaff.

Editing as Landscape and Atmosphere

A more radical approach to creating meaning through editing can be found in Baz Luhrmann's *William Shakespeare's Romeo+Juliet*. Luhrmann uses quicksilver cuts to create both landscape and atmosphere in his film. He also mixes in title cards to identify characters and establish narrative structure in the film's opening sequence, where the play's prologue is delivered by a television newsreader as if the explosive events of the play were subject matter for the local evening newscast. After the newscast, Luhrmann seeks to establish the virtual reality of his cityscape, a mixture of Mexico City, Miami Beach, and Los Angeles. He films from both helicopter and crane to quickly establish the rival corporate headquarters of the Capulet and Montague empires, which are separated by a giant statue of Christ around which swirls a busy traffic circle. In contrast to these spiritual and secular images of authority, Luhrmann creates several spaces that belong exclusively to the young: the Sycamore Grove amusement park located on the beach, the nearby shell of an abandoned theater, and the Globe pool hall. These are the sites where the film first discovers Romeo, where the lads gather before heading to the Capulets' party, where Tybalt confronts and kills Mercutio, and where Romeo seeks the fatal poison on his way to Juliet's bier. These locations are established early in the film in a series of rapid cuts as Luhrmann never allows his camera to settle on a single image for more than ten or fifteen seconds before racing off to the next. His cuts establish the hectic headlong pace and flow of his film, catching his audience up in the same furious dynamic that seizes Romeo and Juliet from the moment of their first encounter.

This violent frenzy is best illustrated by the first extended treatment of material directly taken from Shakespeare's text: the quarrel between the Montagues and Capulets that opens the play. In Luhrmann's film the Montagues roar down the street in a bright yellow convertible and gun past the Capulets, tossing their taunts to the wind. They pull into the Phoenix Gas Station ("More Fuel to the Fire" reads its advertising slogan) and are immediately confronted by Tybalt and the Capulets. Now Luhrmann's cuts come fast and furious—none lasting longer than a few seconds—and **point-of-view** shots ricochet like the bullets from the combatants' "Sword 9 mm Series" handguns. We are bombarded with lightning-fast cuts including **slam zooms**, **tumble shots**, **whip pans**, and **extreme close-ups** (especially of Tybalt's and Benvolio's eyes as they confront each other sighting down the ends of their gun barrels), and finally a crane shot up and over the mayhem, as the gas station ignites like a Gulf War refinery. Luhrmann is clearly creating a version of *Romeo and Juliet* for the MTV generation and he speaks their cinematic language.

He does not retreat from this aggressive style, even when dealing with the few longer speeches his screenplay retains from Shakespeare's text. Luhrmann does make something of a Wellesian transition as he moves from Juliet's pre-party talk about Paris with her mother and the nurse to the exchanges between the Montague lads as they make their way to the Capulets' ball. The Nurse squeezes into the frame next to Claire Danes's Juliet as she encourages her, with a naughty twinkle, to "seek happy nights to happy days." We hear an explosion and cut to Juliet, now in her angel costume, standing on her balcony watching the fireworks from the Sycamore Grove blossom in the sky. Then we cut to the lads at the Grove watching the same sight and listening to Romeo's hesitation about attending the party. When

Harold Perrineau's cross-dressed Mercutio launches into the "Queen Mab" speech, Luhrmann doesn't cut a line, but his anxious camera never settles on a single image for more than a moment. In fact, he gives us thirty cuts in less than two minutes as his camera flashes from Mercutio to Romeo to the ecstasy pill Mercutio offers to his friend to the fireworks exploding overhead to Benvolio then back to the pill and Mercutio's loss of imaginative control as his speech reaches its climax. When Leonardo DiCaprio's Romeo comforts his spaced-out pal and continues to have misgivings of "some conse-quence yet hanging in the stars," Luhrmann can't resist giving us a **flash-forward** to an image of Romeo walking down the candle-lit aisle of a cathedral. We cannot know at this moment in the film, nor can Romeo, that he walks toward Juliet's body on its bier in the film's final sequence. Luhrmann's film is the most aggressively edited of all Shakespeare films and it is in the editing room that his film finds its unique style and pace.

Many conventional filmmakers seek an invisible editing style, one that does not intrude on or compete with the narrative or call atten-tion to the artifice of the medium. James Joyce, in *Portrait of the Artist as a Young Man*, has Stephen Dedalus describe drama as the highest form of art because in it "the artist, like the God of the creation, remains . . . invisible, refined out of existence, indifferent, paring his fingernails." He meant that while the author was clearly the creator of the work, he functioned best when he was invisible in the unfolding of his creation. This quality is true of most film editors, but in some in-stances, as with Luhrmann and his editor Jill Bilcock, the director de-cides that only by making the editing so self-consciously a signal element in the narrative can he effectively capture Shakespeare in the grammar and rhetoric of film. Welles uses his editing to meld text and visual image seeking to capture the multiple plots and resonances of the *Henry IV* material as he reworks it into his own **screenplay** to tell a condensed version of the Hal-Falstaff story. Luhrmann takes a more cinematically aggressive approach in his attempt to capture the de-structive passions released in the Romeo and Juliet story by incorpo-rating some of that violence into his editing style. The editing of most Shakespeare films exists between these two poles, but all will reveal something of the director's approach to reshaping his Shakespearean material for film.

Camera Work and Editing on Television

Shakespeare productions devised for television are made in one of three fashions: as films shot on location with budgets only a fraction of those required for feature films; as productions recorded in theaters during a live performance; and as productions shot in a television studio. The last of these may consist of productions originally mounted on stage and later moved into a television studio or as productions conceived exclusively for television. Televised recordings of live theater performances use multiple television cameras, with one mounted in the first row of the balcony to record a **master shot** of the action and two or three floor-mounted cameras maneuvering on stage on the edge of the action. Studio Shakespeare also employs three or four floor-mounted television cameras to record the action. These cameras are placed at various angles to the playing space and all record the action simultaneously. The director assembles the production as it unfolds by the way he directs the three cameras, selecting only one to record at a time. Most of the action is captured in long or medium shot; the close-up is rare because of the difficulty of sliding one camera in close in the midst of the unfolding action.

Stage productions of Shakespeare recorded live for television rarely offer the special challenges of translating the text into the television medium. Viewers quickly understand that they are in a theater where stage conventions and expectations prevail. However, such productions vary enormously in how they make use of their theatrical audiences. Are they included in any shots? Does the production ever cut to the audience for a specific reaction to a comic or tragic moment in the production? How much of the sound of the audience's reaction is retained on the soundtrack? In the recording of a comedy, does the director ever cut to shots of the audience laughing, and if so, what effect does that have on the television viewer? How are the performances pitched to reach the theatrical audience as opposed to the one watching on television? The New York Public Theater's performance of *King Lear* in Central Park, mentioned in Chapter 4, is a good example for considering these questions, as is the English Shakespeare Company's seven-play television version of *The Wars of the Roses*.

Shakespeare recorded in a television studio does present special problems and opportunities to designer, director, and cast. Because television is such a realistic—as opposed to abstract or symbolic—medium, dominated by "live" events like the nightly news, documentaries, and sporting events, and fictional entertainment series like sitcoms, cop shows, and medical dramas, it has been hard for producers to find a congenial world in which to set Shakespeare on television. Initially the BBC series thought that given the expectations of television viewers, it was necessary to set the plays against realistic backgrounds. But trying to construct a realistic version of Verona or Rome in a television studio proved impossible as the camera quickly exposed the attempt as simply painted sets and backdrops, effectively destroying the attempt at realism.

Because camera work and editing are limited in most studio productions of Shakespeare, they do not reflect the same wide range that can be found in their film equivalents. However, one can still trace a particular television director's rhythm in moving between shots from the three cameras and the way he mixes **long shots**, **medium shots**, and close-ups in his visual telling of the Shakespearean narrative. For example, Philip Casson, who directed Trevor Nunn's production of *Macbeth* (1979) for television, shot most of the production in close-up to capture the intense, claustrophobic, psychological power of the play. His camera closes in to concentrate on the faces of Judi Dench (Lady Macbeth) and Ian McKellen (Macbeth) as they become mentally tormented by their crime. He even uses the extreme close-up on several occasions so that only McKellen's eyes or Dench's hands are visible in the frame.

A television director's style can also be seen in how he arranges his actors in the frame. McKellen and Dench are often captured in a medium two-shot, with each trying to calm or reassure the other by a constant nervous touching. Richard Eyre, in reimagining his *King Lear* (1998) for television, allows the fool (Michael Bryant) to jump up on Lear's council table to deliver his riddling assessment of Lear's reduced status while being sure to keep Lear visible in the rear of the frame—thus visually reinforcing the topsy-turvy nature of the play's universe, as here, fool dominates king. Crowd scenes are difficult to master in the confined space of the television studio. Robert Wise tries to solve this problem in the BBC version of *Julius Caesar* by packing as many actors in the frame of a medium shot as possible to create a sense of mass. Soliloquies, too, are necessarily treated differently in television. For instance, television productions of Shakespeare rarely use voice-over for soliloquies.

Film Scores and Blank Verse: Problems and Solutions

Music is an integral part of film's vocabulary. All major commercial films include a musical soundtrack that is meant to underline emotion, heighten suspense, build tension, and create atmosphere and mood. Often the **film score** will develop unique themes for individual characters, events, ideas, and even objects. Great Hollywood film composers from the past include Alfred Newman, Alex North, Elmer Bernstein, and Bernard Herrmann. Often composers are linked with the work of particular directors: Herrmann with Alfred Hitchcock, Ennio Morricone with Sergio Leone, Maurice Jarre with David Lean, and John Williams with Steven Spielberg and George Lucas. This pattern holds with Shakespeare films as well. Laurence Olivier's films were all scored by William Walton; Grigori Kozintsev's by Dmitri Shostakovich; Franco Zeffirelli's by Nino Rota; and Kenneth Branagh's by Patrick Doyle. Stage productions of Shakespeare usually feature some music but generally only to cover transitions between scenes, or to announce the entrance of a king with trumpet flourishes, or to accompany otherwise silent bits of action like battles or duels. Rarely does a stage production bring in music under the spoken text whereas almost all films do.

The deployment of the film score provides another tricky element for the director of the Shakespeare film to master. Shakespeare's language is so rich and dazzling that it creates its own unique music and rhythm. Deciding when to bring the score in under the dialogue is a delicate art, as the music must enhance the moment rather than work against it. Most Shakespeare films opt for a traditional film score played by a full orchestra and used in association with particular characters, events, and themes in the film. A few recent Shakespeare films (in particular, Luhrmann's *William Shakespeare's Romeo+Juliet* and Branagh's *Love's Labour's Lost*) have followed another musical alternative: the use of popular songs, from a variety of composers, both under and in the action of the narrative. A brief examination of Shostakovich's score for Kozintsev's *Hamlet* and Doyle's for Branagh's film version of the play reveals the resources of the traditional orchestral film score when used in a Shakespeare film.

The Traditional Film Score

Shostakovich's music for Kozintsev's *Hamlet* (1964) reflects the friendship and close professional affinity between the two Russians, who were born within a year of each in the early 1900s. Both the **auteur** cinematographer Kozintsev and the innovative composer Shostakovich witnessed their national history thrown out of joint by the 1917 revolution, felt Stalinist pressure to set it right in the 1930s, and then lived to set it all down in this film and film score during the cultural thaw initiated by Nikita Khrushchev in the 1960s. Like Kozintsev's film, Shostakovich's music projects a deep historical and psychological—and deeply Russian—identification with character and conflict in Shakespeare's *Hamlet*.

Shostakovich's music is often in the foreground rather than the background in the film, from the overture-like musical description of the film's opening stark landscape of sea and stone as Hamlet gallops home for his father's funeral, his long cape billowing out in concert with the waves, to the reprise of this wordless setting, action, and music for Hamlet's funeral at the end. Throughout the film, Shostakovich consistently invokes conflicts both internal and external through striking contrasts of orchestral color and instrumentation and by propulsive or explosive rhythms: unison brass or strings alternating with dissonant hammer chords in the full orchestra; solo woodwind, string, or brass instrumentation above a pulsating drumbeat; busy perpetual motion orchestral textures beneath brass choir, as in the duel scene.

Shostakovich's music also underlines contrast and irony in text and screenplay by theme and variation, cross-referencing tragic and comic scenes. The gavotte theme for Ophelia's dance lesson, for instance, returns—without its elegant Baroque setting for harpsichord (mimed by a lute player onscreen) and with its rhythms simplified and tempo quickened—as the folk song sung by the gravedigger to the labored rhythm of his shovel as he digs Ophelia's grave; here Renaissance dance joins with Soviet work song. A comparable burlesque effect transforms the *Dies irae* dirge first heard for old Hamlet into a demonic *Danse Macabre* reminiscent of Berlioz's *Symphonie Fantastique* in the music for old Hamlet's poisoning by Claudius's surrogate in "The

Mousetrap." And the same prankish spirit gives voice to Yorick in a half-poignant, half-humorous solo flute and violin setting for Hamlet's address to the skull. In addition to these scenes and musical settings, a general juxtaposition of the comic and tragic in the film score reinforces a similar quality in the play.

Patrick Doyle has collaborated on all of Branagh's Shakespeare films. His score for Branagh's first film, *Henry V* (1989), helped to create the dark, gritty, conspiratorial atmosphere established in the opening scenes of the play and the elegiac, rather than triumphant, tone struck by the film after England's victory at Agincourt. Doyle had an even broader musical canvas to work on for *Hamlet* (1996), and his score there is appropriately more subdued, somber, and even lyrical than the insistent, often jagged pounding of the music in *Henry V* or the festive upbeat melodies he provided for *Much Ado about Nothing* (1993). Doyle's score doesn't enter the film until the first appearance of the Ghost, when the music is meant to reinforce the Ghost's size and terrifying impact on Horatio, Marcellus, and Bernardo. Elsewhere, Branagh's pattern is to introduce the score under the spoken text only after a section of dialogue or a soliloquy is well begun, so that the music insinuates itself under the verse after the Shakespearean rhythm has already been established. The most obvious use of this technique comes in the "How all occasions" soliloquy where, by its climax, Doyle's score comes close to overwhelming Hamlet's words. The score's volume and force are meant to comment on Hamlet's overheated rhetoric and posture here as he recklessly insists, "O, from this time forth,/ My thoughts be bloody, or be nothing worth!" (4.4.65–66).

Film scores often include themes for individual characters (think of "Lara's Theme" from David Lean's *Dr. Zhivago* or the "James Bond Theme" used to introduce 007 in the Bond films). Doyle, in his score for *Hamlet*, identifies characters with melodic motifs, which then lend themselves to varied restatement as the tragedy unfolds. Ophelia's theme illustrates Doyle's talent for original uses of classical influences. Her theme is almost a direct quotation from composer Gustav Mahler in its pronounced and repeated resolution of the seventh scale degree downward. Mahlerian too is the theme's progression between the scene in which Polonius reads Hamlet's letter (where Ophelia is present in the film) and Ophelia's later mad scene, from soulful yearning and naiveté to elegiac mourning, scored for dominant horns and woodwind. The Hamlet theme by contrast is small in compass, virtually contained within a fifth; it is short and convoluted, the melodic equivalent to being bounded in a nutshell.

Doyle's big orchestral score, with its classical antecedents, fits the film's nineteenth-century setting and epic ambitions well. The score adds weight and expanse to Branagh's conception of *Hamlet* as occupying a screen world as vast as Lean's *Dr. Zhivago*. Both Shostakovich and Doyle fashion full orchestral scores meant to deepen our emotional response to the characters and events in *Hamlet*, but they also provide, upon reflection, intellectual qualities perfectly in tune with the visual approaches Kozintsev and Branagh take to the play.

The Film Score as Cultural Expression

The score for Baz Luhrmann's *William Shakespeare's Romeo+Juliet* (1996) is more eclectic than traditional film music. Luhrmann has done several productions of Puccini's opera *La Bohéme*, and two of his other films, *Strictly Ballroom* (1992) and *Moulin Rouge!* (2001), both focus on young couples expressing their troubled love in either song or dance. In *Romeo+Juliet*, Luhrmann uses music ranging from Mozart and Wagner to One Inch Punch, Garbage, and Radiohead. Brief strains from Mozart's Symphony no. 25 are heard on the soundtrack when we are first introduced to Claire Danes's Juliet, and the "Liebestod" from Wagner's *Tristan and Isolde* fills the cathedral as Juliet awakes to find Romeo dead on the bier beside her. She takes her own life as Isolde's lament for Tristan sweeps both couples up into an apotheosis of the human fascination with love and death.

As Doyle's *Hamlet* score (following the lead of both Walton and Shostakovich) created individual musical themes for major characters like Hamlet and Ophelia, Luhrmann accomplishes something similar by appropriating certain contemporary (in 1996) popular rock songs to serve as markers for such central characters as Romeo, Juliet, and Mercutio. Radiohead's "Talk Show Host" is Romeo's theme and is heard when we first meet him writing poetry as the dawn rises over the Sycamore Grove. "Angel," sung by Gavin Friday, serves a similar function for Juliet; we hear a brief phrase from it (before the Mozart takes over) in our first shot of her submerged in her bath as she prepares for the party, and another excerpt is heard as she stands on her balcony in her angel costume watching the fireworks explode in the sky overhead. Harold Perrineau's silver-corseted, drag queen Mercutio—a cross between Dennis Rodman and RuPaul—dances down Capulet's grand staircase to Kym Mazelle's "Young Hearts Run Free" and transforms the party into a raucous version of carnival. The manic version of "Young Hearts" soon disappears from the soundtrack, to be replaced by Des'ree singing the ballad "I'm Kissing You," the only song created specifically for the film. As the screenplay notes, "I'm Kissing You" releases its "first pure, achingly beautiful notes" just as DiCaprio's Romeo spies Danes's Juliet for the first time.[2]

The pop song that Luhrmann chooses to fully express Romeo and Juliet's passionate, fatal relationship is Garbage's "#1 Crush." We hear brief snatches from the song at several times in the film, most prominently when Juliet visits Friar Laurence with the news that her father has arranged her immediate marriage to Paris. The song's lyrics include lines like "I would die for you . . . I will cry for you . . . I will burn for you . . . I will twist the knife and bleed my aching heart . . . I believe in you . . . I would die for you."[3] The song reinforces that Juliet's "crush" on Romeo is deadly serious and that she is prepared to risk death to be reunited with him.

Luhrmann handles his film score much as he does the editing of his film: just as he refuses to hold any image for more than a few seconds on the screen, he never allows a single sound to remain for long on the soundtrack. He is bold and brazen in allowing the pulse of modern rock and pop rhythms to coexist with Mozart, Wagner, and Shakespeare's iambics. The only time he allows Shakespeare's verse to speak for itself is in Romeo and Juliet's encounter in the balcony scene, here largely relocated to the Capulet swimming pool. He resists underscoring their exchanges until Romeo's line: "My life were better ended by their hate/Than death prorogued, wanting of thy love" (2.1.119–120), and then only with a solo piano for several beats before bringing in a full orchestra to underline their parting. Luhrmann's soundtrack

2. *William Shakespeare's* Romeo +Juliet: *The Contemporary Film, the Classic Play* (New York: Bantam, 1996), p. 47.
3. I am indebted to Professor Gregory Lanier and his fine paper "#1 Crush: Popular Music in Luhrmann's *Romeo and Juliet*," contributed to the seminar I led titled "Branagh and His Contemporaries" at the 1997 Shakespeare Association of America annual meeting in Washington, D.C.; it offered many telling insights about Luhrmann's use of popular music in his film and the lyrics to Garbage's "#1 Crush."

matches the relentless pace and pressure of his film and his determination to translate Shakespeare's tale of star-crossed lovers into a modern fable of two sweet, round-faced kids who can find peace only in death. Luhrmann's soundtrack, like his editing style, is meant to speak to the MTV generation; both are meant to be bold and "in your face" rather than discrete and Joycean.

The Film Score as Movie Genre

With "Young Hearts Run Free" and "I'm Kissing You," Luhrmann brings the soundtrack directly into the action of the film. Kenneth Branagh takes Luhrmann's move a step further in his film of *Love's Labour's Lost* (2000) by making the songs a crucial element in the narrative; in fact, they become its raison d'être. Branagh transforms Shakespeare's early comedy into a version of the great American musical comedies of the 1930s and 40s. He trims 75 percent of Shakespeare's text, leaving just enough to establish the central characters, the basic action of the plot, and a few key speeches. He then appropriates ten popular songs from the 1930s—many first sung by Fred Astaire in the musicals he made with Ginger Rogers and written by such masters of the genre as Cole Porter, Irving Berlin, George and Ira Gershwin, and Jerome Kern—to re-mount Shakespeare's festive comedy on the wings of song and dance. The songs were selected to seem to spring naturally from their newly planted Shakespearean context, best illustrated by the move from text to song in the film's rendition of Irving Berlin's "Cheek to Cheek."

"Cheek to Cheek," from *Top Hat* (1935), spins gracefully out from Shakespeare's verbal spins and twirls concerning the relationship between love, learning, and the dazzle of a lady's eye. Branagh's Berowne begins his clever lecture on love to his fellow love-smitten pals by tapping out Shakespeare's iambs under the speech's opening lines: "Have at you then, affection's men-at-arms." Branagh circles the great Oxbridge library as Berowne gives full voice to his insistence that love "adds a precious seeing to the eye;/ A lover's eye will stare an eagle blind." When Branagh reaches "And when love speaks, the voice of all the gods/ Make heaven drowsy with the harmony" (4.3. 318–19), the film glides ingeniously from Shakespeare to Irving Berlin as

Branagh begins to croon, "Heaven, I'm in heaven/ And my heart beats so that I can hardly speak," as he and his fellow romantics lift off and up, sailing into the library's great dome, carried aloft by their giddy wooing spirits. The song and Stuart Hopps's choreography are the perfect musical expression of the festive high spirits of Shakespeare's young songsters off on a wooing spree.

The scene continues as the men return to earth, now attired in Fred Astaire's customary white tie and tails, and spill out from the library into the college's courtyard to be met by their respective Gingers. Each woman is dressed in a flowing pastel gown, and we are treated to the fantasy heavenly harmony among the four couples that we are denied in Shakespeare's play. Each woman is allowed a solo dancing entrance; each male appears at one of the library's doors as first Berowne sings "Dance with me," and then Dumain chimes in on "I want my arms around you," followed by Longaville with "Those charms about you" and finally Navarre with the line "will carry me through"; and then the four couples are dancing together strung out in an elegant chorus line across the courtyard. Hopps's choreography gives each couple a turn together before reuniting the group of eight as they "seem to find the happiness we seek / When we're out together dancing cheek to cheek." As the sequence finishes, the film cuts back to the men in the library, and we realize that the entire number has been a fantasy as the men now formally resolve to launch a full-scale wooing assault on the women: "For revels, dances, masks, and merry hours, / Forerun fair love, strewing her way with flowers" (4.3.353–54).

These examples, from filmmakers as diverse as Kozintsev, Luhrmann, and Branagh, reveal the importance and variety of the film score to the Shakespeare film. In some instances the music is newly created to respond to the specific characterizations and images of the individual film; in others it is borrowed from established popular or classical sources to create a contemporary resonance for a modern audience perhaps experiencing a Shakespearean text for the first time. As these examples demonstrate, Shakespearean film scores can range from their traditional roles in establishing mood and defining character to being a vital part of the film's storytelling, even to becoming the film's animating idea and energy.

Film Acting

The power of the actor is as paramount on film as it is on stage, though there are subtle but important differences in acting in the two media. The stage actor is perceived in three dimensions. The audience is always aware of his full physical presence and his movements, gestures, and vocal inflections must be large enough to reach the back of the house and up into the balcony. The film actor's performance is mediated by the camera and the editor. Film acting requires patience and restraint rather than the grand gesture and the raised voice. The film actor understands that the close-up allows him to convey emotion and meaning with a tiny detail (a single tear, an arched eyebrow, a subtle wink) and to speak in a confidential, conversational manner.

The actor in a Shakespeare film is challenged by the special obligations of Shakespeare's text. The typical film script is not written in blank verse. The film actor has to master Shakespeare's iambic pentameters and make them seem natural in the context in which they are uttered. It is perhaps no surprise that three of the greatest Shakespearean film auteurs, Olivier, Welles, and Branagh, began their careers as Shakespearean actors and discovered ways to modulate performances originally conceived for the stage to fit the demands of the screen. While the film actor does not have the freedom to command the production as the stage actor does, his performance remains a crucial ingredient in shaping the audience's response to the film.

Unlike the other three main elements of film—camera work, editing, and music—acting can be difficult to analyze objectively and persuasively. Articulating the power of film acting is tough. It is much easier to track the work of the camera, to pick out patterns of verbal and visual images, to detail the relationship of a film to the cultural moment of its production, to apply theory to performance, or to discuss the *auteur* status of the film's director than to write perceptively (with crucial specific details for support) of the actor's contribution to the finished film. Film acting is even more difficult to analyze than an actor's work on stage because all of the actor's efforts are filtered through the camera and the director's editorial decisions before they reach the audience. It is remarkable how little serious work has been done on describing the work of great film actors. Biographies and gossip abound, but not detailed attention to the art and craft of actors such as Katharine Hepburn, John

Wayne, Catherine Deneuve, Gerard Depardieu, Max von Sydow, Humphrey Bogart, Alec Guinness, Cary Grant, Ingrid Bergman, Paul Newman, Meryl Streep, and Dustin Hoffman. Too often descriptions of film acting end up talking about how the camera "loves" a particular countenance or how an actor projects "quiet energy" on the big screen.

The answer to such amorphous rhetoric is to pick out one or two key details of an actor's performance—the particular delivery of a line or a crucial roll of the eyes or the wry tilt of a head—and then to build an analysis around those very precise moments when the actor seems to be defining the character. Another approach is comparative. In looking at, for example, Julia Stiles's performance of Ophelia in Michael Almereyda's *Hamlet*, it is instructive to compare her performance with that of, say, Jean Simmons in Olivier's *Hamlet*, or Kate Winslet in Branagh's, or Helena Bonham Carter in Zeffirelli's. Such a comparison highlights each actress's unique interpretation of Ophelia and the central details that define her performance. It also helps provide a concrete base for a judgment about the performance, rather than the flabby and unpersuasive "I really liked Kate Winslet in that part. She gave a strong performance." Below are some examples from my own collection of fine performance moments.

Creating Character for and with the Camera

Marlon Brando (1924–2004) was the greatest film actor of his generation. Early in his film career—after his star-making turn in *A Streetcar Named Desire* (1951) but before his iconic performance in *On the Waterfront* (1954)—he stole Joseph Mankiewicz's *Julius Caesar* (1953) from venerable British classical actors James Mason and John Gielgud in a single moment at the climax of Mark Antony's famous funeral oration over Caesar's dead body. Playing Antony, Brando neatly modulates his public rhetoric for the camera as he manipulates the crowd and comes to discover in that manipulation that he has the ability to be a potent political force. When Brando emphatically declares, "Here was a Caesar! When comes such another?" Mankiewicz shoots the resultant frenzy of the mob over the actor's shoulder so that Brando can then turn his back on the crowd and the pandemonium he has created and face the camera, where he treats us to a sly, sardonic smile, his eyes dancing at the discovery of his own newfound demagogic powers.

Mark Antony (Marlon Brando) turns to the camera with a wry smile as the citizens of Rome riot behind him in response to his oration over the body of Julius Caesar in Joseph Mankiewicz's *Julius Caesar* (1953, MGM).

Brando's Antony, cut in the heroic mold, has suddenly revealed, in a single smile, a complex and ambiguous cynicism.[4]

Forty years later Brando passed the Shakespeare-on-film acting torch to Kenneth Branagh when he wrote in his autobiography: "The evolution of the English theater came to full flower in Kenneth Branagh's [film] production of *Henry V*. He did not injure the language; he showed reverence for it, and followed Shakespeare's instructions [to the actors in *Hamlet*] precisely. It was an extraordinary accomplishment of melding the realities of human behavior with the poetry of language. I can't imagine Shakespeare being performed with more refinement."[5] Branagh's *Henry V* was so powerful because it was so grounded in his conception of the character. His Henry was a man of flesh and blood,

4. See Jack Jorgens's *Shakespeare on Film* (Bloomington: Indiana University Press, 1977), pp. 99–100 for a detailed reading of Brando's performance.
5. Marlon Brando, *Songs My Mother Taught Me* (New York: Random House, 1994), p. 204.

not an icon of articulate English invincibility. At the beginning of the film, his youthful Henry is uncertain of his abilities and his claim to the French throne. When the Archbishop of Canterbury offers a long and detailed account of the Salique Law, concluding that it provides justification for Henry's claim, Branagh's king shoots a quick glance at Exeter (his uncle) that says "Is Canterbury on the level?" When Exeter nods affirmatively, Branagh quietly and cautiously responds, "May I with right and conscience make this claim?" (1.2.16), hitting both "right" and "conscience" like a drummer's rim shot.

Branagh expresses himself in this council sequence with a quiet determination, as though he is finding his character through a restrained release of his rhetorical voice. An important aspect of Branagh's style in speaking Shakespeare's verse first emerges in this scene. The actor speaks with a confidential tone, recognizing that the camera is an audience as important as the actors who share the frame with him. He never rushes, and he strikes his consonants with a distinctive force that sustains a crisp delivery. Later, before Harfleur and Agincourt, Branagh does let Shakespeare's rhetoric rip and soar, often underlined by Patrick Doyle's film score, but it always takes off from a quiet moment grounded in the reaction shots of the familiar (and young) faces of his troops.

Small Parts and Veteran Actors

Shakespeare films require large casts. His plays all feature a remarkable range of characters from kings to clowns. The great Russian stage director Konstantin Stanislavsky once said that "there are no small parts, only small actors." Shakespeare's small parts offer actors large opportunities, opportunities that can be magnified on film because of the director's control of what we see on screen and the power of the visual image, as witness what director Kenneth Branagh and the actor Rufus Sewell do with the character of Fortinbras in Branagh's film of *Hamlet*. Film also has the prestige to attract noted actors to play lesser roles for the opportunity to work with Shakespeare without having to commit themselves to an extended series of performances as they would have to do in a stage production. Thus we have the pleasure of watching the great French film actress Jeanne Moreau play Doll Tearsheet in Welle's *Chimes at Midnight*, or Robin Williams play Osric in Branagh's *Hamlet*, or Michelle Pfeiffer try her hand at Titania in Michael Hoffman's *A Mid-*

summer Night's Dream, all giving us Shakespearean performances we would never have the opportunity of ever seeing in the theater.

Another attractive option for exploration when considering the actor's contribution to the success of screen Shakespeare is to follow a veteran actor's work over a series of roles in a variety of Shakespeare films. Richard Briers, Brian Blessed, and Richard Clifford appear in almost all of Branagh's Shakespeare films and provide interesting examples of the actor's craft. Imelda Staunton brings fresh energy to Margaret in Branagh's *Much Ado about Nothing* and Maria in Nunn's *Twelfth Night*. And Kevin Kline reveals his range with his Bottom in Hoffman's *Dream* and his Jaques in Branagh's *As You Like It*. Perhaps the most interesting example of watching an actor at work over a series of Shakespearean roles on film and television spanning three decades is provided by Ian Holm.

Holm began his career with the Royal Shakespeare Company in the 1960s playing lead parts, including Hal and then Henry V in *1* and *2 Henry IV* and *Henry V*. He is unique as an actor for having played interesting major and minor roles (Puck, Fluellen, Polonius, and Lear) in four screen Shakespeares, from Peter Hall's *Dream* in 1968 to Richard Eyre's *King Lear* in 1998. Watching Holm move through roles from Puck to Lear is a rare opportunity to chart the development of a great stage actor moderating and modulating his talents in the world of film. Over time Holm mastered one of the tenets of film acting: less is more. His 1968 Puck over-did exaggerated facial gestures, including wagging his tongue at the camera in eager anticipation of Oberon's next command; his 1998 Lear was perfectly pitched to the reduced screen size and technical limitations of television.

Holm's performance of Fluellen in Branagh's *Henry V* elevates the character to an importance only suggested in the text and rarely achieved on stage or film. Branagh's film climaxes not with Henry's wooing of Katherine, the Princess of France, in its final scene, but in the embrace of Henry and Fluellen, one of his captains, after the battle of Agincourt. Fluellen is a pedantic Welshman who is always reminding his fellow soldiers of the proper rules of war. He is usually played for laughs and gently dismissed as a caricature rather than a fully realized character. Branagh and Holm stand that tradition on its head. When they meet after the battle, Branagh's Henry is smeared with blood and mud, as is Fluellen. When Fluellen launches into his speech identifying the king as his countryman, the exhausted king begins to laugh and then to cry as he proudly confesses that "I am Welsh, you know" and collapses into Fluellen's arms. King and commoner are united. Holm's Fluellen is pesky and persistent but never pedantic, and his union with Branagh's king marks the bond of brotherhood created by their mutual heroism and heritage.

Film and Television Acting: Small Gestures, Big Results

Sometimes an actor can define his performance through a single gesture. Innokenti Smoktunovski's Hamlet, in Kozintsev's film of the play, is tracked down and apprehended by Rosencrantz and Guildenstern and several guards after the murder of Polonius. Hamlet has lost his freedom; he is now in the control of the state. As he is being marched back to his confrontation with Claudius, he suddenly stops, forcing his captors to do likewise. He makes them cool their official heels as he calmly reaches down, removes his boot, shakes out an imaginary pebble, puts his boot back on, and proceeds. This single gesture proclaims Hamlet's freedom (and wit) even in captivity and reinforces the way that Hamlet is always one step ahead of Claudius—and several steps ahead of his adder-fanged schoolmates, Rosencrantz and Guildenstern.

Bill Murray gives a finely nuanced performance of Polonius in Almereyda's *Hamlet*. He refuses to find the easy laughs in the character that have proved irresistible to many actors. Neither does he present Polonius as a distant and overbearing parent concerned only that Ophelia (in her relationship with Hamlet) not embarrass his political and professional relationship with Claudius. He genuinely cares about his children, even when he is misguided in his attempts to shelter or protect them. When Ophelia shares Hamlet's letter with him, he takes it and her off to Claudius's penthouse swimming pool to announce that he has found the source of Hamlet's "lunacy." He gives the letter to Claudius to read and sits down on a pool bench next to his daughter. Almost absent-mindedly, he reaches over and picks up her foot and begins to tie the unlaced shoe-strings of her sneakers. This beautiful gesture of parental solicitude is a perfect expression of Murray's conception of Polonius—perhaps even acknowledging his status as a single parent where a father—not the usual mother—is the one picking and tidying up after a daughter.

Emma Thompson's performance of Beatrice in Branagh's film of *Much Ado about Nothing* exhibits other traits of subtle film acting. She is the film's radiant, sentient center. Intelligence and wit illuminate every corner of her performance. She can register emotion, raise alarm, underline irony, change mood, suppress sorrow, and enhance wit by the mere tilt of her head, the flick of an eyelash, the cock of an eyebrow, or a pucker of the lips. The economy with which she allows us to understand her previous romantic entanglement with Benedick and her embarrassment at unintentionally encouraging Don Pedro's marriage proposal is film acting at its best. Thompson's Beatrice is distinguished not just by her sharp high spirits but by her vulnerability, which she demonstrates in her fierce exchange with Benedick after Claudio's shameful treatment of Hero at their wedding. She's angry, but also exasperated because as a female she cannot directly challenge Claudio. For that she needs a man, and when she blinks back tears in asking that Benedick challenge Claudio, the tears are not just for Hero but for herself and for all women still constrained by the patriarchy.

Trevor Nunn's film of *Twelfth Night* contains several fine performances, especially those by Helena Bonham Carter, Ben Kingsley, and Imogen Stubbs. Bonham Carter provides us with real comic pleasure as we watch her eyes widen and her mouth open in wonder as she first sees that there are two Cesarios, thus explaining in a flash the multiple confusions that have brought the inhabitants of Illyria into "midsummer madness." Kingsley transforms his Feste from a traditional jester into a traveling troubadour and provides him with a sad but knowing smile, best flashed when he places Viola's discarded coin necklace over Cesario's head in the recognition scene. Stubbs is an accomplished romantic comedienne. The way in which her face and body register both curiosity and embarrassment when asked, as Cesario, to scrub Orsino's back as he lounges in his bathtub is a little gem of comic acting. She desperately wants to have a peek at his body even though to do so might betray both of her genders: her male disguise and her female reality.

Speaking Shakespeare

One of the revolutions in stage productions of Shakespeare developed in the 1970s and 80s when major English and North American companies began producing Shakespeare in small, "black box" theaters. Such theaters generally held 150–200 spectators rather than the 1,000–2,000 that could be packed into the Shakespeare Memorial Theatre in Stratford-upon-Avon or the Shakespeare Festival Theatre in Stratford, Ontario. Working in these intimate spaces allowed actors to deliver Shakespeare in a more conversational tone rather than having to project their voices to reach the back rows of the balcony. Consequently, they developed a new style for speaking Shakespeare's verse that stressed its psychological realism rather than its rhetorical power. It is perhaps no surprise that several of these productions, especially Trevor Nunn's *Macbeth* (1979) and *Othello* (1989) and Richard Eyre's *King Lear* (1998), were moved into the television studio and recorded for broadcast. Actors like Ian McKellen, for instance, known for being a mesmerizing and histrionic Shakespearean stage actor, learned to severely modulate and refine their performances when working in a smaller theater. Suddenly it was the subtle inflection of a single word in the iambic pentameter line that could be relished rather than the thunder of the entire speech. The small, telling detail became more prominent than the wide, sweeping gesture. This mode of speaking and playing Shakespeare transferred effectively to the small screen. McKellen's television performances of Macbeth and Iago can be profitably studied from this perspective and provide another example of the "less is more" school of Shakespearean acting.

Kenneth Branagh expresses Shakespeare's music in a lean and muscular tone, which is why it strikes the contemporary ear with such force and understanding. Branagh's approach to speaking Shakespeare's verse avoids the trills and sonorities associated with an earlier generation of British actors, and his Shakespeare performances often strike students as being more "natural" than Olivier's.

When describing and assessing the actor's essential contribution to making Shakespeare live on screen it is necessary to get at the gestures, postures, glances, verbal stresses, and vocal rhythms through which the actor builds his performance and his unique interpretation of the character. The more specific the examples, the more powerful and persuasive the analysis.

7

DEEP FOCUS

Text and Context

Filmmakers often remark that every film gets made at least three times: first in the **screenplay**, second in the shooting, and third in the editing. The screenplay is crucial in the Shakespeare film because it determines the director's approach to the text: what he or she decides to cut and to keep will shape key decisions about the film's form and content.

Text: From Playscript to Screenplay

Shakespeare was deeply embedded in the Elizabethan theater as an actor, playwright, and shareholder. He produced income from all three activities as well as from the publication of his narrative poems and sonnets. He may also have profited from the publication of individual editions of his plays, though the plays were owned by the theatrical companies who paid for their composition.

Shakespeare conceived of his plays as scripts for performance. Scripts, he knew from practice, might be trimmed, amended, or enlarged in the collaborative nature of theatrical rehearsal and performance. As Renaissance scholar Stephen Greenblatt has suggested, "There is an imaginative generosity in many of Shakespeare's scripts, as if he were deliberately offering his fellow actors more than they could use on any one occasion and hence giving them abundant materials with which to re-conceive and revivify each play again and again, as they or their audiences liked it."[1]

1. *The Norton Shakespeare*, (New York: W. W. Norton, 1997), ed. Stephen Greenblatt, Walter Cohen, Jean Howard, and Katharine Maus, p. 67.

Modern editorial scholarship, with only a few dissenters, holds that however rich, suggestive, and provocative we find Shakespeare's texts, they are, like the theater they were created for, more unstable than authoritative. Any edition of a Shakespeare play we hold in our hands comes to us through a long line of intermediaries, including actors, compositors, printers, and editors, who stand between us and the author's originating text. While they complicate the purity of the text we receive, they are also responsible for the text's survival and for making Shakespeare available to the world.

Our reading of a Shakespeare play begins and ends with the text. That reading may provoke journeys into history, philosophy, psychology, politics, sociology, and ultimately ourselves, but we always return to the words on the page. Performance lifts those words from the page and puts them in motion in space and time through an actor's voice and body, a designer's landscape, and a director's vision. Shakespeare's generous text is almost always trimmed and shaped to meet both the performance expectations of the age and the ideas director and cast bring to specific productions. Most stage productions trim 10 percent to 30 percent of the text, and often only Shakespeare scholars with an encyclopedic command of the text notice what is missing.

Screenplays bear an even more problematic relationship to Shakespeare's text than do **playscripts**. While films have the power to transport us to remote and exotic locations (for example, Jutland for Peter Brook's *King Lear*, Cornwall for Trevor Nunn's *Twelfth Night*, Tuscany for Kenneth Branagh's *Much Ado about Nothing*, Venice and Morocco for Welles's *Othello*), they know that they must return us to our quotidian reality in two hours to be commercially viable. This means that screenplays rarely contain more than 40 percent to 50 percent of their Shakespearean source material. As intelligent consumers of film entertainment and as students of the genre, our job is not to lament what has been left out of a Shakespeare film but to understand what has been retained. Does the manner in which the text has been transformed into a screenplay make imaginative connection with the visual dynamics of the film, the director's approach to the play, and the choices made by the actors in their embodiment of Shakespeare's characters?

How Does the Screenplay's Treatment of the Text Determine Interpretation in the Shakespeare Film?

For some solutions, let us examine several film versions of *Hamlet* and *A Midsummer Night's Dream*. The screenplays for Olivier's, Zeffirelli's, and Almereyda's films of *Hamlet* all eliminate Fortinbras. That decision leads them to excise other political dimensions of the play, like Horatio's history of the tension between Denmark and Norway, Claudius's dispatch of Cornelius and Voltemand to resolve the resurfacing of those tensions, Laertes's insurrection, Hamlet's anguish at watching Fortinbras's army march into Poland, and Claudius's call for his "Switzers." These cuts naturally lead each director and the actor playing Hamlet to emphasize the private, psychological complexities of the character, centering more on Hamlet's relationship with Gertrude and the Ghost than on his power struggle with Claudius. With varying degrees of emphasis, these three *Hamlet* films, though set in very different landscapes and shot in radically differing film styles, all reduce the play's political dimension to concentrate on the more private family drama.

In contrast, the screenplays for the *Hamlet* films directed by Grigori Kozintsev and Kenneth Branagh retain the Fortinbras material and lead to approaches that are less Freudian and more Machiavellian in their focus on Hamlet's power struggle with Claudius for the Danish throne. Branagh's film, in particular, makes Fortinbras (played by Rufus Sewell) a vivid visual presence from the beginning of the film because of frequent **flash-cuts** that illustrate Fortinbras's actions while they are being described by Horatio. Branagh's Hamlet (unlike Olivier's or Mel Gibson's) repeatedly appears wearing a military uniform and even practicing swordplay with the palace guard, reinforcing the political (as well as private) threat he represents to Claudius.

Similar decisions about text and screenplay can be seen at work in the world of comedy. In the case of *A Midsummer Night's Dream*, the film script can tip the balance of attention given to the play's four parallel narratives: the wedding of Theseus and Hippolyta, the romantic confusions of the four young lovers, the quarrel between Titania and Oberon, and the efforts of Bottom and company to rehearse and perform "Pyramus and Thisby." It is perhaps no surprise that film is naturally drawn to depict the magical world of Oberon, Puck, and

Bottom (Kevin Kline) at the center of attention in Michael Hoffman's *A Midsummer Night's Dream* (1999, Fox Searchlight Pictures).

Titania and to emphasize the Bottom comedy. The former tries to match the fluid shape-shifting of Shakespeare's flights of Ovidian fancy with film's technological powers while the latter recognizes the ageless invitation for the clown to run away with the show.

In both the 1935 Warner Brothers *Dream*, co-directed by William Dieterle and Max Reinhardt, and the 1999 *Dream* directed by Michael Hoffman, Bottom and the fairies dominate. The two films, in fact, carry on an **intertextual** dialogue as each represents Hollywood's attempt (at two very different moments in its history) to gather Shakespeare into its unique combination of star and spectacle. Bottom is clearly the "star" part in Shakespeare's text, and it is no surprise that his role is played in these two *Dreams* by James Cagney and Kevin Kline. In concentrating on Bottom's story and on making the woods a cinematic mixture of film tricks and exotic creatures, the scripts of both films make deep cuts in the bittersweet comedy expressed by the romantic and emotional confusions of the young lovers as they experience all the agonies of puberty in a single night.

Peter Hall's 1968 film of the play restores the balance between its parts by retaining almost all of the text.[2] Here, the night's crazy

2. Hall cut only six lines from the play when fashioning his film script.

emotional and sexual confusions are given full expression by the lovers (played by Helen Mirren, Diana Rigg, David Warner, and Michael Jayston, young actors nurtured by the Royal Shakespeare Company), and the Helena and Hermia comedy rivals Bottom's. Hall visually reinforces the comic confusion of the lovers by making literal Titania's great speech about the seasons being turned upside down and Puck's remark that he discovers the lovers on "the dank and dirty ground." Hall shot his film on location in a cold and wet Warwickshire woods near the sixteenth-century country estate of Compton Verney, outside of Stratford. Images of the lovers splattered in mud and overseen by the nearly naked Titania (Judi Dench) and Oberon (Ian Richardson), who are conceived more as English folk spirits like Puck (Ian Holm) than as classical Ovidian gods, provide his film with a vivid visual reality.

Thirty years later another Royal Shakespeare Company director, Adrian Noble, attempted to translate his popular stage production of the play into film. The stage production had been a dazzle of rich primary colors: royal blue, scarlet, bright yellow, orange, and lime green. With the entire script giving equal weight to all four narratives, the lovers, the fairies, and the players all shared in a bold energy and humor. Puck descended from above, floating down through a sky of yellow light bulbs and holding onto the handle of a large green umbrella; an even bigger umbrella, this time in shocking pink and turned upside down, served as Titania's Bower. Bottom arrived at rehearsal riding a bike and wearing a helmet and goggles. His fellow hempen homespuns doubled as Titania's fairies. The production had an antic spirit and the lovers were the source of as much farcical humor as the players were in "Pyramus and Thisby."

Only the Bottom comedy translated when the production was reimagined for film. Even though the cast did not feature any "stars" from the world of film, Desmond Barrit's Bottom emerged nevertheless as the film's most compelling figure. As with the Reinhardt-Dieterle and Hoffman *Dreams*, Bottom's gain came at the expense of the lovers. Helena's two great speeches in 1.1 and 3.2 about her relationship with Hermia were severely truncated, eliminating the text's painful recognition of the ways in which heterosexual romantic relationships can puncture the bonds of teenage sisterhood. When I discussed these losses with the director, Noble indicated that he had shot Helena's material but in watching the rough cut in the editing room he kept thinking "Where's Bottom? Where the hell has Bottom gone? I've got to get him back into the film."[3] To speed Bottom's return, now on a motorcycle, Helena and the comic anguish of the rupture of her friendship with Hermia ended up on the cutting room floor.

These examples from several *Hamlet* and *A Midsummer Night's Dream* films illustrate the myriad ways the cutting of the text shapes a director's approach to his Shakespearean material. Though Fortinbras speaks only nineteen lines in *Hamlet*, his removal from the screenplay often triggers a number of other cuts and signals the director's decision to concentrate more on Hamlet's internal struggle to master the shattering losses of father, mother, and lover than on his political battle of wits and wills with Claudius.

The *Dream* films reveal that the attractiveness of the Bottom comedy is likely to result in reduced attention to the plight of the lovers and the feminist issues Shakespeare touchingly visits in exploring the Helena-Hermia relationship and Titania's loyalty to the Indian vot'ress who died giving birth to the little changeling boy. Even in Hall's film, which retains almost all of the text, the visual impact of his conception of the turmoil in the woods and his very earthy presentation of Oberon, Titania, and Puck create a *Dream* world in which landscape and costume often speak even more powerfully than text.

How Do Screenplays Rearrange Shakespeare's Text for Cinematic Purposes?

Sometimes the text isn't only pruned but rearranged, either to heighten an issue the director wishes to emphasize or to quicken the narrative flow of the film. An example of the former is Trevor Nunn's handling of Feste's song "O Mistress Mine" in his film of *Twelfth Night*. Nunn's screenplay foregrounds Feste's role by making him more like a wandering troubadour and omniscient narrator of the tale than a traditional clown or jester. Feste (Ben Kingsley) becomes the viewer's guide to the unfolding of the film's action. Feste is present, on a bluff overlooking the sea, when Viola is washed ashore from the shipwreck. He is also a silent witness to Viola's passion for Orsino, and he peeks in on the wedding of Olivia and Sebastian (after all, he does "live by the church").

3. Unpublished interview conducted by the author, May 14, 2001.

Feste's "O Mistress Mine" is sung in 2.3 by the revelers carrying on late at night in Olivia's kitchen. Through a series of brilliant **cross-cuts**, Nunn expands the song's audience from Sir Toby and crew to include Orsino, Cesario, Malvolio, and Olivia. The film subtly interweaves elements of 2.3 and 2.4 to create a composite portrait of the play's romantic yearners and holiday revelers, all depicted in their varying responses to the song's lyric strain. As Feste begins his song, Nunn cuts to Malvolio sitting in his room in a handsome dressing gown, drinking a brandy and reading the naughty French magazine *L'Amour*—thus visually establishing his bourgeois tastes and fantasies in a flash. When Feste reaches the line "That can sing both high and low," the film cuts to Olivia gently tossing in her sleep with a slight smile playing on her lips, suggesting her own romantic dreams stimulated by her encounter with Cesario, a remarkable creature come from the sea who can sing both high and low.

Then Nunn quickly cuts to Orsino's court and 2.4, where the count asks Cesario about "that old antique song we did hear last night" as we hear the tune of "O Mistress Mine" being played on the piano. The scene continues in this nostalgic atmosphere for several beats as the film interlaces the song's lyrics with the exchange between Orsino and Cesario about the fragile nature of youth, beauty, and love. This melancholy tone is maintained as Nunn cuts back to Olivia's kitchen, where Maria's voice joins Feste's on "In delay there lies no plenty / Then come kiss me, sweet and twenty / Youth's a stuff will not endure" (2.3.46–48). Maria, Toby, Sir Andrew, and Feste are years beyond twenty-something, and it is this knowledge, rather than a desire to torment Malvolio, that leads to the wild outburst of singing and noise-making that ensues as they realize that their revels now are ending.

Nunn extends his imaginative manipulation of the text as he moves from Feste's "O Mistress Mine" to his singing of "Come Away, Death." Nunn mixes in some of the exchanges between Orsino and Cesario early in 2.4 in his version of 2.3. He then delays returning to the end of 2.4 and Feste's sad song and its revealing aftermath so that it follows Malvolio's gulling (2.5), Cesario's second encounter with Olivia (3.1), and Sebastian's reunion with Antonio (3.3). Feste's second song is about not the fragility but the fatality of love. Nunn follows Shakespeare in setting its fatalism against the example of Cesario/Viola, who tries to educate Orsino about a lover who is self-sacrificing rather than self-aggrandizing; a lover who "never told her love" and instead "pined in thought,/And with a green and yellow melancholy,/She sat like Patience on a monument,/Smiling at grief" (2.4.111–14). Nunn repositions Feste's songs to mark the two major turns in the narrative: the abuse of Malvolio and the education of Orsino. Nunn rearranges and repositions the text to take advantage of film's ability to instantly cut back and forth between disparate settings and the musical soundtrack's ability to underscore and reinforce the emotional nuances of the narrative.

Nunn and Peter Hall both studied English literature at Cambridge under the great **formalist** literary critic F. R. Leavis. Much like the American new critics, Leavis believed that a close reading of the literary text was criticism's sole object. He thought that such close readings would reveal the ironies and ambiguities at work in the greatest literature as well as yield important ideas about the cultural moment in which it was produced. Nunn and Hall carried Leavis's critical principles into the world of performance, and their many Shakespearean stage productions and two Shakespeare films are distinguished by a close attention to Shakespeare's text. Hall accomplishes this heightened attention to text by shooting much of his film in **close-up** to highlight Shakespeare's language, and Nunn uses film's ability to cross-cut to add layers of gentle irony to Feste's songs by visually extending the reach of their lyrics to other characters in the play.

Another example, again from a comedy, of a screenplay's rearrangement of Shakespeare's scenic structure can be seen in Kenneth Branagh's treatment of the Dogberry comedy in his film of *Much Ado about Nothing*. Michael Keaton's transformation of Dogberry into a distant cousin of Beetlejuice was one of the most controversial elements in the popular and critical response to Branagh's film. Interestingly, no film critic made reference to the way Branagh's screenplay repositioned the Dogberry scenes in the film. Dogberry appears in four scenes in Shakespeare's text (3.3, 3.5, 4.2, and 5.1). He and the Watch aren't introduced until we are deep into the narrative and have experienced the tricks by which Benedick and Beatrice have been brought to recognize their affection for one another and Don John's counterplot to discredit Hero's love for Claudio.

Branagh introduces Dogberry several moments earlier than Shakespeare does. He appears immediately after the visual display of the giddy romantic spirits suddenly released by the fountain-splashing

Benedick and the high-swinging Beatrice. Branagh inserts the film's version of 3.2 (Don John and Borachio's duping Claudio) into the middle of the first Watch scene (3.3), as the film's plot and its comedy turns into darker colors. Keaton's Dogberry and Ben Elton's Verges are, in Branagh's own description, "charismatically, indomitably mad."[4] Dogberry is thus cleverly linked with Don John, for in the comic world the clown, however dim, will always expose the villain, however crafty. Branagh hastens that exposure by eliminating 3.4 and cutting immediately back to the comic suspense generated by Dogberry's arrest of Conrade and Borachio and his inability to comprehend and report their villainy to Leonato. Branagh's screenplay then combines elements of Dogberry's final appearances in 4.2 and 5.1 into a single scene following Benedick's pledge to Beatrice that he will challenge Claudio as a demonstration of his love for her.

Branagh's screenplay tightens the Dogberry comedy by wrapping it around the slander of Hero, using it as a foil to the two most vibrant scenes between Beatrice and Benedick, and by establishing its comic parallel with Don John's villainy. Our understanding of Branagh's trimming and repositioning of Dogberry does not, of course, fully dismiss the continuing debate about Michael Keaton's conception and embodiment of the character. Every screenplay makes decisions about how to employ Shakespeare's text; our job is to understand those decisions before we judge them.

Context: From the Globe to the Cineplex

Shakespeare films are driven not only by the way the screenplay shapes the text to the director's purposes but also by the historical and cultural moment of their creation. Chapters 2 and 3 discuss in greater depth the ways in which three seminal Shakespeare films, Olivier's *Henry V*, Zeffirelli's *Romeo and Juliet*, and Branagh's *Henry V*, were indelibly stamped by the spirit of the age in which they were conceived: World War II, the 1960s, and the post-Vietnam and Falklands era. Olivier's film was meant to rally his nation as the Allies embarked on the invasion of

---

4. Kenneth Branagh, Much Ado about Nothing *by William Shakespeare: A Screenplay Adaptation* (New York: W. W. Norton, 1993), p. xiii.

France to free Europe from the Nazis; Zeffirelli's heady, explosive film championed a passionate youth culture; and Branagh's dark, gritty, conspiratorial approach to *Henry V* placed it in the company of a host of Vietnam War films from *The Deer Hunter* (1978) to *Platoon* (1986).

The next two sections will provide more detailed readings of how Shakespeare films have been influenced by cultural and political ideas current in the social fabric at the time of their making. By examining films as varied as Laurence Olivier's *Hamlet* (1948), Joseph Mankiewicz's *Julius Caesar* (1953), Peter Hall's *A Midsummer Night's Dream* (1968), Baz Luhrmann's *William Shakespeare's, Romeo + Juliet* (1996), and Michael Almereyda's *Hamlet* (2000), we will see how films set in periods ranging from classical Rome to modern Manhattan all reveal a fascinating mix of issues alive in Shakespeare's age with those circulating in the latter half of the twentieth century.

How Is a Four-Hundred-Year-Old Text Made to Speak in a Modern Medium?: Finding the Present in the Past

Shakespeare films, even if they are set in the Renaissance or the historical period they depict, always reveal something of the cultural and political moment in which they were made. Two noted examples are Laurence Olivier's *Hamlet* and Joseph Mankiewicz's *Julius Caesar*. Each provides an interesting example of the ways in which ideas and events alive at the time each film was made helps to shape the director's approach to his Shakespearean material.

Olivier's *Hamlet* was released in 1948 and was part of the post–World War II celebration of Shakespeare as an icon of the British culture that triumphed in the war. The film's approach to the play and its cinematic style, however, also celebrate an interesting blend of European and American ideas and techniques. Olivier's ideas about *Hamlet* were deeply influenced by Ernest Jones, a psychoanalytic follower of Freud. Olivier had visited with Jones in the late 1930s prior to his stage performance of Hamlet directed by Tyrone Guthrie. Jones, who was later to write *Hamlet and Oedipus* (1949), outlined to Olivier and Guthrie his Freudian approach to the play: Hamlet delays in killing Claudius because he subconsciously identifies with him, as Claudius has enacted Hamlet's own Oedipal desires by murdering Hamlet's father and marrying his mother.

When Olivier made his film of *Hamlet* a decade later, Freud's ideas still gripped his imagination. Freudian psychology appeared to offer new avenues in understanding the human mind and character. Olivier cast as Gertrude Eileen Herlie, who was only twenty-seven—thirteen years younger than Olivier—when the film was made. Traditionally, Gertrude had been played by the senior actress in the theatrical company, one for whom all of us might think "the heyday in her blood was tame." Herlie's Gertrude expressed robust vigor, ample cleavage, and a passionate attachment to her son. Her bed, framed by suggestively folded drapes intended to suggest the vagina, became an obsessive curiosity of Olivier's prowling, probing camera. Olivier meant for the famed confrontation between mother and son following "The Mousetrap" to be sexually charged, though in performance that charge is somewhat dissipated by Hamlet's passivity once the Ghost enters to chastise his son for directing his venom at Gertrude rather than Claudius.

The film's Freudian reading explores the murky waters of Hamlet's troubled subconscious and is reinforced by its cinematic style. Olivier and his cinematographer, Desmond Dickinson, appropriated the black and white **chiaroscuro** play of light and shadow associated with Hollywood's **film noir** and the **deep focus** photography made famous by Orson Welles in *Citizen Kane* (1941). Both elements allowed Olivier to create a gloomy, gothic world for his film that neatly matched Hamlet's suspicious skepticism and his psychological turmoil. Though set in the sixteenth century, the film is, in substance and style, a perfect expression of the intellectual and cultural currents of postwar Britain and America, where Freudian psychology became the dominant paradigm for understanding human development.

Joseph Mankiewicz's *Julius Caesar* (1953), Hollywood's most ambitious attempt to capture Shakespeare on film in the immediate postwar period, also reveals the cultural and political context of its making even though it is set in ancient Rome. Producer John Houseman collaborated with Orson Welles on many of his theatrical productions in New York in the 1930s, including a famed fascist version of *Julius Caesar*. The Welles-Houseman partnership dissolved after *Citizen Kane*, but after the war Houseman was determined to produce a film of *Julius Caesar*, and in 1953 he recruited the Academy Award–winning director Joseph Mankiewicz to direct the film with a cast headed by James

Mason, John Gielgud, Deborah Kerr, and Marlon Brando. Houseman reports that he and Mankiewicz lobbied Metro-Goldwyn-Mayer's studio executives to be allowed to shoot the film in black and white to "stress the historical parallel between the political intrigues of the last years of the Roman Republic and recent European events" captured for the public by press photos and newsreels. Houseman believed the Forum scenes would naturally "invoke memories of the Fuhrer at Nuremberg and of Mussolini ranting from his high balcony overlooking the wildly cheering crowd that would presently spit on his dead body as it hung by its feet outside of a gas station."[5]

These unequivocal images of the lessons of power politics revealed in World War II may have held sway in Houseman's imagination, but by the time Mankiewicz came to shoot his film, other equally powerful black and white images of political turmoil had come to dominate the public's imagination, and the film resonates for more with postwar America than with the rise and fall of the Nazis and fascists in Europe. By the early 1950s the country was being internally consumed by the communist witch-hunts sponsored by the House Un-American Activities Committee and by Senator Joseph McCarthy of Wisconsin. Hollywood was intimately involved in the hysteria about supposed subversives in America. Elia Kazan, the famed stage and film director, was close to both Mankiewicz and Marlon Brando, and both were shocked and troubled by Kazan's decision to cooperate with McCarthy's investigation. As a result, the style and atmosphere of Mankiewicz's film speaks much more to the 1950s American present than to 1940s Europe. Mankiewicz, though filming on the sets discarded from *Quo Vadis* (a Hollywood Roman epic from 1951), explicitly refuses to give us the spectacle version of Rome we might expect from Hollywood and concentrates instead on a tightly focused formalist approach eager to explore the play's irony and ambiguity. Mankiewicz's ironic design is apparent from the film's first cut, as we move from the roar of the MGM lion to a close-up of a military standard bearing the Roman eagle: the symbol of an emerging cultural empire laying claim to the powerful legacy of a political empire long dead.

5. John Houseman, *Unfinished Business: Memoirs: 1902–1988* (New York: Applause Books, 1989), p. 324.

Mankiewicz's film style matches his interpretive intentions. His camera work is distinguished by clean, geometric patterns and movements utilizing, as Shakespeare critic Jack Jorgens notes, circles, triangles, and squares.[6] James Mason's Brutus is conceived as the classic conscientious liberal trapped between his pure ideals and dirty politics. Mankiewicz makes Brutus's nobility ambiguous by shooting his capitulation to Cassius's promptings in a high angle shot looking down over the shoulder of a massive statue of Caesar. The film repeatedly captures Caesar's looming presence and reminds us of his inescapable centrality to the play and to the lives of the conspirators who topple him. Later, Mankiewicz creates a similar visual irony in Brutus's "it must be by his death" soliloquy by shooting Brutus first through the limbs of a barren tree and then with the shadows cast by an overhead arbor falling across his face, both suggesting the dry and tangled nature of Brutus's tortured reasoning.

A production that focuses on the play's irony and ambiguity will inevitably come to concentrate on the play's most ironic and ambiguous figure: Mark Antony. Marlon Brando's performance is intelligent, controlled, and calculating, film acting at its finest. His eyes are the key to his performance. Notice how they absorb Caesar's treatment of Calpurnia at the running of the Lupercal; their refusal to acknowledge the assassins until they have looked long on Caesar's fallen body; their movement up from the corpse to take the measure of each conspirator as Brando shakes each of their hands and then glances down with disgust at his own, now bloody, hand; and their wicked gleam as he turns his back on the mob during the funeral oration. These actor-inspired images are all central to the cool, ironic, formalist intelligence Mankiewicz incorporates into his film version of Shakespeare's text, and they speak more to the irony and ambiguity of Hollywood's flirtation with communism than to the open brutality of the Nazis and fascists in World War II.

Olivier and Mankiewicz set their films in landscapes Shakespeare would recognize—the Renaissance and imperial Rome—but they saturated their films with contemporary ideas and parallels. Peter Hall's 1968 film of *A Midsummer Night's Dream* suggested a different approach to linking the past with the present. The film was shot on loca-

6. See Jack Jorgens, *Shakespeare on Film* (Bloomington: Indiana University Press, 1977), p. 101.

tion at Compton Verney, a seventeenth-century country estate near Stratford-upon-Avon. The estate's neo-classical architecture and patterned marble floors created a witty Warwickshire connection with Theseus's Athenian palace. Hall, however, introduced the flavor of the 1960s, particularly London's Carnaby Street fashions made famous by the designer Mary Quant, by dressing the aristocratic young men (Demetrius and Lysander) in Nehru jackets modified by lace collars and the women (Hermia and Helena) in mini-skirts and knee boots. This design choice firmly placed the spirit of Hall's film neither in classical Athens nor Renaissance London but in the swinging 60s. This spirit was reinforced by Hall's approach to camera work and editing.

Film style in the 1960s was heavily influenced by the French **New Wave** directors such as Jean-Luc Godard, Alan Resnais, and Francois Truffaut. Their style was distinguished by the use of **handheld cameras**, jumpy editing, grainy images, and location shooting using only available light. Hall employed all of these devices in the making of his *Dream*, mirroring the edgy, experimental, anti-authoritarian, youth-dominated cultural energy of the 1960s. Hall's film was most radical in its use of **jump-cuts**, an editing device that rapidly flashed from one actor to another, or from one part of the woods to another, without logical transitions. In several instances, most notably the long exchange between Hermia and Lysander about the course of true love not running smoothly and Helena's first soliloquy, Hall effectively broke up lengthy patches of Shakespeare's verse by rapidly changing the landscape of the shot. Thus Hermia and Lysander begin their exchange within Compton Verney, then a jump-cut finds them continuing their dialogue outside near a small pond, and a final jump-cut takes them to a rowboat on the pond, where they conclude their exchange. Hall's film reveals how a specific cultural context can be suggested through costume and cinematic style rather than through historical period parallels.

Olivier, Mankiewicz, and Hall all set their films against a past historical landscape, but they all, in differing fashions, find ways to link the past with the present by employing certain markers that allow their Shakespeare films to speak to our world as well as Shakespeare's. Let us turn now to examine briefly what happens when the filmmaker decides to set Shakespeare squarely in the modern age, where he risks having Shakespeare's rich blank verse seem an anachronism in our more prosaic culture.

How Is a Four-Hundred-Year-Old Text Made to Speak in a Modern Medium?: Finding the Past in the Present

Two films from the 1990s boldly set Shakespeare in the modern world: Baz Luhrmann's *William Shakespeare's Romeo +Juliet* (1996) and Michael Almereyda's *Hamlet* (2000). In screenplay, setting, style, **film score**, and casting, both films express a **postmodern** aesthetic. Luhrmann's film is framed by a television newscast and is thoroughly saturated with contemporary media overkill. Luhrmann creates his own virtual reality of a modern cityscape: part Los Angeles, part Mexico City, part Miami Beach. He sets his film in the world of the movies and borrows his techniques from everything between *Rebel without a Cause* and John Woo action films. These elements provoked Barbara Hodgdon to playfully confess about Luhrmann's **slam zooms** and jump-cuts: "If this be post-modernism, give me excess of it."[7]

The media saturation, the MTV-style rapid cuts and edits, the repeated visual references to the movies, even the Shakespearean tags that show up on advertising billboards are Luhrmann's way of demonstrating that contemporary corporate mass media's constant mingling of text and image, high culture and low, is just as hyperbolic as Shakespeare's heightened and dense rhetoric and thus a fitting landscape for its expression.

Luhrmann's Verona Beach is a multicultural gathering place where Latinos, African Americans, and Anglos rub up against one another and eventually combust. The film score pulsates with rock, hip-hop, gangsta rap, ballads, a gospel rendition of Prince's "When Doves Cry," and the plaintive strains of Wagner's "Liebestod," reminding us that Luhrmann is as much a creature of Shakespeare and the opera as he is of the pop charts and the streets. In fact, Luhrmann's film, for all its restless contemporary teenage cultural savvy, is at heart even more of a fantasy than Zeffirelli's gloriously romantic *Romeo and Juliet* from the late 60s. Luhrmann's potent mix of Shakespeare, Prince, Mozart, Wagner, and John Woo, all wrapped around two very conventional young Hollywood stars (Claire Danes and Leonardo DiCaprio), is what

---

7. Barbara Hodgdon, "*William Shakespeare's* Romeo +Juliet: Everything's Nice in America?", *Shakespeare Survey* 52 (1999), p. 90.

Hamlet (Ethan Hawke) watches footage of his home movie, in which he recites the beginning of the "To be or not to be" soliloquy with a gun to his head, in Michael Almereyda's *Hamlet* (2000, Miramax Films).

marks his film as a product of the postmodern aesthetic that champions pastiche and hybridity.

Michael Almereyda's *Hamlet* also has an urban and corporate setting, this time modern Manhattan. Like Luhrmann, Almereyda senses that modern media holds the key to making Shakespeare's language work in a contemporary setting. Picking up on Hamlet's interest in plays and players and the text's **metatheatrical** qualities, Almereyda fashions his Hamlet (Ethan Hawke) as an amateur filmmaker absorbed with making a home movie of his emotional angst and dysfunctional family. This allows Hawke's Hamlet to incorporate an enormous range of visual images as he edits, re-edits, plays, and replays snippets from his life shot on a Pixelvision video recorder (a toy made by Fisher-Price). These images include shots of burning oil fields, stealth bombers, James Dean in *East of Eden*, John Gielgud as Hamlet, Vietnamese monk Thich Nhat Hanh, a pornographic film of *Hamlet*, Claudius and Gertrude ice-skating, Ophelia in a variety of settings, and endless head-shots of Hamlet himself (including one in which he holds a gun to his temple).

Almereyda wants to immerse Hamlet and *Hamlet* deep in film's technologies and images. He fractures and fragments what his screenplay retains of Shakespeare's text just as he repeatedly fractures and fragments the visual narrative of his film. Hawke's introspective, melancholy, brooding Hamlet is a thing of shreds and patches. He's trapped in a corporate world of surveillance images and sounds controlled by Claudius and Polonius, and his attempt to find and define himself through a recording and restructuring of visual images of himself and his world is doomed to failure. The glass and steel Manhattan universe Almereyda creates for his Hamlet neatly mirrors the character's sense of imprisonment, and by breaking up Hamlet's soliloquies and making them another part of Hamlet's home movie, Almereyda interrupts and thus contains the spontaneous overflow of Hamlet's emotional rhetoric. In Almereyda's editing and Hawke's performance, *Hamlet* and Hamlet emerge as perfect paradigms of postmodernism.

Luhrmann and Almereyda both see Shakespeare as our contemporary and find in *Romeo and Juliet* and *Hamlet* narratives that not only speak powerfully over time to our own age but, even more important, seem to spring naturally from our own cultural milieu.

Examining a Shakespeare film's screenplay can lead to an important understanding of the particular approach a director takes to his Shakespearean material. By concentrating on what the screenplay retains of Shakespeare's text, we can chart what the director wants to emphasize in his or her cinematic version of the play. By being alert to the cultural and historical moment of the film's making, we can see how Shakespeare films are shaped by the ideas and issues of the age in which they were made. The inevitable dialogue between past and present provoked by every Shakespeare film also becomes a vital avenue of exploration for the student of Shakespeare on film.

8

DEPTH OF FIELD

Text and Image

Shakespeare was a great theater-poet whose genius was to shape language into character and action that fueled a compelling dramatic narrative. The sparkling dazzle, multiple layers, and powerful intelligence of that language are what continue to attract actors and audiences to his work. Shakespeare wrote for an audience that was intoxicated by language. The language was "fire-new" and Shakespeare and his fellow playwrights were helping to create and extend its power. The crowds who flowed over London Bridge and into the Rose and Globe theaters on an Elizabethan summer's afternoon came to hear even more than to see: they were more audience than spectators, in the root sense of those words. How much of the deep textures and images of Shakespeare's language they absorbed and retained will forever be a mystery to us. We do know that hearing him led many to seek to read him as well, allowing them the opportunity to savor his language in a private rather than a public space.

Film is a swift medium, a rush of image, action, and language sweeping before our eyes. Elizabethans, with their focus on language, might well be baffled by our ability to absorb and comprehend images that flash before us in rapid sequences. The filmmaker's great challenge is to find a successful way to synthesize Shakespeare's verbal dexterity and film's visual power. Sensory translation is one part of the transaction, but not all. The filmmaker must retain enough of Shakespeare's text to maintain the charge and flow of the play's verbal narrative while also establishing some key visual parallels for the seminal images at work in Shakespeare's language.

How Does the Visual Medium of Film Treat Shakespeare's Rich Verbal Images in the Creation of Character?

Mise en scène is a French term widely used in film studies. It encompasses all the elements that go into the staging of the action before the camera: setting, costume, lighting, and acting. It defines the landscape of a Shakespeare film: the intelligent interaction between action and setting. Laurence Olivier's *Richard III* (1955) provides a classic example of this method for translating a Shakespearean verbal image into a visual one.

Olivier creates an interaction between action and setting by picking up on Richard III's repeated use of the image of the shadow to describe an ironic appropriation of his own self-image. In his famous opening soliloquy ("Now is the winter of our discontent"), he contrasts his own situation with that of his older brother Edward who has recently been crowned king, by reminding us that "I have no delight to pass away the time,/Unless to spy my shadow in the sun/And descant on my own deformity" (1.1.25–26). Later, after he has brazenly (and successfully) wooed Princess Anne (after killing both her husband, Prince Edward, and her father-in-law, Henry VI), he takes a different sort of delight in the shadow he casts: "Shine out, fair sun, till I have bought a glass/That I may see my shadow as I pass" (1.2.262–63).

Olivier lifts these images and makes them central to his visual presentation of Richard III. In his filming of Richard's long opening soliloquy (made even longer in the film with fifteen lines added from another Richard soliloquy in *Henry VI, Part Three*), he places Richard alone in the throne room and has him move in and out of light and shadow as he moves toward and then retreats from the camera in a cunning maneuver to woo the film audience. When he moves away from the camera we become conscious of his shadow, particularly at those moments in the soliloquy when Richard is proudly proclaiming his own duplicitous nature (for example, "Why I can change colors like the chameleon"). At certain moments the lighting creates several shadows for Richard, projecting out to his side as well as to his front or back. Olivier's Richard is a sharp, ironic, and mercurial con artist who projects a variety of personalities as he works his way through layers of family opposition to gain the crown.

Richard III (Laurence Olivier) and his ever-present shadow in Olivier's *Richard III* (1955, London Films).

As Richard begins to bustle in his world, Olivier's camera uses Richard's shadow repeatedly to announce his presence or to bring a lethal closure to his exit from the scene. Richard's shadow precedes him before he breaks in on Lady Anne for the first time and then is even more ominously cast across her door as he enters to claim her as his sexual prize after he has wooed her for his wife. His shadow plays down over his brother's court as he plots his next move against Clarence and then falls over the barred window of Clarence's cell as he arrives to recruit his brother's murderers; this visual imagery allows Olivier to underline Richard's shadowy control over the events that lead up to his usurpation of the crown. The shadow imagery never becomes a melodramatic movie cliché because it is always balanced by Olivier's tart delivery of Richard's mocking yet strategic rhetoric. Olivier's use of shadow imagery is overt and theatrical, and it is one way he extends his talent as an actor into his role as the film's director.

How Does the Visual Medium of Film Treat Shakespeare's Rich Verbal Images in the Creation of Landscape and Atmosphere?

Roman Polanski's film of *Macbeth* (1971) contains several examples of visual imagery used in a different manner from that of Olivier in *Richard III*. *Macbeth* is a violent and bloody play packed with images of horror. Macbeth is an unconventional figure: an ambitious, murderous tyrant with a hyperactive moral conscience. Images of bats, beetles, snakes, scorpions, and ferocious animals occupy his tortured imagination. After Macbeth has killed Duncan and been crowned, the new king and his queen plan a banquet ostensibly to honor his dear friend Banquo. In Polanski's film, Macbeth welcomes "our chief guest" Banquo while the camera focuses on a caged bear in the foreground of the shot. Later, Polanski will give us a quick shot of the dead bear being dragged out of the great hall after he has been killed by dogs at the end of the banquet. The bear works on many imaginative levels here. First, he provides a symbol of the entertainment Polanski's Macbeth imagines suitable for a state occasion. Second, he becomes an image of Macbeth's own ravenous lust for power willing to feed on others (Duncan and soon Banquo) to satisfy his appetite. And third, he is an ironic reminder that Macbeth will become his own trapped animal, a man "cabined, cribbed, confined" by "saucy doubts and fears" (3.4.23–24). Ultimately Macbeth will even identify himself with a chained animal in the bear-pit in his final moments in the play: "They have tied me to a stake; I cannot fly,/But bear-like, I must fight the course" (5.7.1–2). The bear is an organic image that Polanski lifts from the end of Shakespeare's text and replants at the center of his film to become an important comment on Macbeth and his reign of terror. The image provokes and resonates with Shakespeare's text, merging image, landscape, and character.

Earlier in the film, when Macbeth hesitates to confide in Lady Macbeth about his plans to have Banquo murdered ("Be innocent of the knowledge, dearest Chuck,/Till thou applaud the deed" (3.2.45–46), Jon Finch as Macbeth gazes out as the sun begins to set and observes in his gloomy, gothic manner, "Light thickens; and the crow/Makes wing to the rooky wood" (3.2.50–51). Polanski's camera follows his gaze and tracks a single crow making its flight to the rooky wood. Here the visual image is perhaps too pointed. It simply repeats Shakespeare's image without enlarging or commenting on it. The bear belongs to both Shakespeare and Polanski; the crow never takes resonant flight from Shakespeare's text into Polanski's film. Shakespeare's crow is a creature of Macbeth's murky imagination; Polanski makes it literal and diminishes its effectiveness.

How Does Television Shakespeare Relate
Verbal Image to Landscape?

The BBC television series of Shakespeare's plays experimented with three approaches to the problem of verbal image and mise en scène. These approaches might be defined as the realistic or representational, the painterly or pictorial, and the abstract or symbolic. Because television, as mentioned in Chapter 4, is so closely tethered to reality by its broadcast of the news, sporting events, documentaries, investigative reporting programs, cop shows, hospital dramas, and situation comedies, the original producers of the BBC series believed that Shakespeare should be set against a realistic background. The first productions were either shot on location (*As You Like It*, *Henry VIII*) or in a television studio with representational sets (*Julius Caesar*, *Romeo and Juliet*). The former suffered from the lack of a budget large enough to take true film advantage of shooting on location, and the latter stumbled on the difficulty of establishing believable versions of Rome and Verona with painted flats constructed in the small space of a television studio.

The second producer of the series, Jonathan Miller, was more successful when he turned to a painterly style for establishing a production's mise en scène. Miller took his visual inspiration from the colors, costumes, and fabrics featured in the Renaissance period paintings he admired in London's National Gallery of Art. Sets became less important than costume and the "look" of the production was inspired by a famous painter like Veronese or Vermeer. These productions took a step away from realism to locate Shakespeare in a painter's version of period rather than an architect's.

Finally, Jane Howell, in the *Henry VI* plays and *Richard III*, moved the BBC Series Shakespeare into a more abstract and symbolic landscape using, in a nod to the design of the permanent stage at Ontario's Shakespeare Festival Theatre, the same unified open set for all four plays. The progression of the series neatly mirrored the way in which television drama is caught between film and theater: it began by trying to take productions in the direction of film and ended by pulling back toward the stage without ever finding a consistently successful approach to televising Shakespeare.

How Does Film Give Extra Resonance to a Shakespearean Image or Important Prop?

Sometimes the language of film can lift an image or important prop from its Shakespearean context and give it a prominence far beyond its mention in the text or its use in a stage production. Michael Radford's film of *The Merchant of Venice* (2004) provides a stunning example of what a **flash-cut** and **close-up** can accomplish in making an important detail in the text visually vivid and psychologically revealing. Shylock's daughter Jessica has eloped with her Christian lover, Lorenzo. Shylock's friend Tubal inquires about their flight and reports to Shylock that they were seen in Genoa where one of his informants "showed me a ring that he had of your daughter for a monkey" (3.1.23–24). Shylock, in one of the most painful and poignant moments in the play, responds: "Out upon her! Thou torturest me, Tubal: it was my turquoise; I had it of Leah when I was a bachelor: I would not have given it for a wilderness of monkeys" (3.1.126–28).

When Al Pacino utters this lament in Radford's film, we are given a flash-cut where Pacino's Shylock imagines seeing the ring being exchanged for the monkey in lewd circumstances. Only film could provide us with a close-up of such a tiny prop and deeply imprint this specific ring, with its turquoise stone placed in a unique gold latticework setting, in our imaginations. At the end of the film, after the lovers and Antonio have all returned to Belmont and been reconciled, Radford returns to Leah's ring and reinforces the importance of rings and bonds to Shakespeare's play. As the newlyweds head off to bed, Radford's camera follows a solitary female figure out from the villa and down a path in its formal gardens. She stops at a railing overlooking a tranquil bay at sunrise. The camera captures her melancholy face in close-up and we see that it is Jessica. The camera pans down her body to focus on her right hand, and we see the turquoise ring her mother gave her father on her finger. Jessica has not given Shylock's ring away; she has kept it as a reminder of what she gave up for this wilderness of Christians. The power of this vivid detail is created by film's ability to

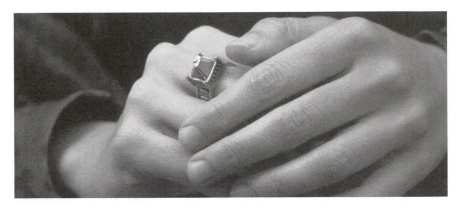

Jessica (Zuleika Robinson) wears the ring her mother, Leah, gave to her father, Shylock, in Michael Radford's *The Merchant of Venice* (2004, Sony Pictures Classics).

concentrate our attention on the smallest object via the close-up and to magnify its importance by locking it in our imagination.

Olivier's *Hamlet* provides another interesting example of the way film can underline the relationship between a character and a particular prop. In the duel between Hamlet and Laertes, Olivier's camera repeatedly cross-cuts between Gertrude and the goblet into which Claudius promises to dissolve an expensive pearl if Hamlet scores the first hit. The film silently traces Gertrude's interest in the cup through a series of close-ups. Once Claudius deposits the pearl in the goblet, the film makes it clear that Gertrude knows her husband has poisoned the wine. When she drinks from the cup she does so intentionally, believing that she is saving her son's life. The cross-cut and the close-up provide Olivier with the film technique to add an important dimension to Eileen Herlie's portrait of Gertrude: her self-sacrificial love for her son.

Examples of props taking on a special significance like Shylock's ring and Claudius's goblet abound in Shakespeare films, and they can be intelligently explored as indicating ways that film can visually suggest Shakespearean subtext.

How Does Film Find Visual Inspiration in an Extended Passage of Shakespeare's Blank Verse?

Polanski's bear, Radford's ring, and Olivier's goblet are visual details that become central to each director's translation of Shakespeare's verbal images or props into images that work on film. Alternatively, sometimes directors will focus on a long speech, rather than a small detail, as the source of their visual inspiration. Peter Hall's 1968 film of *A Midsummer Night's Dream* rewrote generations of stage and film *Dreams* that were conceived as idyllic fantasies dominated by fairies dressed in tutus and wrapped in Mendelssohn's familiar score. Hall plopped his cast down in a cold, wet Warwickshire woods in September and had his lovers battle the elements as well as their own volatile emotions. Hall takes his visual cue from Titania's great "These are the forgeries of jealousy" speech, in which she describes at length the disorder in the natural world emanating from her quarrel with Oberon about the raising of her little changeling boy. As she describes them, their brawls have sucked up contagious fogs from the sea, causing rivers to flood, corn to rot, animals to starve, and seasons to alter so that "hoary-headed frosts/Fall in the fresh lap of the crimson rose" (2.1.107–108).

Hall anticipates Titania's speech in the **montage** that opens his film. As the credits roll, the camera captures the quick seasonal changes in the weather, from sun to rain to storm, reflected in the small pond on Theseus's estate. These quicksilver changes in nature are then contrasted with the rational and solid architecture of Theseus's neo-classical villa, neatly capturing the play's movement from Theseus's world of law and order to the chaos and confusion of the woods.

When the film reaches Titania's "forgeries of jealousy" speech in the narrative, Judi Dench delivers it in medium close-up as Hall's camera rotates several filters, from blue to red to green, over the lens. In the background of the shot we see the seasons alter, as in the film's opening montage. The film later revisits the chaos of nature and links it to love's confusion when Puck exclaims that he found the lovers asleep on the "dank and dirty ground." As Hermia, Helena, Lysander, and Demetrius grow more perplexed and pained by the night's agonies, Hall shows in their muddy faces and torn clothing that they have become entangled in an unruly and inhospitable world.

Titania's speech provides Hall the license to explore the play's darker and more erotic elements, usually overlooked by productions that seek to emphasize dream over nightmare in the lovers' experience in the woods.

How Do Films Use Shakespeare's Images as Narrative Devices?

Orson Welles's *Othello* provides an example of the way film can organically appropriate an image or series of images from Shakespeare's text to visualize the translation of the text into the film's narrative. Welles understands visually how Shakespeare's images chart Othello's descent from "an unhoused free condition" to a "cistern for foul toads/To knot and gender in" (4.2.63–64). From the film's opening overhead **iris shot** of Othello's face on his funeral bier, to the final overhead shot of Othello and Desdemona on their marriage-murder bed, the key perspective of Welles's camera is downward, often peering into underground vaults and sewers. The camera is most frequently placed above the action, forcing us to peer down through circular openings, or windows, or twisting staircases to try to see what is submerged. We are placed in the same relationship to the action as Othello is to his own psyche. Just as Othello is manipulated by Iago, we are manipulated by Welles's camera to look down and in to discover something ugly.

This process starts in the film's treatment of the long arc of Shakespeare's second act, which begins with the reunion of Othello and Desdemona on Cyprus's battlements and ends with Cassio and Roderigo sloshing through a sewer in the drunken brawl precipitated by Iago. Othello and Desdemona are roused from their lovemaking to silence the riot below, and Welles cuts quickly and repeatedly between the two lovers framed against the night sky and Cassio, Roderigo, Montanto, and Iago pursuing one another in a Byzantine sewer. Welles extends this "foul rout" through a maze of pillars to become a nightmare image of Othello's honeymoon. The fighting and sloshing concludes with an overhead shot down into the sewer where we see Roderigo's little Maltese terrier wandering through the water in search of his master. By framing the awakened lovers with the sewer shots of Roderigo's forlorn dog, Welles makes a wickedly playful association of gulls and their pets that will lead to the release of destructive powers much greater than those required to drown cats and blind puppies.

This image pattern is extended into the famous Turkish bath scene, Welles's version of 5.1. The film score's mandolins underline the frenzied excitement of the scene, which contains thirty-seven **cuts** in just two minutes of film time. The atmosphere of the Turkish bath shares the dankness of the sewer scene, the sense of water dripping everywhere, and violence exploding in an enclosed space. The latticework of the cistern cover in the earlier scene is here echoed by the wooden slats in the floor, through which Iago repeatedly stabs his sword, trying to kill Roderigo scurrying for safety beneath. Shots of Iago's sword plunging through the slats, accompanied by the frenzied mandolins mixing with the sounds of water oozing in the close atmosphere, recall the earlier cistern scene and prepare for Welles's handling of Desdemona's murder immediately after the Turkish bath scene.

We hear Welles intone "It is the cause" as the camera slowly pans to Othello's face as he approaches the sleeping Desdemona. In that movement he passes through the visual devices Welles has used to establish the landscape of the play: shadows, windows, and a many-pillared subterranean room that bears an eerie resemblance to the pillars and ceiling of the Moroccan cistern. Othello moves in and out of the shadows to the bed, where he suffocates Desdemona with the spotted handkerchief and where we see yet another overhead shot, this time of Desdemona's surreal face beneath the handkerchief, struggling for breath.

After the murder, we see a quick series of shots that the film has associated with Othello's progressive and accelerating circumscription: Welles is framed by shadows, archways, and bars as the camera spins out of control in a manner similar to its treatment of Othello's epileptic fit, but this time capturing the chamber's vaulted ceilings as Othello recovers his equilibrium and lifts Desdemona from the floor and places her on the bed. He looks up and sees Cassio peering down at him through a large round opening in the crypt's ceiling. We now join Cassio's perspective and look down into Othello's sewer-cistern-dungeon. Welles shoots the entire "soft you, a word or two" speech from this overhead perspective. Othello's face becomes entirely swallowed in shadows as the speech ends and the cover is slowly pushed across the opening, shutting off the camera's access to Othello's ruined world. Othello, determined not to "Keep a corner in a thing I love/For other's uses" (3.3.276–77), ends up, in the visual daring of Welles's film, creating just such a foul cistern as the final image of his tragic marriage.

Welles's *Othello* is an example of the way a masterful filmmaker reaches into his Shakespearean text and finds there a series of related images (in this case of ego circumscription and sexual corruption; of expanse and impasse) that stimulate his cinematic imagination. Welles's images drive and define the narrative in equal force with what remains of Shakespeare's dialogue in the finished film. One can see why Welles's Shakespeare films were so popular with European **cinèastes;** they read his visual images with the same relish that an English-speaking audience reserves for Shakespeare's words. For the French, in particular, Welles's images told the story; English speakers gain the benefit of seeing how successfully Welles's visual images reinforce Shakespeare's verbal narrative.

How Does Film Translate a Shakespearean Metaphor into a Movie Genre?

Sometimes an element in Shakespeare's text—an image, metaphor, character, or atmosphere—will evoke in the film director a resonance with a particular movie genre. Richard III's character and rise to power suggested to director Richard Loncraine parallels with the great Hollywood gangster films of the 1930s and 40s. Similarly, Laurence Olivier and Orson Welles both incorporated elements of film noir in their versions of *Hamlet* and *Othello*. Kenneth Branagh went even further than these directors in finding his inspiration for his film version of *Love's Labour's Lost* in the great American movie musicals of the 1930s where, particularly in the Fred Astaire–Ginger Rogers films, dance carried the narrative as much as dialogue and song.

Like all of Shakespeare's festive comedies, *Love's Labour's Lost* is highly patterned. The group experience, rather than the individual, is paramount. In his comedies, Shakespeare often likes to take several pairs of aristocratic lovers and follow their progress through the follies and confusions of romantic awakening. He intertwines their experiences with those of a series of clowns who intentionally or unintentionally parody and mock the aristocrats' behavior. Shakespeare develops these interrelationships like an elaborate and elegant dance that goes awry when emotional rhythms trump rational patterns. Early in *Love's Labour's Lost*, when the four pairs of potential partners are first brought together, the leading young man (Berowne) asks the woman (Rosaline) he seeks to woo: "Did I not dance with you in Brabant once?" She replies by echoing his question: "Did I not dance with you in Brabant once?" (2.1.114–15). Scholars and directors, most prominently

Harley Granville-Barker, have noted that *Love's Labour's Lost*, in particular, is "never very far from the actual formalities of song and dance."[1]

Kenneth Branagh, inspired by Berowne's query and Granville-Barker's insight, saw the potential to make a film of *Love's Labour's Lost* by linking it to the genre of the American movie musical, which reached its zenith in the 1930s with the films of Fred Astaire and Ginger Rogers. The implied metaphor of dance in Shakespeare's play becomes literal in Branagh's film, as the lovers sing and dance to the popular songs of the period composed and written by Cole Porter, George and Ira Gershwin, Irving Berlin, and Jerome Kern.

Shakespeare's play ends unconventionally for a comedy. Just as the wooing games are reaching their climax, the Princess of France receives word that her father has died. The women end the festivities by determining to return to France to mourn the dead king. The men press their desires to marry, but the women make them promise to withhold any future courtship for a year to test the sincerity of their romantic sentiments. The play ends with a parting rather than a wedding. Branagh's buoyant film, like Shakespeare's festive play, takes a melancholy turn at its end.

Branagh, already committed to the 1930s period because of his movie musical genre choice, seizes on the further opportunity to set his film in 1939 so that not only the king's death but the advent of World War II breaks off the romantic fun (and the song and dance) and sends the men to war to prove their valor and worth. Branagh captures the poignancy of the ending in a sequence that features the four lovers singing George and Ira Gershwin's "They Can't Take That Away from Me" and culminates in their parting at a foggy airport (a scene lifted from *Casablanca*).

Branagh's film finds in the American movie musical a patterned grace, elegance, and wit that serve as a twentieth-century equivalent to Elizabethan romantic comedy. The movement of dance, implied by the interaction of the lovers and clowns in Shakespeare's play and made literal in the great Astaire-Rogers films, becomes Branagh's way of translating a sixteenth-century comedy into a twentieth-century idiom.

1. Harley Granville-Barker, *Prefaces to Shakespeare* Vol. II (Princeton: Princeton University Press, 1947), p. 442.

How Do Shakespeare Films Visually Engage with Critical Idea and Theory?

Sometimes films find their way into a visual language for Shakespeare through prominent critical ideas about the plays alive in any given era. Many of the most interesting Shakespeare films from the 1990s— Luhrmann's *William Shakespeare's Romeo+Juliet*, Taymor's *Titus*, and Almereyda's *Hamlet*, for example—all share certain visual elements that point to concepts at the heart of the postmodern aesthetic, concepts such as indeterminancy, fragmentation, pastiche, and hybridization. All three of these films reflect the influence of such prominent postmodern theorists as Jacques Derrida, Michel Foucault, Slavoj Žižek, and Fredric Jameson, and they have inspired provocative essays from such prominent contemporary film and cultural critics as Barbara Hodgdon, Peter Donaldson, and W. B. Worthen.

The relationship between film productions of Shakespeare and literary criticism is not a new one. Joseph Mankiewicz's film of *Julius Caesar* was heavily influenced by formalist ideas about the text that sought to capture the subtle irony and ambiguity of Shakespeare's form and content. Peter Hall has credited the ideas of famed formalist English literary critic F. R. Leavis for his use of many close-ups in his film of *A Midsummer Night's Dream* to "scrutinize the marked ambiguity of the text."[2] An important generation of Shakespeare stage and film directors, including Peter Hall and Peter Brook, were influenced by the work of a Polish critic and stage director, Jan Kott. Kott's *Shakespeare Our Contemporary* (1964) was very much a product of his middle-European upbringing at a time when Poland was under the heavy boot of first the Nazis and then the Soviets. Kott found Shakespeare a theatrical companion to such contemporary playwrights as Samuel Beckett and Eugene Ionesco, leading practitioners of the Theater of the Absurd.

Kott's ideas infiltrated the worlds of theater and film a decade before they were absorbed by the academy, influencing directors from Orson Welles to Peter Brook and Roman Polanski. Kott did not read Shakespeare as a nineteenth-century romantic but as a mid-twentieth-century realist dramatizing a violent Eros in the comedies and a brutal

2. Quoted in Roger Manvell, *Shakespeare and the Film* (New York: Praeger, 1971), p. 121.

power politics in the histories and tragedies. Kott's phrase for the relentless jackboot of authoritarianism was "The Grand Mechanism." For Kott, history was more like a giant wheel (as it is imagined by Shakespeare in *King Lear*) endlessly turning and repeating itself, rather than, as the Marxists thought, a linear process working toward a preordained goal. Kott identified with Shakespeare's clowns rather than his kings and saw them, as existential humanists rather than ideological utopians. He linked them with figures like Charlie Chaplin's little tramp and Samuel Beckett's Vladimir, Estragon, Hamm, and Clov (the lead characters in *Waiting for Godot* and *Endgame*), characters who struggle and persevere in the absence of grand theories about historical progress and the meaning of life. Such figures, exemplified by Falstaff and Lear's Fool, are realists who possess a skeptical eye and ear for the dangers of hollow rhetoric and propaganda. "I like not such grinning honor as Sir Walter hath," says Falstaff, dismissing Hotspur's fatal attraction to abstract honor, "give me life." (1HIV.5.357–58)

Kott wanted to strip away the veneer of authority and elitism that had been attached to Shakespeare over several centuries to confront the hard realities at the core of his plays: the rapacious power struggles in tragedies like *Macbeth* and *King Lear* and the bestial, sometimes even masochistic, expression of our animal instincts in comedies like *A Midsummer Night's Dream* and *As You Like It*. Kott's view was pragmatic and tough-minded, forged by the events in Europe including the rise of the Nazis, the devastation of World War II, the institution of the Holocaust, and the postwar Soviet imposition of the Iron Curtain. Kott's bleak influence can be seen in number of Shakespeare films shot in the 1960s and 70s by directors as diverse as Orson Welles, Roman Polanski, and Peter Brook.

Peter Brook's film of *King Lear* (1971), like his stage production of the play for the Royal Shakespeare Company (RSC), was deeply influenced by Kott's essay *"King Lear or Endgame,"* in which Kott explored the parallels between Shakespeare and Beckett. Kott found in Lear's banter with the Fool the rhythms of the English music hall comedians that had inspired Beckett's tramps. He also found in Lear's mad encounter with Gloucester on the beach at Dover echoes of the nihilistic, if often piercingly comic, exchanges between Hamm and Clov in Beckett's *Endgame*. Lear's universe, like Beckett's, is grotesque and absurd. Brook tried to capture this atmosphere by setting his film in the barren snow-covered landscape of Jutland and shooting in a grainy black and white to stress the text's cruelty rather than the power of its poetry. Brook cast the Irish actor Jack MacGowran, known for his work in Beckett's plays, as the Fool, and the film highlighted his relationship with Lear. Paul Scofield played the king as a cold, stern, repressed figure rather than following the more traditional interpretation of the king as an angry Old Testament prophet. Brook's film is short, nasty, and grotesque, combining elements of Hobbes, Darwin, and Kott.

Brook's cinematic technique linked Kott with Brecht by using a series of alienation devices that repeatedly disrupted the flow of the narrative. As film scholar Kenneth Rothwell notes, Brook "employs discontinuities, zoom-fades, accelerated motion, freeze frames, shock editing, complex reverse-angle and over-the-shoulder shots, jump cuts, overhead shots, silent screen titles, eyes-only close-ups, and hand-held as well as immobile cameras."[3] The texture of the film, the nature of the performances, and its radical style all support Kott's thesis that *King Lear* is about the decay and fall of the world; a decay and fall we experience in Brook's film as searing and ultimately cruelly absurd.

Though Orson Welles did not share Kott's bleak sensibility, his *Chimes at Midnight* does become very Kottian in its treatment of the encounter between Hal and Hotspur at the Battle of Shrewsbury. The clash between these two vibrant young warriors is the heroic climax of *1 Henry IV*, but Welles takes his inspiration for filming the battle from the play's great clown, Falstaff. Falstaff is one of Kott's realists, wary of the absolutist rhetoric that leads men to battle and potentially to death.

Welles's battle is an exercise in horror rather than heroics. Mud-covered soldiers hack away at one another in a devastating visualization of Kott's crushing view of war as the Grand Mechanism. Welles shot the scene with a big crane, very low to the ground, moving fast against the action. He then cut these takes into shorter segments so that, as he has remarked, "every cut seemed to be a blow, a counter blow, a blow received, a blow returned."[4] During this grotesque mayhem, Welles's film repeatedly cuts away to shots of Falstaff scurrying in and out of

3. Kenneth Rothwell, *A History of Shakespeare on Screen* (Cambridge: Cambridge University Press, 1999), p. 151.
4. Juan Cobos and Miguel Rubio, "Welles and Falstaff," *Sight and Sound* 35 (Autumn 1966), p. 161.

harm's way on the edge of the action, wisely preserving his life while those around him are being turned into "food for powder." The brutality of Welles's battle scene has the effect of turning us all into Falstaffs.

Finally, Kott's influence provides several key visual metaphors in Polanski's *Macbeth*. Kott's ideas about Shakespeare's universe directly challenged those of E. M. W. Tillyard, whose *Shakespeare's History Plays* (1944) and *Elizabethan World Picture* (1947) read Shakespeare's images of chaos and brutality as part of a larger cosmic vision whose ultimate end was the reestablishment of a proper hierarchial order implied in the concept of the great chain of being. Tillyard's stress on the return to order in the final moments of the tragedies and the working-out of Tudor providence in the histories was challenged by Kott's reading of the tragedies as experiences dominated by the savage and absurd and the histories as instances of unending power struggles.

Polanski's *Macbeth* does not end with Macduff's "The time is free" and Malcolm's pledge to perform the correct political rituals "That calls upon us, by the grace of Grace," which are the pieties of restored order and harmony that Tillyard championed. Rather, in keeping with Kott's view of power, Polanski cuts from Macbeth's severed head being swirled like a soccer ball through a crowd of cheering soldiers, to Donalbain riding and then limping (his hunchback and limp having been established early in the film to imprint Donalbain in our memory so as to be instantly recognized and recalled at this moment) to *his* appointment with the weird sisters. For the two Poles, Polanski and Kott, saturated by the experience of German and Russian domination, *Macbeth* is more about its brutal core than its optimistic ending.

These examples reveal how directors discover key visual images for their films not only from within Shakespeare's text but also from the ideas generated by leading critics of the plays and those provided by the cultural moment in which the films were imagined and created. Students familiar with postmodernism will quickly see how its ideas are reflected in many of the Shakespeare films of the 1990s, and those who read some of the essays in Kott's *Shakespeare Our Contemporary* will readily see its influence on Shakespeare films in the late 1960s and early 1970s.

9

MONTAGE

Beginnings and Signature Shots

The next two chapters will examine specific devices filmmakers employ to translate their Shakespearean material into the grammar and rhetoric of film and to put their own artistic imprint on the films they are creating. Directors of Shakespeare films understand that they must put their stamp quickly on narrative material already familiar to many in their audiences. They need to create a visual landscape, tone, and atmosphere that imaginatively express the film's Shakespearean narrative. They also want to establish the formal elements (camera work, editing, music) that will come to distinguish their personal style in translating Shakespeare into film.

Directors often establish their approach to style and narrative by the way they decide to open their films. Orson Welles noted that films often begin with what he termed "a riderless horse shot."[1] Welles knew that while stage plays often open slowly, allowing the audience time to adjust to the aesthetic environment they are entering and the pitch and timbre of the actor's voice, films tend to open quickly to immediately absorb us in the visual world on the screen. The opening of a Shakespeare film is particularly critical because it requires the director to establish the visual world of the action and to link that world to images or ideas suggested by Shakespeare's text. It also provides the opportunity for the director to reveal his stylistic approach to his Shakespearean material. The opening shot or sequence must grab our attention, pique our curiosity, and establish a Shakespearean resonance for the film that follows. In many instances, these beginning sequences have no dialogue, allowing the director **film time** to create a landscape and universe with visual images and film score before a word of the screenplay is spoken.

1. Welles made this remark in the program "Filming *Othello*," which he made for German television in 1978.

If opening sequences are crucial in moving us into the world of the film, signature shots define the director's combination of treatment and technique in moving Shakespeare from script to screen. Most Shakespeare films contain three or four signature shots or sequences, defining moments in the director's work, and they can be as robust as Olivier's long tracking shot of the French cavalry's charge in his *Henry V* or as subtle as Branagh's mirror shot for the "To be or not to be" soliloquy in his film of *Hamlet*.[2] Sometimes the signature shot becomes associated with a particular camera perspective that's repeatedly employed in the film, like Welles's use of the **overhead** shot in his *Othello* or **low angle** shots in his *Chimes at Midnight*.

How Do Directors Use Shots and Sequences to Establish Their Approach to Opening a Shakespearean Comedy?

Shakespeare's most popular comedies, *A Midsummer Night's Dream*, *As You Like It, Much Ado about Nothing*, and *Twelfth Night*, are all distinguished by their festive, holiday atmosphere, but Shakespeare always shades that festivity with darker elements tempering the genre's traditional happy ending. To trace a director's approach to handling the light and dark elements in Shakespearean comedy, let's look at examples of how filmmakers as diverse as Max Reinhardt and William Dieterle, Franco Zeffirelli, Kenneth Branagh, and Trevor Nunn have signaled their intentions to emphasize either the festive or melancholy qualities of the comedy in the opening sequences of their films.

The 1935 Warner Brothers *A Midsummer Night's Dream*, directed by Max Reinhardt and William Dieterle, opens with a grand triumphal progression as Theseus leads his conquered prize, Hippolyta, into Athens. The frame is packed with a throng of cheering spectators and the camera picks out Hermia and Lysander waving to each other through the crowd before moving on to discover Helena searching for Demetrius in the tumult. We are clearly being treated to a Hollywood

2. Kenneth Branagh defines such shots in his own work as "anchor shots" and they are the only shots he plans out in advance of rehearsing the screenplay with his cast. See my interview with Branagh, "Communicating Shakespeare: An Interview with Kenneth Branagh," *Shakespeare Bulletin* 20, no. 3 (Summer 2002), p. 25.

spectacle, establishing Reinhardt and Dieterle's intent to bring all of early sound film's resources to the task of capturing Shakespeare on film.

This intent is reinforced when the film moves from Athens's marble columns and expansive sets into the forest world dominated by Oberon, Puck, and Titania. There we again find ourselves surrounded by spectacle: an orchestra of gnomes; rabbits, stags, and unicorns roaming the woods; a black-clad, sexually threatening Oberon mounted on a black stallion; a changeling boy dressed like a little maharaja; and fairies in tutus streaming down from the night sky on moonbeams. This powerful fantasy is all suggested in the film's desire to sweep Shakespeare (and the audience) up into the Hollywood world established in the film's opening sequence.

In 1964 Franco Zeffirelli employed a similar approach, though to a somewhat different purpose, to open his film of *The Taming of the Shrew*. Zeffirelli dispatches Shakespeare's Christopher Sly frame and replaces it with his own cinematic preface. His camera follows Lucentio and Tranio as they enter Padua. The city is caught up in the holiday festival accompanying the opening of the new term at the university: streets are packed with revelers; prostitutes fill every window and doorway; carnival masks are ubiquitous; and Lucentio and Tranio are transfixed by the display. Zeffirelli is creating a festive spirit of the world that is to contain his Petruchio and Kate. In his film, their excessive behavior is akin to the release of festive energies where norms, rules, and established social routines are routed in favor of holiday exuberance. Zeffirelli's opening creates the context for the hyperbolic farce that characterizes the clash of Richard Burton's manic Petruchio with Elizabeth Taylor's fiery Kate.

Almost thirty years later, Kenneth Branagh may have had Zeffirelli's colorful opening in mind when he came to fashion the opening of *Much Ado about Nothing*. Branagh begins with text, printing out on the screen the opening stanza of Balthazar's song about the fickle nature of men, plucked from the middle of the play, as Emma Thompson's voice speaks the song's lyrics: "Sigh no more, ladies, Sigh no more/Men were deceivers ever,/One foot in sea, and one on shore,/To one thing constant never" (2.3.56–59). Branagh then cuts from the stark white words on the black screen to a painting-in-progress of an Italian villa. He then pulls his camera back from the canvas to reveal

The Magnificent Seven gallop into Tuscany in Kenneth Branagh's *Much Ado about Nothing* (1993, the Samuel Goldwyn Company).

the actual villa and countryside filled with picnickers enjoying the Tuscan sun while listening to Emma Thompson finish Balthazar's lyric as she reclines in a tree and eats a grape.

This idyll is broken by the arrival, on horseback, of a messenger who presents the group's patriarch with a letter, and the film segues into the opening lines of Shakespeare's text. In a few quick exchanges the principals are established—Leonato, Hero, Claudio, Beatrice, and Benedick—and suddenly the camera zooms down into the valley to discover the men returning from war. Seven men on horseback, strung out in a line across the screen, thunder toward the camera and punch their fists in the air as Patrick Doyle's film score reaches a bright crescendo and the credits begin to roll. Branagh brings the Magnificent Seven charging into Shakespeareland and in the process not only announces his festive approach to Shakespeare's comedy but also reminds us of the influence of the popular Hollywood film on the Shakespeare films of the 1990s.

The giddy opening sequence continues as the women race down the hill and into the villa to prepare themselves for the men's arrival. The men, layered with the grime and dust of the long ride home from war, leap from their horses, shed their clothes, and plunge into outdoor tubs to bathe. Finally, scrubbed and spruced up, the two groups move to encounter each other in the villa's courtyard, where an over-head shot captures them forming a giant X in an indication of the bat-tle of the sexes to follow, just as the credits finish rolling. Branagh clearly places his cinematic stamp on his Shakespearean material here by creating an inviting opening to a film targeted for the largest group of regular moviegoers—those between the ages of fifteen and twenty-five. He also declares his intention to emphasize what *Much Ado* shares with Shakespeare's festive comedies rather than what it shares with the darker problem comedies like *Measure for Measure* and *All's Well That Ends Well*. He transfers the setting from an urban Messina to a Tuscan green world and in so doing privileges the triumph of Beatrice and Benedick's skeptical, but healthy, wit over Claudio and Don Pe-dro's shallow and conventional social attitudes about women and woo-ing and Don John's wooden villainy.

Branagh's opening sequence establishes mood, atmosphere, land-scape, and approach. Trevor Nunn's prologue to his film of *Twelfth Night* is more concerned with establishing relationships and clarifying narrative storytelling. Before our eyes are engaged by images, our ears hear Ben Kingsley's voice lightly singing:

> *I'll tell thee a tale, now list to me,*
> *With heigh ho, the wind and the rain.*
> *But merry or sad, which shall it be,*
> *For the rain it raineth every day.*

The words are a mixture of Nunn's and Shakespeare's. By bor-rowing from Feste's bittersweet song about the wind and the rain that closes Shakespeare's play, Nunn chooses to open his film by emphasizing *Twelfth Night*'s melancholy rather than its festive spirit. Nunn employs Kingsley's Feste as an omniscient presence in the film, and his wry sensibility comes to dominate Nunn's approach to the play.

Nunn uses Feste's song to insist on the everyday experience that festive comedy both sweetens and threatens. *Twelfth Night* tests the limits of holiday release; the play both inscribes and incriminates fes-tive abuse. Nunn wants to balance holiday and everyday in his film. The film's late-nineteenth-century setting and landscape help to foreground an autumnal melancholy associated more with Chekhov than with

Shakespeare's midsummer madness, both in the upstairs romance plot and the downstairs class plot. The poles of everyday and holiday are captured in Feste's songs, "The Wind and the Rain" and "O Mistress Mine," and Nunn uses both in his opening sequence to frame the film's depiction of everyday travail and holiday romance.

Immediately after Feste's "The Wind and the Rain" establishes the opening narrative mood, "O Mistress Mine" helps to explain the action that, in the film, precedes the first two scenes of Shakespeare's text. The film opens on a steamship, rolling on the high seas, with passengers enjoying a Twelfth Night entertainment provided by twins wearing identical oriental costumes. One is playing the piano, the other a concertina, and both are singing "O Mistress Mine." Both performers are wearing identical yashmaks and, as the song builds, they begin a comic process of self-exposure. As each pulls the other's veil down, we see that each also has a mustache. One twin reaches out and pulls off the other's mustache; as the other begins to make a similar move, the storm suddenly intensifies, the ship is rocked from side to side, and the entertainment abruptly ends as the passengers try to scurry to safety. During this sequence the camera has repeatedly cut to a solitary male figure intently watching the performance. As the storm batters the tiny ship, the twins are swept overboard, reaching out to one another as they sink in the sea. The lonely observer clings to the ship as his eyes search for the two bodies in the turbulent sea.

In these opening images, Nunn not only establishes the film's narrative line but also incorporates the play's lyrical nature, its gender confusions, its latent homoeroticism (the solitary onlooker is, of course, Antonio), its literal and metaphorical motif of a rescue from drowning, and its association of the sea with various ideas (expressed in the text by Orsino) about the romantic appetite of the male ego. Nunn's opening creates a version of that enigmatic creature, come from the sea, who can "sing both high and low" and who, in the disguised figure of Viola/Cesario, miraculously both destabilizes and harmonizes the Illyrian world into which she/he is reborn. Action, image, text, and film score all collaborate here to provide both atmospheric and narrative clues to Nunn's intentions as he translates *Twelfth Night* into film.

Each director seeks a different approach to his comic material (spectacle, Dionysian energy, festive romance, and Chekhovian melancholy) and clearly establishes the visual markers of that approach in his film's beginning sequence.

How Do Directors Use Opening Shots and Sequences to Establish Their Approach to Shakespearean Tragedy?

As we have seen, directors of films of Shakespearean comedies signal their interpretive approach to the text by the tone and atmosphere they establish in the opening shots of their films. A similar practice holds for films of the tragedies. Directors want quickly to create the setting and landscape within which the narrative will unfold and the key visual images that will establish their approach to the text of the play. The range of options open to directors can be revealed by examining the open sequences of three noted film adaptations of *Hamlet* made by Laurence Olivier, Grigori Kozintsev, and Franco Zeffirelli.

Olivier's *Hamlet* opens with the camera holding a steady long shot of a castle shrouded in fog, perched on a rocky crag above violent waves crashing against the shore. The **soundtrack** features William Walton's score for Hamlet's funeral march as Olivier cuts to an overhead shot of the castle's ramparts; an edited version of Hamlet's speech beginning "So, oft it chances in particular men" and continuing through "take corruption/From that particular fault" (1.4. 18.7–18.20) appears on the screen, as the words are spoken by Olivier in a slow and measured cadence. At the conclusion of Hamlet's lines, Olivier intones: "This is a tragedy (pause) of a man (pause) who could not make up (pause) his mind." As the text disappears from the screen, the camera zooms down on the rampart's central platform, where four soldiers hold Hamlet's dead body on their shoulders. The shot dissolves and Olivier cuts to a low angle shot of Barnardo climbing up a set of steep, winding, interior stone steps to relieve Francisco from his watch as **chiaroscuro** patterns of light and dark shadows flicker on the castle's walls. As Walton's score swells with busy violins building suspense, Barnardo cries out the first words of the play: "Who's there?"

All of these details of form, technique, landscape, and image are central to Olivier's approach. As discussed at greater length in Chapter 8, Olivier was heavily influenced by Freud's ideas about *Hamlet*. Here the image of the violent sea crashing against the base of a gloomy, fog-enshrouded castle speaks immediately to the turmoil and confusion of Hamlet's psychological state as he reels from the double blow of his father's death and his mother's remarriage. Olivier reinforces this visual image by describing Hamlet's character by lifting a passage from the play that is actually about Claudius. This adds a further confusion and identification of Hamlet and Claudius to Freud's famous pairing of the two men (based on the idea that Hamlet had an Oedipal desire to kill his father and marry his mother, as Claudius has done). Olivier drives the point home with the addition of his own succinct definition of Hamlet as a "man who could not make up his mind," hitting the final word "mind" for emphasis, preparing us for a film production that will focus on a psychological approach to the prince and the play.

Kozintsev's opening to *Hamlet* borrows from Olivier's even as it opens up new visual avenues to the play. Kozintsev's sequence runs for five minutes before a word of the text is spoken. Like Olivier, Kozintsev opens with a shot of waves pounding against the base of Elsinore's walls. He doesn't introduce Dmitri Shostakovich's film score until the credits have finished rolling over the sounds of the sea, punctured by a bell tolling twenty-four times, and the flames of a massive torch flickering against the castle's wall. Then we hear the abrupt, staccato percussive opening of the film score as a series of shots reveal black flags and banners being unfurled from the castle's outer walls and interior courtyard, visually announcing Old Hamlet's death. As the violins join the score, Kozintsev cuts to Hamlet, mounted on a white stallion, riding home over a barren terrain with his cape flying out behind him. His horse speeds toward the castle, clatters over its wooden drawbridge, and enters Elsinore's courtyard. Hamlet dismounts and dashes up an exterior staircase and into the castle and his mother's arms as black drapes tumble down to cover the windows. Gertrude is all in black, and Kozintsev's camera focuses on her black-gloved right hand pressed against Hamlet's back as she pulls him into her embrace. The camera then cuts to a giant wheel being turned laboriously by a host of men as we watch the drawbridge rise and the portcullis lower. Kozintsev shoots the raising of the drawbridge from a low angle and holds the shot until the bridge has completely blotted out the light from the sky.

The sea, the stone, and the fire are all images Kozintsev returns to throughout his film, a series of images that illustrates Hamlet's understanding that "Denmark's a prison." Kozintsev's Hamlet (Innokenti Smoktunovski) is more aggressive than Olivier's (as witness his romantic entrance in the film thundering home on that white charger) and more committed to opposing Claudius than to challenging Gertrude. His Hamlet enters a political world dominated by Claudius, rather than a psychological world dominated by his mother. Kozintsev's Elsinore is a house of death defined by those black flags and drapes into which Hamlet will attempt to bring both fire and light.

The opening of Zeffirelli's *Hamlet* offers yet another visual version of Shakespeare's landscape and narrative. Zeffirelli begins, like Olivier and Kozintsev, with a shot of castle and sea. This time the film is in Technicolor, but the castle is shot through a blue filter and the sea is tranquil. Zeffirelli then cuts to Elsinore's courtyard and a crowd of silent soldiers, some of them mounted, patiently waiting as the camera pans their expectant faces before entering the castle's crypt. We quickly realize we are at Old Hamlet's entombment. We hear Gertrude's sobs as she approaches the bier and removes a silver rose ornament from her hair and places it on the dead king's chest. Her blue eyes swell with tears as the camera quickly cuts to Claudius and then back to the **close-up** of a hand reaching into a bowl of dust. The camera follows the hand, now closed into a fist, as it moves over Old Hamlet's body and releases its contents. The camera moves from the fist to the face of Mel Gibson as Hamlet, shrouded in the hood of his cape. Gertrude's sobs continue to be heard on the soundtrack as the cover is placed on the coffin and the camera cuts to Gibson's Hamlet beating a retreat from this awkward little family drama.

Zeffirelli's opening prepares for his concentration on the private, family dynamic at work in Shakespeare's play. Deeply influenced by Olivier's Freudian reading of *Hamlet*, Zeffirelli jettisons the play's political and philosophical layers to zero in on Hamlet's relationship with his mother. Alan Bates's weak Claudius and Paul Scofield's weary Ghost are completely overshadowed by Glenn Close's Gertrude in Hamlet's emotional life. While Zeffirelli surrounds his two American Hollywood stars with a host of English classical actors like Bates, Scofield, and Ian Holm (Polonius), Gibson and Close are always the main and, ultimately, fatal, attraction. Much of this emphasis on the complicated emotional relationship between mother and son is suggested in the dumb show that Zeffirelli invents to open his film. Olivier, Kozintsev, and Zeffirelli all begin their *Hamlet* films with strong visual and stylistic clues about their approach to Shakespeare's text.

Television productions generally take fewer visual liberties than films do in self-consciously generating images and ideas in their opening moments meant to provoke the viewer's interest. Richard Eyre's production of *King Lear* (1998) is an exception to this practice. Eyre begins his television version of *Lear* with a silent scene added to the production when it moved from stage to screen. The credits are shot over an image of a solar eclipse. Eyre then segues to a close-up of a burning candle and pulls the camera back so that we see Edgar staining a glass slide by holding it over the candle's flame. Edgar then observes the eclipse through his smoky glass and records his observations in a journal while he, in turn, is observed by his brother Edmund, who is studying how to achieve another kind of eclipse. After he finishes his entry, Edgar rises and exits, while Edmund emerges from the shadows as the council chamber doors open to admit Gloucester and Kent and the opening exchanges of the play. Eyre seizes on Gloucester's subsequent insistence "that these late eclipses of the sun and moon portend no good to us" (1.2.96–97) as a key image for the chaos that is to explode after Lear's rash decision to banish Cordelia and turn his governing powers over to his two other daughters. This brief dumb show also establishes Edgar's scientific curiosity about the world and his brother Edmund's role as an undercover agent in his own family. The scene quickly but effectively sets up issues about man and nature that the play explores in depth.

How Do Signature Shots Become the Signposts for the Director's Personal Style?

Signature shots, defining moments in a director's work, can be as robust as the charge of the French cavalry in Olivier's *Henry V* or as subtle as Branagh's mirror shot for the delivery of the "To be or not to be" soliloquy in his film of *Hamlet*.

Olivier's famous **tracking shot** defines his heroic approach to *Henry V* as well as the move into the language and action of film his treatment of the play has been building toward. Olivier begins his film in a replica of the Globe theater, thereby acknowledging the stage roots of his material. The movie then shifts to the background of painted studio sets for the scenes set at the French court. Only when Olivier reaches the Battle of Agincourt does he take his film on location and abandon dialogue for action.

The charge and subsequent battle sequence occupy only ten minutes of film time, but it took Olivier six weeks to shoot at Powerscourt, a great landed estate in Ireland. The sequence begins with a four-minute tracking shot of the French charge that builds momentum and gathers speed as the camera begins slowly and eventually races down a two-mile track built for the shot. William Walton's rousing score, filled with percussion and brass, imitates the thrilling beat of the charge. Olivier brings the charge to a climax as the film cuts from the French cavalry to the English long-bow archers who, at Henry V's signal, release a torrent of arrows at the enemy. Olivier cuts off Walton's score so that the sudden silence is punctured only by the release of the arrows and their high-arcing path toward the French. The long tracking shot and the extended battle sequence that follows capture Olivier's heroic intentions as the elegant French horsemen, dressed in full body armor, are shot from their mounts by the common English bowmen. As they struggle to rise in their heavy gear, they are easily dispatched by Henry's infantry. This sequence visually defines Olivier's cinematic approach to *Henry V*. The French charge is stirring but doomed as the outnumbered English outwit their superior opponent through Henry's clever military strategy and the pluck and ingenuity of his troops. This sequence captures the bold bright energy of Oliver's interpretation of the Battle of Agincourt and reinforces his inspiring and uplifting intention to create a film to rally his nation at a time of crisis.

An equally effective signature shot, though from the opposite spectrum of film's technical repertory, is Kenneth Branagh's handling of Hamlet's most famous soliloquy. The interior space of Branagh's Elsinore is defined by a sparkling great room, lined with mirrored doors, and trimmed in white and gold: a version of the Winter Palace's famed Hall of Mirrors. The mirrors and the doors reflect the values of Claudius's court: dazzling surfaces disguise impenetrable mazes within. Branagh's Hamlet enters the room and, thinking that he is alone, moves to one of the mirrored doors to begin his famous disquisition on suicide and death. He is unaware that Claudius and Polonius are behind that door staring back at him behind a two-way mirror.

In a deceptively tricky shot, the camera peers over Hamlet's right shoulder, catching his full-length reflection in the mirrored door. As the speech builds, the camera closes in until Hamlet is present in the shot only in reflection, as if trying to discover in that narcissistic image some clue to his impasse in moving against his "uncle-father." Branagh's intelligent Hamlet is interrogating his own psychological complicity in Claudius's crime (Branagh's Hamlet bears a striking physical resemblance to Derek Jacobi's smooth, handsome Claudius) as well as puzzling out the whips and scorns of time. The image of Hamlet framed and trapped in the mirror is the film's most stunning merger of text and technique. The mirrored doors pick up and extend the play's many mirror images, from Ophelia's description of Hamlet as "the glass of fashion and the mould of form" to the "mirror [held] up to nature" that Hamlet insists is at the heart of the actor's craft, to the "glass" into which he intends to transform himself in order to show Gertrude her "innermost part" in the closet scene. Hamlet has been pushed from the center of his world to its periphery; he's on the outside looking in, and Branagh's Hamlet is dislocated not only by that marginal perspective but also by the way he both opposes and re-flects Claudius. When he tries to hold a mirror up to Claudius's and Gertrude's corruption, it insists on throwing back images of his own turmoil rather than their transgression.

Olivier's tracking shot is robust and captures the vivid action of a battle charge; Branagh's mirror shot, by contrast, is almost static and privileges word over action. Olivier's shot opens up; Branagh's closes in; yet both are emblematic of the myriad ways film can translate Shakespeare into its own unique grammar and rhetoric.

How Do Signature Shots Merge Landscape and Character?

The successful Shakespeare film, particularly of a tragedy, needs to create a landscape and setting that corresponds with the complex psychological reality of the hero at its center. The film's visual tex-ture must include several signature shots where character, setting, and action all cooperate to release Shakespeare's power in cinematic terms. Orson Welles's *Othello* and Julie Taymor's *Titus* provide com-pelling examples of such moments where the exterior landscape and the movement of the camera become a perfect expression of the psy-chological dynamics unfolding in the tragic hero's troubled imagi-nation.

Orson Welles combines both the action and the stasis at work in Olivier's and Branagh's shots in a remarkable signature sequence in his film of *Othello*. Welles begins his version of the play's famous "seduction scene" (3.3) with Othello and Iago walking along the ramparts of the fortress at Cyprus with the camera tracking their movement mounted on a Jeep. The shot, Jack Jorgens argues, is "the centerpiece of the film" and develops its rhythm by the way the two men walk side by side with their movement interrupted by Iago's persistent questions, followed by ambiguous pauses, followed by more leading questions. As Jorgens points out,

> it is a great shot because of its overlaying of several *aural* and *visual* rhythms, each in conflict with the others, which builds to a growing sense of unease in the viewer: the regular *beat* of the boots on the stone and the accompanying movements of their bodies, the rhythm of the waves *beating* against the shore, the uneven bursts of speech and silence, the irregular appearances of cannon in the notches of the wall, the regular patches of sunlight thrown on the walker's feet, and the pattern of the irregularly spaced rocks in the sea beyond the ramparts.[3]

Welles has those foot beats carefully punctuate the two key words Iago plants in Othello's mind and which Othello repeatedly echoes back to him: "honest" and "think." Then Welles cuts to a quick series of close-ups with first Othello and then Iago alone in the frame and finally both captured together with Iago's face in sunlight and Othello's in shadows as Iago warns Othello to "beware, my lord, of jealousy/It is a green-eyed monster. . . ." (3.3.169–70). Welles then cuts to a low angle shot with Othello's face framed against the sky—the last time we will see him in this sequence framed against light and space.

Othello now plunges down a narrow staircase into the fortress, declaring Iago his lieutenant even as he tries to rid his imagination of the ugly images of Desdemona's infidelity Iago has planted there. Othello stops to remove his robe, and Welles's camera, in a final shot, captures Iago, Othello, and Othello's image reflected in an oddly shaped mirror resembling that in Jan Van Eyck's painting, "The Marriage of Arnolfini."

3. Jack Jorgens, *Shakespeare on Film* (Bloomington: Indiana University Press, 1977), p. 184.

Othello (Orson Welles) and Iago (Michael MacLiammoir) captured in a tricky mirror shot in Welles's *Othello* (1952, Mogador Films).

The textual and visual layers of truth and illusion at work here as Othello succumbs to Iago's rancid imagination are remarkable. Welles, by beginning the sequence up on the ramparts with Iago and Othello outlined against the sky, then moving them into a mix of sunlight and shadow, and finally plunging them into the dark fortress, neatly mirrors the nature of their relationship as Iago transforms Othello from a great military commander secure in his own identity to a man ravaged by suspicion and doubt—a victim of his own psychological confusion expressed in his anguished cry: "Othello's occupation's gone"(3.3.362).

Another vivid sequence capturing the fall of a proud Shakespearean general can be found in Julie Taymor's ambitious film *Titus*. Taymor, like Peter Brook and Deborah Warner in their stage productions for the Royal Shakespeare Company, dares to take Shakespeare's *Titus Andronicus* seriously. Most modern directors, confronted by the play's horror and violence, treat Shakespeare's material with Grand Guignol hyperbole bordering on camp. Taymor instead sees the play as a commentary on empire and violence stretching from ancient Rome to contemporary America. At the center of her film is Anthony Hopkins's performance of Titus. Hopkins takes us on Titus's remarkable journey from being the empire's great general to becoming its mad outcast and victim. A crucial moment in that journey is when two of his sons are falsely accused of a brutal murder and sent to prison to await execution.

This scene (3.3) is set at a crossroads where Titus confronts the guards taking his sons to prison. Taymor repeatedly shoots Hopkins's Titus against the background of the ruins and remnants of the Roman civilization he idealizes. An ancient aqueduct stretches out behind the garden of Titus's house, and the skeletons of classical buildings dot the landscape surrounding the crossroads scene, where Taymor shoots the prostrate Hopkins recounting his sorrows to a stone as his sons are carted off to their deaths. At this moment Titus confronts his stunning fall from the center of the Roman world. Once the head of Rome's great military force marching in triumph into the Colosseum early in the film, Titus now watches helplessly as another military progression passes him by.

Taymor's camera frames Hopkins, his face pressed against a paving stone, through the spokes of the wheel on the cart carrying his sons to their deaths. Titus's own wheel has come half-circle. He has moved from the top to the bottom of his world, and now it is this proud warrior who is forced to plead for mercy, with rough "bitter tears" filling "the ancient wrinkles" in his cheeks. Titus rises from the ground to be greeted by his two remaining children, Lucius and Lavinia, and his brother, Marcus. The family is ruined. Lucius has been banished; Lavinia raped and mutilated; Marcus devastated by Lavinia's treatment. The Andronici are now the outcasts. In a poignantly beautiful shot, the faces of this ruined family are captured reflected in a puddle, where they have knelt to join Titus as he laments, "[Look how we] sit round about some fountain/Looking all downwards to behold our cheeks/How they are stained, like meadows yet not dry/With miry slime left on them by a flood?" (3.1.123–26). Taymor holds their reflected images in the water as the rain begins to beat against the puddle's surface, obliterating the outlines of their faces.

Another significant visual image in Taymor's *Titus*, sparked by Shakespeare's poetry, is found in her presentation of Lavinia after she has been brutally raped and mutilated by Tamora's sons, Chiron and Demetrius. Shakespeare lifts this incident from Ovid, where a woman is raped and then her tongue is cut out and her hands cut off so that she cannot reveal her attackers. Shakespeare does not directly depict this horrific crime but has Lavinia's uncle (Marcus) discover her after the attack. Taymor instead gives us an initial **long shot** of Lavinia. She is standing on a stump on the edge of a swamp, dressed only in a flimsy white slip. In a surreal masterstroke, merging text and design, the stumps of her hands are represented by a tangle of gnarly twigs. Taymor is boldly making literal Marcus's description of Lavinia: "Speak, gently niece, what stern ungentle hands/Hath lopped and hewed and made thy body bare/Of her two branches" (2.3.16–18). The camera edges closer to Lavinia as Marcus's description of her condition becomes more graphic: her stationary position, fixed on the pedestal of her charred stump, reminds us that her body is an object made (or at least refashioned) by the culture of violence that defines Titus's world. This moment is yet another example of film's ability to merge text, image, and action to capture and enhance the Shakespearean dynamic.

How Can Signature Shots Define a Film's End?

We have examined how directors often invest the opening shots of their Shakespeare films with images and techniques that will extend throughout the film and come to define their approach to the text. In some instances directors will rely on such signature shots to bring closure to their films as well. Orson Welles has his camera linger on Falstaff's gigantic coffin as it is pushed out of the Boar's Head Tavern's inn yard as the last shot of his *Chimes at Midnight*. Laurence Olivier's camera fixes on an overhead shot of Hamlet's dead body being carried by the guards up the winding staircase that has defined his Elsinore to the platform high above the castle. But the most flamboyant closing shot in the history of Shakespeare on film may be the long uncut **steadicam** and **crane** shot that closes Kenneth Branagh's film of *Much Ado about Nothing*.

Branagh's *Much Ado* is distinguished by its cinematic exuberance, from the dash and energy of the film's opening, to the overlapping images of Benedick splashing in the fountain and Beatrice flying high on her swing at the romantic center of the film, to Claudio's savage tantrum in viciously attacking Hero at their wedding. Once Benedick has pledged to honor Beatrice's outrage at Hero's treatment by challenging Claudio, Dogberry has bumbled his way into exposing Don John's villainy, and the lovers have been reunited, Branagh wants to cap his film with a dazzlingly festive moment.

To do so he constructs a single complicated steadicam and crane shot that intends to set our spirits soaring in response to the successful resolution of the play's exposure of the darker side of romance and courtship. The community has gathered in front of the villa's small chapel to witness the reconciliation of Hero and Claudio and the happy outcome of the mutual tricks played on Benedick and Beatrice. When these matters have been concluded and Benedick, true to his unconventional spirit, insists on dancing before wedding, the entire cast begins singing Balthazar's song, which has been featured prominently in the film. As they sing, they begin to dance out from the space in front of the chapel, through the villa's inner courtyard, and out again into the estate's front gardens. At first, they are filmed from behind by the steadicam operator. In the villa's courtyard, he pivots and passes them so he is now walking backward while filming their whirling progress toward him and into the front garden. He then backs up to the crane seat, sits, and is lifted up high in the air to give us an overhead shot of the dancers swirling in the garden while song and score soar on the soundtrack and confetti pirouettes in the summer air.

Finally, when the crane reaches its apogee, the camera looks out over the romantic Tuscan countryside as the film ends. This single, unbroken shot, lasts over four minutes and encapsulates all the festive and romantic energy Branagh, and his cast, have loaded into the film. Branagh's film takes risks by wearing its comic populism so proudly in its style and substance. This final extravagant shot, matching atmosphere with technique, is meant to send the audience home happy, humming the refrain of Balthazar's song, "Hey nonny, nonny," in celebration of film's power to make one of Shakespeare's comedies succeed for the large teenage film audience.

These examples reveal the ways individual shots and extended sequences can come to define how any given film director works with Shakespeare's text. In each case the shot or sequence grows from something in the text (an image already present in Shakespeare's poetry), or in Shakespeare's conception of character or action, or in the play's atmosphere or spirit. These signature shots are most effective when they issue organically from the director's encounter with Shakespeare and his instinctive understanding of how Shakespeare speaks in the language of film.

10

SOLILOQUIES AND SCENES

Adapting Stage Conventions to the Screen

The shape and structure of Shakespeare's Globe theatre allowed the actor to have a unique and intimate relationship with an audience of two thousand or more. The audience, surrounding the thrust stage on three sides, became an acknowledged and vital element in the unfolding of the action. Actor and spectator not only shared the same space but also the same light. The film audience, by contrast, is always in the dark and has no tangible relationship with the actors, who are giant (and powerful) images flickering on a screen beyond our reach. Conventions natural to Shakespeare's theater, like the soliloquy and the aside, are foreign to film's dominant realism, where the actors almost never break the fourth wall to address the audience directly. Shakespeare's basic unit of dramatic construction is the scene. His scenes are generally rooted in a specific landscape or setting, though because he worked in a nonpresentational theater without scenery or sets, his drama shares film's power to cut rapidly from one locale (say, Rome) to another (say, Alexandria) in a flash. Shakespeare's dramaturgy can create special challenges for filmmakers as they devise means to translate his soliloquies and scenes into the language of film.

How Do Filmmakers Adapt Hamlet's Soliloquies to Film?

The soliloquy is a convention foreign to film. Film dialogue can be poignant and witty, but it is rarely prolix. Because of film's restless realism, characters are almost never allowed extended speeches, and certainly not when they are the only person present in the scene. Actors in the Elizabethan theater repeatedly acknowledge the audience; film actors never do unless they are intentionally violating film convention. Soliloquies thus present a special problem to the directors of

Shakespeare films. Filmmakers have employed several creative solutions when translating the soliloquy into the language of film. Because the soliloquy is so central to *Hamlet*, let's examine some of the solutions to the soliloquy problem that Laurence Olivier, Kenneth Branagh, and Michael Almereyda have experimented with in their films of the play.

The prime film device Olivier appropriates for his treatment of Hamlet's soliloquies is the **voice-over**. While film rarely uses direct address, it has made a standard convention of the voice-over, where we overhear a character's thoughts on the soundtrack while he acts but remains speechless on screen. This device, which would seem unnatural used on stage, works on film. Olivier employs it immediately in Hamlet's first soliloquy and also adds his own unique twist to the convention. His camera shoots Hamlet sitting passively in a chair as Claudius, Gertrude, and the court exit after the first court scene (1.2). As the camera cranes down into a medium close-up, we hear Olivier's voice on the soundtrack softly utter the soliloquy's opening line: "O, that this too, too solid flesh would melt / Thaw and resolve itself into a dew" (1.2.129–30). Then Olivier rises and begins to prowl the empty council chamber and, after several more lines recorded in voice-over, he breaks into spoken address on "Nay, not so much, not two." He repeats the pattern of breaking from thought to speech at several later moments in the soliloquy (and with special invective on "O God, a beast that wants discourse of reason / Would have mourn'd longer!" [1.2.150–51]), thus dramatizing the psychological effect of Hamlet's simultaneous struggle both to repress and to release his outrage at his mother's remarriage.

Olivier effectively melds a theatrical convention (the soliloquy) and a film convention (the voice-over) to provide a novel touch of psychological realism to Hamlet's emotional turmoil in dealing with the rapid loss of both father and mother. The conflict between internal and external realities so central to Hamlet's anguish is precisely in keeping with Olivier's Freudian approach to the play. He employs this same division, though with a significant variation, when he comes to film Hamlet's most famous soliloquy.

Olivier shoots the "To be or not to be" soliloquy on a high platform above Elsinore with Hamlet posed precariously on its edge, gazing down into a turbulent sea pounding on the rocks below. This time

Olivier's Hamlet speaks aloud the opening five lines, up to "to die."
He then moves into voice-over for:

> to sleep—
> No more—and by a sleep to say we end
> The heartache, and the thousand natural shocks
> That flesh is heir to! 'Tis a consumation
> Devoutly to be wished. To die, to sleep—
> To sleep.
> (3.1.62–66)

Hamlet then returns to direct speech on "Perchance to dream" and
continues in that fashion until the end of the soliloquy. In the first soliloquy Olivier's Hamlet broke out of thought and into speech when
his rage at his mother's remarriage could no longer be contained; in
"To be or not to be" he moves from speech to thought when he confronts the idea of death and suicide, an idea so powerful that Hamlet
must repress its spoken expression. Olivier deftly counters the stage
convention of the soliloquy with the film convention of the voice-over
to capture Hamlet's inner turmoil and his passivity.

Branagh's film of *Hamlet* takes another approach. Branagh the actor
gives full voice to each of Hamlet's soliloquies, and Branagh the director shoots each in one long continuous take. Branagh's film is relentlessly text-driven; he wants us to hear all of Hamlet's words, giving
them their full emotional expression as we might encounter them in
the theater. Branagh's cinematic challenge is to employ his camera in a
manner that engages our eyes as the actor shapes and builds each soliloquy in one unbroken moment of expression. The tricky mirror shot
he uses for the "To be or not to be" soliloquy (which places Hamlet,
through the device of the two-way mirror, in the presence of one of
his alter egos, Claudius) is discussed in Chapter 9. The speech, in
Branagh's treatment, suggests something of Hamlet's self-absorption
and narcissism, and the way he not only opposes but reflects Derek Jacobi's smooth and polished Claudius.

Branagh is equally daring in his treatment of the "How all occasions
do inform against me" soliloquy. Here the figure in the background is
another of Hamlet's alter egos, Fortinbras. The image of Fortinbras
marching off to fight for a worthless piece of Poland provokes Hamlet

into a lacerating self-examination of his own inaction. The soliloquy begins with Hamlet captured in medium close-up in the tight center of the frame. Over his shoulder we see a bit of the snow-covered terrain over which Fortinbras's army is marching. As the soliloquy builds, Hamlet remains frozen in the frame except to curl his right arm up into a fist on "I do not know / Why yet I live to say, this thing's to do" (4.4. 9.33–9.34). The camera, mounted on a crane, slowly begins to pull back on "What is a man" and continues to do so until Hamlet's full figure is revealed in the frame as he utters "How stand I then." This pattern reverses the camera's movement in the "To be or not to be" soliloquy, where it slowly closes in on Hamlet until only his reflected image in the mirror is included in the shot. Here, more extravagantly, and matching the extravagance of Hamlet's rhetoric, the camera continues its backward motion and suddenly cranes up and away, reducing Hamlet to a tiny black stick figure thrusting his arms out from his sides as he cries out, "O, from this time forth, / My thoughts be bloody, or be nothing worth!" (4.4.9.55–9.56).

This shot is a revealing example of Branagh's cinematic flamboyance, memorable for its daring as well as its intelligence. Here Branagh gives his Hamlet a huge screen moment, a moment that pays homage to Olivier's film grammar for treating Shakespeare's soliloquies (start in close and pull the camera back as the speech builds, reversing film's normal pattern of movement from **long shot** to close-up). The shot counters any charge of directorial self-indulgence because of its intelligent, searing critique of the character. Hamlet, in this vast expanse of landscape, is reduced to little more than a tiny black dot making theatrically grand but empty gestures. Branagh's Hamlet is less passive than Olivier's, which is why he speaks his soliloquies rather than reverting to voice-over, but Branagh's cinematic handling of the soliloquies still manages visually to capture the ways that Hamlet is not only trapped in a corrupt world but incapable of summoning the heroic action that might cleanse it.

If Branagh's film dares to give us all of Hamlet's soliloquies, each filmed in one long uncut take, Michael Almereyda's *Hamlet* proposes a very different cinematic response to those speeches. Almereyda's film makes a wonderful contrast to Branagh's, a charcoal sketch rather than an illuminated manuscript. Almereyda combines elements used by

Olivier and Branagh to provide his own unique solution to filming Hamlet's soliloquies.

Almereyda sets his film in contemporary Manhattan. Claudius is conceived as the CEO of a giant media company, Denmark Corporation. Hamlet (Ethan Hawke) is a moody, introspective media artist, almost always with a camcorder in hand, either shooting or editing a home movie. This device allows Almereyda to use a variety of **metacinematic** strategies to capture a text that is itself highly **metatheatrical**. Hamlet's first soliloquy is spoken by Hawke in voice-over as he watches clips from his home movie on his video editing machine. Almereyda cuts back and forth between Hamlet's film and his own, often shooting Hawke in a tight close-up that contains only his brow and eyes. Almereyda lifts the voice-over technique from Olivier and brilliantly transforms Branagh's two-way mirror into the screen of Hamlet's movie. As Hawke reaches the lines that idealize (and idolize) his father—"So excellent a king, that was to this / Hyperion to a satyr, so loving to my mother / That he might not beteem the winds of heaven / Visit her face too roughly" (1.2.139–42)—the editing machine projects images of Old Hamlet and Gertrude ice-skating, during which she slips and loses her balance and the king steadies her progress. Almereyda's editing of this sequence chops up Hamlet's soliloquy by providing a series of visual images that illustrate his anguished memory and translate Hamlet's rhetoric from a theatrical convention into a cinematic one.

Almereyda returns to this device and expands on it in his treatment of the "To be or not to be" soliloquy. This sequence begins with Hamlet watching an image of himself with a gun at his temple and then in his mouth on his television monitor as we hear the beginning of the soliloquy in voice-over. The **soundtrack** stops as Hawke pushes first the reverse and then the replay button, creating the impression that the ideas in this soliloquy are repeatedly looping through Hamlet's mind. Almereyda then cuts to a shot of Hamlet standing in the action-film aisle of a Blockbuster video store as once again we hear the famous soliloquy's opening lines in voice-over. Now we are back in the master narrative, not Hamlet's private media meditation on his tormented ennui. But both filmmakers (Almereyda and Hamlet) are searching in the world of films, and particularly the popular genre of action films, for a solution to Hamlet's dilemma.

Interestingly, Hawke's Hamlet breaks out of thought and into speech at the precise moment in the soliloquy where Olivier made the opposite move. Hawke's Hamlet is more obsessed with his own death than either Olivier's or Branagh's, as is revealed in the earlier images of the gun pressed to his temple and his later decision to turn the gun on himself after his failure to kill Claudius in the "Now I might do it pat" scene. This morbid melancholy is part of the modern angst-ridden despair, unleavened by wit, Hawke brings to the character. As Hawke's Hamlet continues to move through the Blockbuster aisle, puzzling out why his will keeps losing the name of action, Almereyda's camera repeatedly cuts to scenes from *The Crow: City of Angels* showing on the store's monitor. The screen shows a figure emerging from an inferno—in marked contrast to Hawke's Hamlet searching among past films for images with which to create his cinematic version of "The Mousetrap."

Olivier, Branagh, and Almereyda each employ innovative cinematic strategies to translate the theatrical convention of the soliloquy into the language of film. We can even see an interesting progression from one *Hamlet* film to another as each director picks up a device used by his predecessor and couples it with an innovation of his own. Outside of *Hamlet*, other filmmakers have found imaginative techniques for translating Shakespeare's soliloquys to film.

How do Filmmakers Solve the Soliloquy Problem in Plays other than *Hamlet*?

In *Chimes at Midnight*, Orson Welles's reshaping of the Hal-Falstaff story dramatized in *1* and *2 Henry IV*, Welles complicates two central soliloquies by including other characters in the frame with the speaker. Hal's famous "I know you all" soliloquy at the end of 1.2 is situated by Welles as the first of five "farewell" moments between Hal and Falstaff around which he structures his film. In this first instance, Falstaff trails Hal (Keith Baxter) as he moves out through the crowded and boisterous tavern. Hal continues across the inn yard and stops at its gates while we see the ramparts of his father's castle in the rear of the frame. Welles's Falstaff stops at the tavern's doorway so that we have Hal strategically posed between Falstaff's world (the tavern) and his father's (the castle). Welles provides a shot looking out at Hal from

Falstaff's perspective and then reverses it, so that Hal is looking directly into the camera (with Falstaff caught in the rear of the frame) as he quietly speaks the soliloquy directly to us. When he reaches its penultimate line, "I'll so offend to make offense a skill" (1.2.194), he pivots to face Falstaff, and underlines "offend" with a wink to which Falstaff responds with a smile. Then Hal turns back to the camera and confides to us in a whisper: "Redeeming time when men least think I will" (1.2.145).

This moment is a rich one. Here Welles transforms Hal's soliloquy from a moment meant solely for one audience—us—into a moment where he is playing to several audiences, confiding to us that he will use Falstaff as an instrument of his reformation even as he allows Falstaff to think that he remains in an offending mood. Welles here removes the soliloquy from its solitary status in Shakespeare's text and embeds it in Hal and Falstaff's complex relationship.

Another imaginative adaptation of the Shakespearean soliloquy can be found in Roman Polanski's film of *Macbeth*. Macbeth is the most claustrophobic, self-absorbed, and fantastical of Shakespeare's tragic heroes; he can be transported into the inner workings of his imagination and conscience at the slightest suggestion. Polanski effectively works with these elements of Macbeth's character in his treatment of his great early soliloquy contemplating his assassination of Duncan: "If it were done when 'tis done, then 'twere well / It were done quickly" (1.7.1–2). Polanski has his Macbeth (Jon Finch) begin the soliloquy in voice-over as he is seated next to Duncan at the feast honoring the king's visit to Inverness. The soliloquy is prompted by Duncan's physical proximity to Macbeth and by Macbeth's divided nature as host and potential assassin. When Macbeth's private thoughts reach "surcease, success" they are interrupted by a general toast being lifted by Duncan in Macbeth's honor. Macbeth responds with a nod and immediately returns to his train of thought. As his mind races on to "we'd jump the life to come," a powerful wind suddenly blows through the room, rattling the shutters and extinguishing the candles, suggesting a wicked visual joke by Polanski on the power outage Macbeth is contemplating.

When light is restored, we realize that Macbeth has left the banquet hall and is now standing on the balcony that rings the castle's inner courtyard. He continues his internal debate, still in voice-over, that "in these cases / We still have judgment here." Suddenly, horses break loose from the stable and clatter out through the castle's gates; thunder rumbles; lightning cracks; and rain begins to fall as Macbeth insists that Duncan's here "in double trust." Finch then breaks his long voice-over to speak out loud for the first time on "Then, as his host, / Who should against the murder shut the door, / Not bear the knife myself" (1.7.14–16). Polanski uses both voice-over and a landscape switch here (from banquet hall to balcony) to capture the inner/outer, foul/fair alternating impulses that define Macbeth and the vivid power of his imagination. Finch breaks into speech again on "I have no spur" just as that spur, Lady Macbeth, appears at his side to scold him back to the party, where after-dinner dancing has begun. Francesca Annis's Lady Macbeth moves her husband back inside as they speak their famous dare/doubt exchange in whispers without looking at each other as both pretend to be absorbed by the dancers' performance. Polanski's handling of Macbeth's soliloquy subtly captures the character's ambitious envy of Duncan's power, his own agonizing private doubts about catching "the nearest way" to the crown, and his ambiguous relationship with Lady Macbeth.

Shakespeare's tragedies feature more soliloquies than do his comedies, where the focus is more often on group and social experiences than on those that are personal and private. A key exception is Viola's soliloquy at the end of 2.2 in *Twelfth Night*, where she explores the various confusions and complications, including her own love for Orsino, that have resulted from her disguise as Cesario. Viola is in a precarious romantic predicament: she is simultaneously, in her interactions with Orsino and Olivia, caught in both homoerotic and heterosexual relationships.

Trevor Nunn, in his film of *Twelfth Night*, visually underlines Viola's emotional depth and pain by splitting her soliloquy into two parts as something of a before-and-after frame to the text's major romantic confusions involving Olivia, Malvolio, Orsino, and Viola/Cesario. Imogen Stubbs speaks the first nine lines (down to "I am the man") in context after her encounter with Malvolio; the film then returns to conclude the soliloquy after the events of 2.3 and 2.4 have transpired. At this moment, the film discovers Viola (disguised as Cesario) alone in her attic room, staring at herself in a small table mirror as she takes off her uniform, unbinds her breasts, and removes her

Viola (Imogen Stubbs) contemplates gender confusion in a mirror shot in Trevor Nunn's *Twelfth Night* (1995, Fine Line Features).

mustache. As she explores the midsummer madness created by her masculine attire ("Disguise, I see thou art a wickedness," originally 2.2.24), she picks up a photograph of her twin brother, Sebastian. Her memory of him has been preserved, as though by the salt waves of the sea, and she shares her predicament with him. She faces a cross-gendered double-bind: as a man she has sparked Olivia's passion and Orsino's friendship; as a woman she has fallen in love with Orsino. By visually reuniting sister and brother, male and female, Nunn at this moment reminds us of the separation that is at the core of *Twelfth Night*'s narrative, a separation saturated with as much tragic potential as comic possibility. Nunn employs the mirror device (as Branagh and Almereyda do) as a means of visually capturing a character on film having a conversation with herself; he uses the photograph of Sebastian to introduce into the moment yet another character intimately involved with Viola's situation and melancholy reflection.

Olivier, Branagh, Welles, Polanski, and Nunn all find imaginative cinematic solutions to the problem of translating a stage convention into the language and landscape of film. Examining a film's response to the Shakespearean soliloquy or investigating the handling of the same soliloquy in a variety of films can be productive avenues of exploration when thinking and writing about Shakespeare on film. Such comparisons illuminate the differences between stage and film; they remind us that both art forms rely on conventions that seem natural within their worlds and can lose their power when transplanted—unless filmmakers find creative solutions to problems of stage-to-film translation and provide new resonances to the conventions of Shakespeare's theater.

The Soliloquy on Television

Television productions of Shakespeare have been less adventurous in their treatment of the soliloquy. As mentioned in Chapter 4, television is essentially a conservative medium. It emerged from radio, where the word is paramount, rather than from photography, where the image is all. Most television productions of Shakespeare have limited budgets, often less than 30 percent of the budgets for even the most modest of Shakespeare films. Sets are minimal and camera work is restricted by the use of three or four floor-bound cameras. However, television does allow the actor greater freedom to move through the soliloquy in one continuous arc rather than film's usual attempt to chop the speech up into discrete segments.

A typical example of television's handling of the soliloquy can be found in the BBC production of *Hamlet*, where the soliloquies are shot in medium close-up from the perspective of a single camera. In the first soliloquy, for example, the camera finds Derek Jacobi's Hamlet seated on a bench in front of Claudius's throne. The shot captures Jacobi's face in profile as he looks off to his left, but then he pivots, looks into the camera, and directly addresses us as he begins the speech. About a third of the way through the soliloquy, Jacobi rises and moves several steps toward Claudius's empty chair where the camera captures his full body in the frame. Jacobi then moves back to the bench, sits, and finishes the soliloquy. The production's director, Rodney Bennett, follows a similar pattern with the second soliloquy: Jacobi begins while seated with his eyes directly engaging the camera; again he rises about a third of the way through the soliloquy, which allows him to make effective use of the Player King's prop sword when expressing his self-disgust at his passive behavior. He returns to the bench and sits for the last segment of the soliloquy, where he fashions the plan to let his revised version of "The Murder of Gonzago" catch the conscience of the king.

In the BBC version of *Henry IV, Part One*, Prince Hal's "I know you all" soliloquy is handled in a similar fashion, though the production was directed by David Giles, not Bennett. David Gwillim, the actor playing Hal, is seated at a tavern table. The camera, again in a medium shot, captures the actor in profile, and then Gwillim turns to the camera to begin his soliloquy. In this instance, however, the actor's eyes do not directly engage with the camera. He looks up, then down, then back off to his left without acknowledging our existence or making us complicit in his decision to use Falstaff and his companions as a means of his transformation from prodigal son to responsible prince. Gwillim isn't allowed to address the camera directly; Giles reserves that convention for Anthony Quayles's Falstaff, who repeatedly turns and addresses his witticisms to us as though he were taking us into his confidence—part of the art of all great con men.

Trevor Nunn's television production of *Macbeth*, with Ian McKellen as Macbeth, creates a few variations on the BBC pattern of shooting the soliloquy. Nunn moves his camera in tight on McKellen's face, catching the actor from the neck rather than the waist up. He also frequently shoots from a low angle perspective. McKellen stares directly into the camera; when he moves his eyes away from that direct engagement—or even, as he does at one point, actually closes them—it is because he has reached a moment in the soliloquy where he is imagining something so fearful (Duncan's death, before and after) that he is too embarrassed or frightened to share it as a confidence with us. McKellen reinforces this idea by speaking Macbeth's early soliloquies in a whisper, as though the ideas they express are secrets almost too terrible to utter.

Television's most radical approach to treating Shakespeare's soliloquies is simply to excise them; impossible, of course, for plays like *Hamlet* or *Macbeth* where they are central to Shakespeare's conception of the title character, but not so for a play like *King Lear*, where the lengthy soliloquies are given to the villain Edmund. Richard Eyre's production cuts both of Edmund's soliloquies, leaving only a line or two from each to use as closure for the scenes that conclude in the text with Edmund's extended reflections on his bastardy and his Machiavellian schemes.

Television productions don't try to translate the stage convention of the soliloquy into conventions unique to the medium. They try to make a conservative compromise with the soliloquy's stage origins by shooting the actor in a constant landscape and from the perspective of a single camera but moving the audience into a more intimate relationship with the actor by shooting him as he delivers the soliloquy in medium shot or close-up.

How Do the Conventions of Film Cooperate in Creating a Shakespeare Scene on Film?

A single film scene can bring together several film conventions, from camera position and movement, to **cutting**, to spatial relationships between actors in the frame, to **film score**. Examining in detail a film's treatment of a crucial scene from the text allows for an understanding of how a filmmaker can employ a variety of devices to create the emotional and thematic essence of a single scene. Let's examine two crucial examples of how film uses its particular resources to compose and capture the vitality or pathos of a particular extended Shakespearean moment to provide some ideas about the artistry that goes into the construction of meaning and the prompting of emotion in film.

The two plots of *Much Ado about Nothing*, Don John's scheme to drive Claudio and Hero apart and Don Pedro's to bring Benedick and Beatrice together, culminate in 4.1. The scene is the climax of the narrative and is divided into two sections. The first involves almost all of the play's major characters gathered for Hero and Claudio's wedding; the second features just Beatrice and Benedick. The first comprises about 255 lines of text; the second only 80. In Kenneth Branagh's film of *Much Ado* (1993), the first section focuses on Claudio's immature behavior in viciously attacking Hero at the moment their union is to be celebrated while the second section provides us with that moment's counterpoint when Benedick, moved by Beatrice's outrage at Hero's treatment, agrees to challenge Claudio to a duel. I want to concentrate on the second, shorter segment of the scene but need to prepare for it with a few remarks about Branagh's handling of the scene's first section.

Branagh sets Claudio and Hero's wedding in the open air in front of the Tuscan villa's small chapel. He gives ample space to Claudio's petulant tantrum by shooting much of the scene in long shot, only **zooming** in to capture Hero's shocked and innocent reaction. Claudio savagely shoves his bride to the ground and makes a triumphant circuit of the scene, overturning benches and ripping away the wedding decorations before nestling in next to Denzel Washington's elegant Don Pedro to reestablish what he smugly believes is the primacy of the male order. By contrast, Branagh's camera slowly closes in on Beatrice and Benedick as they immediately go to their knees to provide support to the fallen Hero. They look on in amazement as even Hero's father, Leonato, joins the attack on his daughter's virtue and aligns himself with the male hierarchy. By allowing Robert Sean Leonard's Claudio the physical space to express his callow and callous anger, Branagh's film provides a searing image of his ugly treatment of his intended bride.

The shocked wedding party retreats into the villa while Beatrice and Benedick move into the chapel as the scene's counterpoint begins. In this cramped and enclosed space, Beatrice and Benedick create a private ceremony and construct a unique vow that issues not from social practice and convention but from their own emotional and imaginative response to Hero's crisis. The scene lasts only four minutes but, as Michael Anderegg has observed, involves six camera set-ups arranged in forty-one shots.[1] The scene is constructed in a series of over-the-shoulder shots/reverse shots, and the editing keeps the couple separate but together with a series of shots focused on a single character but containing a sign—a shadow, a wisp of hair, a part of a shoulder—indicating the presence of the other.

Branagh shoots a kneeling Beatrice in profile over Benedick's left shoulder so that we see and react to her through his perspective. They are not squared to the camera because they are not yet square with each other. Beatrice's anger, and her frustration with her gender's limitations when it comes to taking action in the male world of honor, lead her to respond to Benedick's offer to "bid me do anything for thee" with a line that shatters the romantic mood: "Kill Claudio" (4.1.287).

Branagh's Benedick is transformed by her passion. Earlier we had seen his cocky jester melt into the comic romantic in the gulling scene. Now both of these hyperbolic portraits darken and mature as we watch him absorb and understand the issue that spurs Beatrice's fury.

---

1. See Michael Anderegg's *Cinematic Shakespeare* (Lanham, Md.: Rowman and Littlefield, 2004), pp. 125–26, for a detailed and intelligent analysis of this scene.

For the first time in the film, Branagh allows Benedick to look directly into the camera as he confronts his commitment to Beatrice. He now steadies and fixes his gaze: to engage the camera is to pledge his engagement to Beatrice. Branagh's Benedick plucks out the word "soul" to underscore his quiet determination, "Think you in your soul that Count Claudio hath wronged Hero?" (4.1.322–23). Thompson's Beatrice, in her reply, chooses to emphasize "thought": "Yea, as sure as I have a thought or a soul" (4.1.324), thus completing the marriage of mind and heart, thought and soul, between them. Their pact is then sealed by the vow that the entire sequence has moved toward: "Enough. I am engaged; I will challenge him" (4.1.325).

Benedick's commitment to action complements Beatrice's outrage and conjures a hitherto unknown phenomenon: a constant man. The words that lead man to woo and wed will now be as significant as those that lead him to war. Throughout this exchange Branagh has kept the camera in tight on the characters, underlining the scene's emotional intensity. He has deftly cut from a series of shot/reverse shots in which the characters are separated from each other in the frame, just as they are separated from each other over the issue of Claudio's behavior, until Benedick engages himself to Beatrice by promising to challenge Claudio. Branagh's handling of this scene is subtle, intelligent filmmaking where dialogue, action, and camera all collaborate to capture the serious and deeply relevant gender issues at work in Shakespeare's text.

The Merchant of Venice is another Shakespearean comedy that has a bitter underside and is also dependent on the interaction between two plot lines: Antonio's bond (loan agreement) with Shylock and Bassanio's courtship of Portia, with the first providing the resources for the second. The climax of the first plot comes at the famous trial scene in 4.1, where Shylock demands his pound of flesh, awarded to him by the law when Antonio is unable to repay Shylock's loan. The scene is the play's longest and is deftly constructed and acted in Michael Radford's recent film (2004) of the play. A detailed analysis reveals the way in which setting, pace, acting, music, and editing all contribute to the scene's power to challenge and disturb.

The scene lasts twenty-seven minutes and consists of two hundred forty separate cuts. Radford divides the long scene into four major sections, each lasting about six minutes, followed by a brief coda. The first section consists of Shylock's arrival in court and his demand for

Shylock (Al Pacino) surrounded in the theatrical space of the trial scene in Michael Radford's *The Merchant of Venice* (2004, Sony Pictures Classics).

justice; the second focuses on Portia's appearance, disguised as the young lawyer Balthazar, and her delivery of the famous "The quality of mercy is not strained" speech; the third builds to the moment when Shylock moves to extract the pound of flesh from Antonio's chest; the fourth dramatizes Shylock's defeat; and the coda consists of Bassanio's expression of gratitude to Balthazar for saving Antonio's life and Balthazar's request of the ring Portia has given Bassanio as a reward.

Radford uses two stationary camera positions for long shots, one shooting across the crowded courtroom toward the duke and the Venetian senators, the other shooting back in the other direction over the duke's shoulder. However, Radford shoots the majority of the scene with a handheld camera. The crowd is packed in tight around Shylock, and the use of the handheld camera captures the claustrophobic intensity of the situation. Radford seeks here to recreate on film the atmosphere of the theater as a cousin to the bear-baiting pit. The throng is an integral player in the scene: it must be forced to part to allow first Shylock and then Balthazar to enter the tiny circle of space at the center of the action; Radford repeatedly cuts to the crowd for reaction shots, including Tubal and other Venetian Jews marked by their red caps, and the crowd joins in the ugly treatment of Shylock, spitting on him and ripping his yarmulke off his head, as he departs, humiliated, at the end of the scene.

Radford allows the camera to be bumped and jostled once or twice by the spectators to underscore technically the tense atmosphere. Radford repeatedly shoots Al Pacino's Shylock in the left side of the frame with either the crowd, Antonio, or, later, Balthazar on the right. Radford allows Pacino to deliver all of his demand "to have the due and forfeit of my bond" without interruption except for a single cut that acknowledges Bassanio and Gratiano's arrival in the courtroom. Then multiple cuts quicken the pace, technically reinforcing the irrational inevitability of Shylock's insistence on judgment even after a chest full of ducats has been placed at his feet as payment for the bond. The camera again cuts from Shylock to the crowd on "you have among you many a purchased slave" (4.1.89) to illustrate his example, but then returns to focus exclusively on Shylock as he reaches "The pound of flesh which I demand of him / Is clearly bought. 'Tis mine, and I will have it" (4.1.98–99). Radford allows Pacino to add two extra "mines" in the second line. Pacino utters the first " 'Tis mine" in a normal tone, the second with pronounced force, and the third in a guttural whisper underlining his fierce determination to have Antonio's life (his by force of law) as compensation for the loss of something that he also has regarded as "mine"—his daughter, Jessica.

As Portia, Lynn Collins is at her best in the trial scene. She plays the determined young Doctor of Rome better than the golden girl of Belmont. Her delivery of Portia's most famous line makes it seem fresh and natural, the spontaneous response to the rapid-fire naturalistic exchanges that precede it, rather than the beginning of a well-worn Shakespearean speech:

> PORTIA: Do you confess the bond?
> ANTONIO: I do.
> PORTIA: Then must the Jew be merciful.
> SHYLOCK: On what compulsion must I?
>   Tell me that.
> PORTIA: The quality of mercy is not strained. . . . (4.1.177–80)

Collins's matter-of-fact cadence, lightly hitting "mercy" and "strained" and "droppeth" with a pause after each, directs the line

back at Pacino's Shylock with a natural authority, and the contest between them begins. Just prior to the beginning of the speech, Radford
cuts quickly back and forth between Portia, Shylock, and Antonio.
Once Portia launches into her big courtroom speech, Radford's camera
holds both Portia and Shylock in the frame in a tight two-shot. She circles around behind him and for a moment supplants his dominant position in the left side of the frame as she reaches "But mercy is above
this scept'red sway," and then completes the circle, returning to the
right side of the frame as she delivers her third evocation of mercy, reminding Shylock that "mercy seasons justice" (4.1.192).

Now the third section of the scene begins, and Radford quickens the
pace with rapid cuts between Shylock, Portia, and the crowd as Antonio
is strapped—legs, arms, and chest—into his chair in preparation for
Shylock's knife. Till now, Radford has wisely resisted the temptation to
use music to cue our emotional response to Shylock's demand for the
law or Portia's plea for mercy. He has let Shakespeare's verbal music do
that work, contrasting Shylock's sharp plosives and consonants (pig,
bagpipe, rat, hate, urine) with the vowel-dominated, gentler flow of Portia's rhetoric (mercy, heaven, shows, seasons, pray, plea). But now, to in-
crease the tension, Radford introduces the film score under Portia's final
request that Shylock "Be merciful./Take thrice thy money; bid me tear
the bond" (4.1.228–29). We first hear faint violin strings, soon accompanied by the more prominent sound of a lute striking a single chord. As
Antonio is bound in his chair, the melancholy lute is joined by the muf-
fled rumble of the kettledrum. Radford quietly slides the music under
the dialogue, never letting it dominate, but allowing it to propel the action and the tension as Shylock raises his knife to Antonio's bosom, until Portia suddenly cries out "Tarry a little," which startles Shylock (and
the rest of us as well) and the action is suspended and the music stops.

Radford now moves into the last section of the scene in which the
tables (and the law) are turned on Shylock and he is not simply defeated but destroyed: stripped not only of his wealth but of his religion
and identity as well. In certainly the cruelest moment in any Shakespearean comedy, Venice's famed cosmopolitan tolerance evaporates,
revealing the dominant Christian culture wielding its power over an
"alien" while piously calling it "charity." Portia has forced Shylock to
his knees during this sequence, and when he finally rises to depart,
Radford allows the camera to watch the crowd first victimize him—

spit on him, rip his cap off his head—and then swallow him up. Radford, with muted restraint, does not allow Shylock a tragic or defiant exit: suddenly he's just gone, erased like his property and identity.

Shakespeare ends 4.1 by returning to the Portia-Bassanio plot, which in the text takes place in the courtroom. Radford moves the scene to a passageway leading out from the Ducal Palace to the Grand Canal, preserving the courtroom as Shylock's space. This tiny coda looks back on the Shylock plot and Bassanio's insistence that the young Doctor "take some remembrance of us as a tribute" (the ring given to him by Portia) and forward to the resolution of the Antonio-Bassanio-Portia triangle (also accomplished by another exchange of rings) in Belmont in the final act.

These thick descriptions of two discrete scenes in *Much Ado about Nothing* and *The Merchant of Venice* illustrate how filmmakers utilize the full range of their technical craft in making Shakespeare live on the screen. Both scenes occupy similar structural positions in the unfolding of each play's narrative; both dramatize the darker elements that are always at work even in Shakespeare's brightest comedies; and both reveal the directorial strategies that distinguish Branagh's work from Radford's. Branagh is the more flamboyant filmmaker of the two; he is attracted to bright, bold colors and extravagant shots. Radford prefers to work in darker colors (his Venice bears little resemblance to the sparkling city beloved of painters and tourists), more muted tones, and less dramatic cinematic flourishes. But both employ a variety of effective film devices to deliver the emotional impact of these two crucial scenes, and both trust their actors by allowing them the time and space to communicate Shakespeare's dialogue and rhetoric to a film audience. You will discover that Shakespeare films abound in such rich and complex scenes ripe for exploration and analysis.

Glossary of Basic Film and Critical Terminology

Aspect ratio: The correlation between the width and height of the cinema image conveyed as a ratio. A square image would be 1:1 with rectangular projections expressing various ratios between their width and height. A standard screen is 1.37:1 and a Cinemascope screen is 2.33:1.

Auteur: (French, "author") A theory of film criticism which emphasizes the director as author of a film. This theory privileges the singular achievements of the director as artist and creator of a film, in contrast to methods of analyzing films as collaborative constructions.

Chiaroscuro: A term borrowed from the visual arts which refers to the distribution of light and shade to enhance the dramatic effect of a pictorial image.

Cinèaste: A film aficionado; someone interested in film and filmmaking.

Close-up: The projection of a cinematic image which takes up a large portion of the screen, achieved through the close proximity of the subject and the camera's lens.

Crane shot: A shot achieved through the mounting of the camera on a flexible crane.

Cross-cutting: The alternate display of different tangents of action in a film to heighten the relationship between them and to create suspense.

Cut: The shift, whether abrupt or smooth, from one shot to another by the connection of two different pieces of film.

Daily rushes: The immediately processed prints of a day's shooting, viewed to closely monitor the film's progress.

Deep focus: The distant focusing of a lens which allows both close and distant planes in the camera's field of view to remain in sharp focus.

Depth of field: The complete area of sharp focus, both in front of and behind the specific plane of depth, in the camera's field of view.

Dissolve: The transition between two shots through the gradual fade out of one simultaneously with the fade in of the other.

Dolly shot: The camera moves laterally on a track or maneuvers in and around the actions on a cart.

Establishing shot: A shot (typically a long shot) that establishes a subject in a given context, orienting the viewer to a specific locale.

Extreme close-up: A shot that is taken closer than a close-up, usually showing the viewer less of the subject but in greater detail.

Fade in, fade out: A transition method whereby the amount of light projected is controlled to produce the gradual illumination of a scene (fade in), or its gradual diminution (fade out).

Film noir: (French, "dark film") A film made with subdued lighting and a somber tone, usually set in an urban environment, and the effects of which produce an overall sense of despair and fatalism.

Film score: The musical soundtrack that accompanies the film.

Film time: A term used by some directors to describe film action without dialogue.

Filmic mode: A mode of Shakespeare film constructed by the director's own meditation on his Shakespearean material, self-consciously employing the devices of filmmaking to create a cinema poem as expressive of the director's preoccupations as Shakespeare's. See also *hybrid mode, realistic mode, theatrical mode*.

First-person narrator: A narrator recounting a story from his or her individual perspective who speaks in the first person.

Flashback: The modification of a storyline in returning to events prior to that time depicted as present in the chronological development of a film.

Flash-cut: The projection of different shots of very short duration following one another in rapid succession.

Flash-forward: The modification of a storyline in moving forward to events that take place after that time depicted as present in the chronological development of a film.

Formalism: A term in literary criticism to describe the cultivation of artistic style and technique over subject matter.

Frame: (1) A single photographic image in a sequence of images, the rapid display of which produces the illusion of movement. (2) The area of an isolated screen projection.

Handheld camera: A camera that is held by the cameraman rather than placed on a fixed support.

High angle shot: A camera angle whereby the position of the lens is higher than subject, producing a distorted view that diminishes the physical presence of the figure.

Hybrid mode: A mode of Shakespeare film that strives to link their Shakespearean material with the established modes and genres of popular Hollywood films. See also *filmic mode, realistic mode, theatrical mode*.

Intertextuality: A term that describes the various relationships a given text may have with other texts; the conversations that works of art have with one another.

Iris-in: The gradual adjustment of a lens to allow a pinpoint circular projection to concentrically widen to the full screen. Iris-out is the reverse; a wide screen projection narrowing concentrically to a pinpoint spot.

Jump cut: The juxtaposition of two shots, similar in figures or background, which allows a jump in the continuity of the film in what appears to be a single shot. The action toward a destination, for example, can be compressed by the contiguity of an actor in one space instantly represented in another.

Long shot: A shot that projects the subject at a distance, typically, at minimum a full-screen representation of a complete human figure.

Low angle shot: A camera angle whereby the position of the lens is lower than subject, producing a distorted view that magnifies the physical presence of the figure.

Master shot: A single shot, usually a long shot, that incorporates an entire scene from beginning to end.

Medium shot: A shot taken at moderate distance, approximately defined to include the full-screen representation of a human figure from the waist up.

Metacinematic: The condition of action or narrative in a film commenting on itself, thereby exposing its inherent mimesis.

Metatheatrical: The condition of action or narrative in a play commenting on itself, thereby exposing its inherent mimesis. Reference to the audience is one example.

Mise-en-scène: (French, approx. "placed on scene") The setting of a film or play; all of the elements (actors, scenery, etc.) that comprise a specific shot or scene.

Montage: A process of editing that juxtaposes disparate shots and images in a condensed, sequential projection, and that suggests abstract ideas through the representation of the resulting visual mosaic.

New Criticism: The prevailing method of American literary analysis from the 1930s to the 1960s that concentrated on the verbal complexities and ambiguities of poems, plays, and novels without attention to their origins or context.

New Wave: Name attached to a group of French filmmakers (especially Jean-Luc Godard, François Truffaut, and Claude Chabrol) who came to prominence in the 1960s and who were influenced by existentialism, the history of the movies, and the liberating joys of filmmaking.

Omniscient narrator: A term borrowed from literature whereby the narrator of the story is aware of everything that is occurring in it—all of the action, circumstances, and events, including all of the characters' thoughts.

Outtakes: Scenes or moments shot but not included in the final print of the film.

Overhead shot: The camera, mounted on a platform or a crane, looks directly down on the action below.

Pan shot: The movement of a fixed camera along a horizontal axis to produce a smooth projection of images or subjects by scanning the field of view.

Playscript: The written version of a play or film used to prepare for a performance.

Point-of-view shot: A shot taken from the perspective of a character's visual perception showing us what the character would see.

Postmodernism: This term encompasses the range of theories challenging formalism and the new criticism and their championing of the coherent work of art expressed in such traditional forms as the poem, play, or novel. Postmodernism heralds a wide range of cultural expression from advertising and architecture to film, television, and pop art and sees it as reflecting a fragmented and fractured world.

Rack shot: A shot achieved by the shift in focus from one subject to another as a means of drawing the viewer's attention.

Reaction shot: Usually the silent close-up of a character registering a reaction to action or dialogue.

Realistic mode: A mode of Shakespeare film dominated by the sweep, agility, and mobility of the camera to move from a broad panorama to a tiny detail in an instant. Such films are usually shot on location reinforcing their realistic mode of presentation. See also *filmic mode, hybrid mode, theatrical mode*.

Reel: A standard-size spool and the amount of film that can be wound onto it; about eleven minutes of projection time.

Screenplay: A script including the dialogue and essential action of the characters from which a director can create a film.

Sequence: A discrete section of film portraying scenes, which in their contiguity describe a complete cinematic action.

Slam zoom: A zoom shot achieved at high speed.

Soundstage: Film studio facility where the interiors of most films are shot.

Soundtrack: All the sound contained in the film including dialogue, music, and sound effects.

Steadicam: A stabilizing camera mount, or the camera thereby stabilized, which allows a smooth cinematic projection from a potentially uneven handheld position.

Theatrical mode: A mode of Shakespeare film that acknowledges Shakespeare's theatrical roots by employing many long takes, allowing the actor to build a performance as in the theater, and framing the playing space as in a proscenium theater. See also *filmic mode, hybrid mode, realistic mode*.

Thrust stage: A type of theatre, like Shakespeare's Globe, where the stage projects out into the audience that surrounds the actors and action on three sides.

Tracking shot: A fluid, kinetic camera shot produced by the attachment of the camera to a mobile dolly or hand-held in unison with the motion of a filmed subject.

Tumble shot: A shot where the camera rotates 360 degrees as inside the cockpit of a fighter plane or a car turning over in a crash.

Two shot; three shot: Shots, usually in medium close-up, of two or three characters captured in the frame.

Voice-over: A voice in a film that is not synchronized with the projected speech of a character, but is spoken as a narrator outside the context of the cinematic action. Often the voice articulates a character's thoughts, which remain unspoken in the action of the film.

Whip pan: A panning shot whereby the camera is moved very quickly to briefly produce a set of horizontal blurred lines. This technique can be used as a method of transitioning from one shot to the next.

Wide angle shot: A shot taken with a lens with a short focal length which provides a distorted but extensive view of a wide area.

Wipe: A transition whereby a line moves across the screen removing one shot while it reveals another.

Zoom: The shift in focal length from a long shot to a close-up through the use of a camera with a variable focal length lens.

Selective Bibliography

I. Book-Length Studies

Aebischer, Pascale. *Shakespeare's Violated Bodies: Stage and Screen Performance.* Cambridge: Cambridge University Press, 2004.

Anderegg, Michael. *Orson Welles, Shakespeare, and Popular Culture.* New York: Columbia University Press, 1999.

———. *Cinematic Shakespeare.* Lanham: Rowman and Littlefield, 2004.

Ball, Robert Hamilton. *Shakespeare on Silent Film: A Strange Eventful History.* New York: Theatre Art Books, 1968.

Brode, Douglas. *Shakespeare in the Movies.* New York: Oxford University Press, 2000.

Buchanan, Judith. *Shakespeare on Film.* Edinburgh: Pearson Education, 2005.

Buchman, Lorne. *Still in Movement: Shakespeare on Screen.* New York: Oxford University Press, 1991.

Buhler, Stephen. *Shakespeare in the Cinema: Ocular Proof.* Albany: State University of New York Press, 2002.

Burnett, Mark Thornton. *Filming Shakespeare in the Global Marketplace.* Basingstoke: Palgrave, 2007.

Burt, Richard. *Unspeakable ShaXXXspeares: Queer Theory and American Kiddie Culture.* New York: St. Martin's, 1998.

Cartelli, Thomas and Katherine Rowe. *New Wave Shakespeare on Screen.* Cambridge, UK and Malden, MA: Polity Press, 2007.

Cartmell, Deborah. *Interpreting Shakespeare on Screen.* Houndmills: Macmillan, 2000.

Collick, John. *Shakespeare, Cinema and Society.* Manchester: Manchester University Press, 1989.

Coursen, H. R. *Shakespearean Performance as Interpretation.* Newark: University of Delaware Press, 1992.

———. *Watching Shakespeare on Television.* Rutherford: Fairleigh Dickinson University Press, 1993.

———. *Shakespeare in Production: Whose History?* Athens: Ohio University Press, 1996.

———. *Teaching Shakespeare with Film and Television.* Westport: Greenwood Press, 1997.

———. *Shakespeare: The Two Traditions.* Madison: Fairleigh Dickinson University Press, 1999.

————. *Shakespeare in Space: Recent Shakespeare Productions on Screen*. New York: Peter Lang, 2002.

————. *Shakespeare Translated: Derivatives on Film and Television*. New York: Peter Lang, 2005.

Crowl, Samuel. *Shakespeare Observed: Studies in Performance on Stage and Screen*. Athens: Ohio University Press, 1992.

————. *Shakespeare at the Cineplex: The Kenneth Branagh Era*. Athens: Ohio University Press, 2003.

————. *The Films of Kenneth Branagh*. Westport: Praeger, 2006.

Davies, Anthony. *Filming Shakespeare's Plays: The Adaptations of Laurence Olivier, Orson Welles, Peter Brook, and Akira Kurosawa*. Cambridge: Cambridge University Press, 1988.

Donaldson, Peter S. *Shakespearean Films/Shakespearean Directors*. Boston: Unwin Hyman, 1990.

Geduld, Harry. *Film Guide to* Henry V. Bloomington: Indiana University Press, 1973.

Greer, Michael. *Screening Shakespeare: Using Film to Understand the Plays*. New York: Pearson Longman, 2004.

Hatchuel, Sarah. *A Companion to the Shakespeare Films of Kenneth Branagh*. Winnipeg: Blizzard, 2000.

————. *Shakespeare from Stage to Screen*. Cambridge: Cambridge University Press, 2004.

Hindle, Maurice. *Studying Shakespeare on Film*. Houndmills: Palgrave, 2007.

Hodgdon, Barbara. *The Shakespeare Trade*. Philadelphia: University of Pennsylvania Press, 1998.

Holderness, Graham. *Visual Shakespeare: Essays in Film and Television*. Hatfield: University of Hertfordshire Press, 2002.

Howlett, Kathy. *Framing Shakespeare on Film*. Athens: Ohio University Press, 2000.

Jorgens, Jack. *Shakespeare on Film*. Bloomington: Indiana University Press, 1977.

Kliman, Bernice. *Hamlet: Film, Television, and Audio Performance*. Rutherford: Fairleigh Dickinson Press, 1988.

Kozintsev, Grigori. *Shakespeare: Time and Conscience*. Trans. Joyce Vining. New York: Hill and Wang, 1966.

————. King Lear: *The Space of Tragedy; the Diary of a Film Director*. Trans. Mary MacKintosh. Berkeley: California University Press, 1977.

Lanier, Douglas. *Shakespeare and Modern Popular Culture*. Oxford: Oxford University Press, 2002.

Lehmann, Courtney. *Shakespeare Remains: Theater to Film, Early Modern to Postmodern*. Ithaca: Cornell University Press, 2002.

MacLiammoir, Michael. *Put Money in Thy Purse: The Filming of Orson Welles's* Othello. London: Methuen, 1952. 2nd ed. London: Methuen, 1976.

Maher, Mary. *Modern Hamlets and Their Soliloquies*. Rev. ed. Iowa City: University of Iowa Press, 2003.

Manvell, Roger. *Shakespeare and the Film*. London: Dent; New York: Praeger, 1971.

————. *Theatre and Film*. Rutherford: Fairleigh Dickinson University Press, 1979.

Pilkington, Ace. *Screening Shakespeare from* Richard II *to* Henry V. Newark: University of Delaware Press, 1991.

Prince, Stephen. *The Warrior's Camera: The Cinema of Akira Kurosawa*. Princeton: Princeton University Press, 1991.

Reynolds, Bryan. *Performing Transversally: Reimagining Shakespeare and the Critical Future*. Houndmills: Palgrave, 2003.

Rosenthal, Daniel. *Shakespeare on Screen*. London: Hamlyn, 2000.

Rothwell, Kenneth. *A History of Shakespeare on Screen: A Century of Film and Television*. 2nd ed. Cambridge: Cambridge University Press, 2004. [The definitive history of the genre.]

Rutter, Carol Chillington. *Enter the Body: Women and Representation on Shakespeare's Stage*. London: Routledge, 2001.

Willis, Susan. *The BBC Shakespeare Plays: Making the Televised Canon*. Chapel Hill: University of North Carolina Press, 1991.

Willson, Robert F., Jr. *Shakespeare in Hollywood: 1929–1956*. Madison: Fairleigh Dickinson University Press, 2000.

II. Essay Collections

Aebischer, Pascale, Edward Esche, and Nigel Wheale, eds. *Remaking Shakespeare: Performance across Media, Genres, and Cultures*. Houndmills: Palgrave, 2003.

Boose, Lynda and Richard Burt, eds. *Shakespeare, the Movie: Popularizing the Plays on Film, TV, and Video*. London: Routledge, 1997.

———. *Shakespeare, the Movie II*. London: Routledge, 2003.

Bulman, J. C. and H. R. Coursen, eds. *Shakespeare on Television: An Anthology of Essays and Reviews*. Hanover: University Press of New England, 1988.

Burnett, Mark Thornton and Ramona Wray, eds. *Shakespeare, Film, Fin de Siècle*. Houndmills: Macmillan; New York: St. Martin's, 2000.

———. *Screening Shakespeare in the Twenty-First Century*. Edinburgh: Edinburgh University Press, 2006.

Burt, Richard, ed., *Shakespeare after Mass Media*. Houndmills: Palgrave, 2002.

Davies, Anthony and Stanley Wells, eds. *Shakespeare and the Moving Image: The Plays on Film and Television*. Cambridge: Cambridge University Press, 1994.

Eckert, Charles, ed. *Focus on Shakespearean Films*. Englewood Cliffs: Prentice Hall, 1973.

Hatchuel, Sarah and Nathalie Vienne-Guerrin, eds. *Shakespeare on Screen: A Midsummer Night's Dream*. Rouen: Publications de l'Université de Rouen, 2004.

Jackson, Russell, ed. *The Cambridge Companion to Shakespeare on Film*. Cambridge: Cambridge University Press, 2000; 2nd ed., 2007.

Lehmann, Courtney and Lisa Starks, eds. *The Reel Shakespeare: Alternative Cinema and Theory*. Madison: Fairleigh Dickinson University Press, 2002.

———. *Spectacular Shakespeare: Critical Theory and Popular Cinema*. Madison: Fairleigh Dickinson University Press, 2002.

Occhiogrosso, Frank, ed. *Shakespeare in Performance: A Collection of Essays*. Newark: University of Delaware Press, 2003.

Shaughnessy, Robert, ed. *Shakespeare on Film*. Houndmills: Macmillan; New York: St. Martin's, 1998.

Skovmand, Michael, ed. *Screen Shakespeare*. Aarhus: Aarhus University Press, 1994.

Welsh, James, Richard Vela, and John Tibbets, eds. *Shakespeare into Film*. New York: Checkmark Books, 2002.

Willems, Michèle, ed. *Shakespeare á la television*. Rouen: Publications de l'Université de Rouen, 1987.

III. Screenplays and Related Materials

Almereyda, Michael. *William Shakespeare's* Hamlet: *A Screenplay Adaptation*. London: Faber and Faber, 2000.

Branagh, Kenneth. *Beginning*. London: Chatto & Windus, 1989.

———. Much Ado about Nothing *by William Shakespeare: A Screenplay Adaptation*. New York: W. W. Norton, 1993.

———. *In the Bleak Midwinter*. London: Nick Hern Books, 1995. [Published in the United States as *A Midwinter's Tale*. New York: Newmarket, 1995.]

———. Hamlet *by William Shakespeare: Screenplay, Introduction, and Film Diary. London: Chatto & Windus, 1996; New York: Norton, 1996.* [The diary was written by Russell Jackson.]

———. Henry V *by William Shakespeare: A Screenplay Adaptation*. London: Chatto & Windus, 1989; New York: Norton, 1997.

Dent, Alan, ed. Hamlet: *The Fim and the Play*. London: World Film Publishers, 1948. [Includes Olivier's screenplay for the film.]

Greenaway, Peter. *Prospero's Books: A Film of Shakespeare's* The Tempest. London: Chatto & Windus, 1991.

Heston, Charlton. *In the Area: The Autobiography*. London: HarperCollins, 1995.

Hoffman, Michael. *William Shakespeare's* A Midsummer Night's Dream. London: HarperCollins, 1999.

Kurosawa, Akira. *Something Like an Autobiography*. Trans. Audie E. Bock. New York: Vintage Books, 1983.

———. Hideo Oguni, and Ide Masato. *Ran*. Trans. Tadashi Shishido. Boston: Shambhala, 1986.

———. Seven Samurai *and Other Screenplays*. London: Faber, 1992. [Includes the screenplay for *Throne of Blood*.]

Lyons, Bridget Gellert, ed. *Chimes at Midnight*. New Brunswick: Rutgers University Press, 1988.

Masterworks of the British Cinema: Brief Encounter, Henry V, The Lady Vanishes. London: Faber and Faber, 1990. [Includes the screenplay for Olivier's film of *Henry V*.]

McKellen, Ian. *William Shakespeare's* Richard III: *A Screenplay*. London: Doubleday, 1996.

A Midsummer Night's Dream. Foreword by Max Reinhardt. New York: Grosset & Dunlap, 1935. [The screenplay for the Warner Bros. film of the play.]

Nunn, Trevor. *William Shakespeare's* Twelfth Night: *A Screenplay*. London: Metheun Drama, 1996.

Olivier, Laurence. *Henry V*. Classic Film Scripts. London: Lorrimer, 1984.

————. *On Acting*. New York: Simon & Schuster, 1986.

Polanski, Roman. *Roman*. New York: William Morrow, 1984.

Romeo and Juliet *by William Shakespeare: A Motion Picture Edition*. New York: Random House, 1936. [Includes the screenplay for George Cukor's film of the play.]

Taymor, Julie. *Titus: The Illustrated Screenplay*. New York: Newmarket, 2000.

Van Sant, Gus. *Even Cowgirls Get the Blues* and *My Own Private Idaho*. Boston: Faber and Faber, 1993.

Welles, Orson and Peter Bogdanovich. *This Is Orson Welles*. Ed. Jonathan Rosenbaum. New York: HarperCollins, 1992.

White, Mark. *Kenneth Branagh*. London: Faber and Faber, 2005.

William Shakespeare's Romeo & Juliet: *The Contemporary Film, the Classic Play*. New York: Bantam Doubleday, 1996. [Includes the screenplay for Luhrmann's film written by Craig Pearce and Baz Luhrmann.]

Zeffirelli, Franco. *The Autobiography of Franco Zeffirelli*. New York: Weidenfeld & Nicolson, 1986.

IV: Research Aids

Díaz Fernández, José Ramón. "Shakespeare on Screen: A Bibliography of Critical Studies." *Post Script: Essays in Film and the Humanities* 17.1 (Fall 1997): 91–146. [Lists 1,000 references of books, chapters from books, articles, essays, and reviews of Shakespeare films excluding derivatives.]

————. "Shakespeare on Television: A Bibliography of Criticism." *Early Modern Literary Studies* 6.1 (May 2000): 4.

Harner, James L, ed. *The World Shakespeare Bibliography. 1949–* . [Includes a film and television section for each play. Published annually as a separate issue of *Shakespeare Quarterly* and online at www.worldshakesbib.org.

McKernan, Luke and Olwen Terris, eds. *Walking Shadows: Shakespeare in the National Film and Television Archive*. London: British Film Institute, 1994.

Parker, Barry. *The Folger Fimography: A Directory of Feature Films Based on the Works of William Shakespeare*. Washington: Folger Shakespeare Library, 1979.

Rothwell, Kenneth and Annabelle Melzer. *Shakespeare on Screen: An International Filmography and Videography*. New York: Neal-Schuman, 1990. [The definitive listing, in the process of being updated].

Selective Filmography

This filmography contains the film and television productions mentioned or discussed in *Shakespeare and Film* as well as other productions likely to be included in courses on Shakespeare and film. For the convenience of students, I have provided cast lists for each production. Many videotape and DVD versions of the plays can be purchased from Amazon.com, but the most comprehensive listing of available Shakespeare productions and related material can be found in the catalogue produced by Poor Yorick of Stratford, Canada. Poor Yorick can be located on the web at www.bardcentral.com.

Antony and Cleopatra (Film, UK, Spain, Switzerland, 1972)
> Director: Charlton Heston, Designer: Maurice Pelling, Cinematographer: Rafael Pacheco, Composer: John Scott.
> Cast: Charlton Heston (Antony), Hildegarde Neil (Cleopatra), Eric Porter (Enobarbus), John Castle (Octavius Caesar), Fernando Rey (Lepidus), Juan Luis Galiardo (Alexas), Carmen Sevilla (Octavia), Freddie Jones (Pompey), Peter Arne (Menas), Luis Barboo (Varrius).

Antony and Cleopatra (Television, UK, 1974)
> Directors: Jon Scoffield and Trevor Nunn, Designer: Michael Bailey, Composer: Guy Woolfenden.
> Cast: Richard Johnson (Marc Antony), Janet Suzman (Cleopatra), Rosemary McHale (Charmian), Mavis Taylor Blake (Iras), Darien Angadi (Alexas), Sydney Livingstone (Mardian), Loftus Burton (Diomedes), Patrick Stewart (Enobarbus), Constantin De Goguel (Ventidius), Raymond Westwell (Lepidus), Mary Rutherford (Octavia), Philip Locke (Agrippa), Ben Kingsley (Thidias).

As You Like It (Film, UK, 1936)
> Director: Paul Czinner, Designer: Lazare Meerson, Cinematographer: Harold Rosson, Composer: William Walton.
> Cast: J. Fisher White (Adam), Leon Quartermaine (Jaques), Felix Aylmer (Duke Frederick), Elisabeth Bergner (Rosalind), Sophie Stewart (Celia), Laurence Olivier (Orlando), Richard Ainley (Sylvius), Austin Trevor (Le Beau), Mackenzie Ward (Touchstone), Dorice Fordred (Audrey), Joan White (Phoebe).

As You Like It (Film, UK, 1992)

Director: Christine Edzard, Cinematographer: Robin Vidgeon, Composer:
Michel Sanvoisin.

Cast: Cyril Cusack (Adam), James Fox (Jaques), Don Henderson (Duke
Senior/Duke Frederick), Emma Croft (Rosalind), Celia Bannerman
(Celia), Andrew Tiernan (Orlando/Oliver), Ewen Bremner (Silvius),
Roger Hammond (Corin/Le Beau), Griff Rhys Jones (Touchstone),
Miriam Margoyles (Audrey), Valerie Gogan (Phebe).

As You Like It (Film, UK, USA, 2007)

Director: Kenneth Branagh, Designer: Tim Harvey, Cinematographer: Roger
Lanser, Composer: Patrick Doyle.

Cast: Richard Briers (Adam), Kevin Kline (Jaques), Brian Blessed (Duke
Frederick/Duke Senior), Bryce Dallas Howard (Rosalind), Romola Garai
(Celia), Adrian Lester (Oliver), David Oyelowo (Orlando), Alex
Wyndham (Sylvius), Jimmy Yuill (Corin), Alfred Molina (Touchstone).

Chimes at Midnight (Film, Spain, Switzerland, 1966)

Director: Orson Welles, Designer: José Antonio de la Guerra and Mariano
Erdorza, Cinematographer: Edmond Richard, Composer: Francesco
Lavagnino.

Cast: Orson Welles (Falstaff), Keith Baxter (Prince Hal), John Gielgud (Henry
IV), Margaret Rutherford (Mistress Quickly), Jeanne Moreau (Doll
Tearsheet), Norman Rodway (Henry Percy), Marina Vlady (Kate), Alan
Webb (Shallow), Tony Beckley (Poins), Fernando Rey (Worcester), Walter
Chiari (Silence), Michael Aldridge (Pistol), Beatrice Welles (Child).

Hamlet (Film, Germany, 1920)

Director: Svend Gade and Heinz Schall, Designer: Sven Gade and Siegfried
Wroblewsky, Cinematographers: Curt Courant and Axel Graatkjaer,
Composer: Giuseppe Becce.

Cast: Asta Nielsen (Hamlet), Lilly Jacobson (Ophelia), Eduard von
Winterstein (Claudius), Mathilde Brandt (Gertrude), Hans Junkermann
(Polonius), Heinz Stieda (Horatio), Anton De Verdier (Laertes), Fritz
Achterberg (Fortinbras).

Hamlet (Film, UK, 1948)

Director: Laurence Olivier, Designers: Carmen Dillon and Roger Furse,
Cinematographer: Desmond Dickinson, Composer: William Walton.

Cast: Laurence Olivier (Hamlet), Jean Simmons (Ophelia), Basil Sydney
(Claudius), Eileen Herlie (Gertrude), Felix Aylmer (Polonius), Norman
Wooland (Horatio), Terence Morgan (Laertes), Peter Cushing (Osric),
Anthony Quayle (Marcellus), Esmond Knight (Bernardo), Stanley
Holloway (Gravedigger), John Laurie (Francisco), Russell Thorndyke
(Priest), Harcourt Williams (First Player).

Hamlet (Film, USSR, 1964)

Directors: Grigori Kozintsev, Designer: E. Ene, G. Kropachev, and S. Virsaladze, Cinematographer: I. Gritsyus, Composer: Dmitri Shostakovich.

Cast: Innokenti Smoktunovski (Hamlet), Michail Nazwanov (Claudius), Eliza Radzin-Szolkonis (Gertrude), Anastasia Vertinskaya (Ophelia), Yuri Tolubeyev (Polonius), S. Oleksenko (Laertes), A. Krevald (Fortinbras), I. Dmitriev (Rosencrantz), V. Medvedev (Guildenstern), V. Erenberg (Horatio), V. Kolpakor (Gravedigger), A. Chekaerskii, R. Aren and Y. Berkun (Actors), A. Lauter (Priest).

Hamlet (Film, UK, 1969)

Director: Tony Richardson, Designer: Jocelyn Herbert, Cinematographer: Gerry Fisher, Composer: Patrick Gowers.

Cast: Nicol Williamson (Hamlet), Judy Parfitt (Gertrude), Anthony Hopkins (Claudius), Marianne Faithfull (Ophelia), Mark Dignam (Polonius), Michael Pennington (Laertes), Gordon Jackson (Horatio), Ben Aris (Rosencrantz), Clive Graham (Guildenstern), Peter Gale (Osric), Roger Livesey (Lucianus/Gravedigger).

Hamlet (Film, UK, 1990)

Director: Franco Zeffirelli, Designer: Dante Ferretti, Cinematographer: David Watkin, Composer: Ennio Morricone.

Cast: Mel Gibson (Hamlet), Glenn Close (Gertrude), Alan Bates (Claudius), Nathaniel Parker (Laertes), Paul Scofield (Ghost), Ian Holm (Polonius), Helena Bonham Carter (Ophelia), Stephen Dillane (Horatio), Sean Murray (Guildenstern), Michael Maloney (Rosencrantz), Trevor Peacock (Gravedigger), John McEnery (Osric).

Hamlet (Television, USA, 1990)

Director: Kevin Kline, Designers: John Arnone and Robin Wagner, Composer: Bob James.

Cast: Peter Francis James (Horatio), Robert Murch (Ghost/Priest), Dana Ivey (Gertrude), Brian Murray (Claudius), Josef Sommer (Polonius), Michael Cumpsty (Laertes), Diane Venora (Ophelia), Kevin Kline (Hamlet), Phillip Goodwin (Rosencrantz), Reg E. Cathey (Guildenstern), Don Reilly (Fortinbras), Leo Burmester (Osric).

Hamlet (Film, UK, 1996)

Director: Kenneth Branagh, Designer: Tim Harvey, Cinematographer: Alex Thomson B.S.C., Composer: Patrick Doyle.

Cast: Riz Abbasi (Attendant to Claudius), Richard Attenborough (English Ambassador), David Blair (Attendant to Claudius), Brian Blessed (Ghost), Kenneth Branagh (Hamlet), Richard Briers (Polonius), Julie Christie (Gertrude), Billy Crystal (First Gravedigger), Judi Dench (Hecuba), Gerard Depardieu (Reynaldo), Reece Dinsdale (Guildenstern), Ken Dodd (Yorick), Rob Edwards (Lucianus), Nicholas Farrell (Horatio), John Gielgud (Priam), Rosemary Harris (Player Queen), Charlton Heston

(Player King), Derek Jacobi (Claudius), Jack Lemmon (Marcellus), Ian
McElhinney (Barnardo), Michael Maloney (Laertes), John Mills (Old
Norway), Melanie Ramsay (Prostitute), Simon Russell Beale (Second
Gravedigger), Rufus Sewell (Fortinbras), Timothy Spall (Rosencrantz),
Robin Williams (Osric), Kate Winslet (Ophelia).

Hamlet (Film, USA, 2000)

Director: Michael Almereyda, Designer: Gideon Ponte, Cinematographer:
John de Borman, Composer: Carter Burwell.

Cast: Ethan Hawke (Hamlet), Kyle MacLachlan (Claudius), Sam Shepard
(Ghost), Diane Venora (Gertrude), Bill Murray (Polonius), Liev Schreiber
(Laertes), Julia Stiles (Ophelia), Karl Geary (Horatio), Steve Zahn
(Rosencrantz), Dechen Thurman (Guildenstern), Paula Malcomson
(Marcella), Rome Neal (Bernardo), Robert Thurman (Priest), Jeffrey
Wright (Gravedigger), Paul Bartel (Osric).

Hamlet (Film, USA, 2001)

Directors: Campbell Scott and Eric Simonson, Designer: Chris Shriver,
Cinematographer: Dan Gillham, Composer: Gary DeMichele.

Cast: Blair Brown (Gertrude), Roscoe Lee Browne (Polonius), Marcus Giamatti
(Guildenstern), Lisa Gay Hamilton (Ophelia), John Benjamin Hickey
(Horatio), Michael Imperioli (Rosencrantz), Byron Jennings (Ghost and
Player King), Dan Moran (First Gravedigger), Denis O'Hare (Osric), Sam
Robards (Fortinbras), Campbell Scott (Hamlet), Jamey Sheridan (Claudius),
Eric Simonson (Second Gravedigger), Roger Guenveur Smith (Laertes).

Henry V (Film, UK, 1944)

Director: Laurence Olivier, Designers: Paul Sheriff and Carmen Dillon,
Cinematographers: Robert Krasker and Jack Hildyard, Composer:
William Walton.

Cast: Laurence Olivier (Henry V), Renée Asherson (Katharine), Felix Aylmer
(Canterbury), Robert Helpman (Ely), Harcourt Williams (Charles VI),
Janet Burnell (Queen Isabel), Max Adrian (Lewis, the Dauphin), Ivy St.
Helier (Alice), Jonathan Field (Montjoy), George Robey (Falstaff), Freda
Jackson (Dame Quickly), Robert Newton (Pistol), Esmond Knight
(Fluellen), Jamey Hanley (Williams), Brian Nissen (Court), Arthur
Hambling (Bates), Leslie Banks (Chorus).

Henry V (Film, UK, 1989)

Director: Kenneth Branagh, Designer: Tim Harvey, Cinematographer:
Kenneth MacMillan B.S.C., Composer: Patrick Doyle.

Cast: Derek Jacobi (Chorus), Kenneth Branagh (Henry V), Brian Blessed
(Exeter), Charles Kay (Canterbury), Alec McCowen (Ely), Fabian
Cartwright (Cambridge), Stephen Simms (Scroop), Jay Villiers (Grey), Ian
Holm (Fluellen), Shaun Prendergast (Bates), Pat Doyle (Court), Michael
Williams (Williams), Richard Briers (Bardolph), Geoffrey Hutchings
(Nym), Robert Stephens (Pistol), Robbie Coltrane (Falstaff), Christian Bale

(Boy), Judi Dench (Mistress Quickly), Paul Scofield (French King), Michael Maloney (Dauphin), Christopher Ravenscroft (Mountjoy), Emma Thompson (Katherine), Geraldine McEwan (Alice).

Julius Caesar (Film, USA, 1953)

Director: Joseph Mankiewicz, Designers: Edward Carfagno and Cedric Gibbons, Cinematographer: Joseph Ruttenberg, Composer: Miklós Rózsa.

Cast: Marlon Brando (Marc Antony), James Mason (Brutus), John Gielgud (Cassius), Louis Calhern (Julius Caesar), Edmond O'Brien (Casca), Greer Garson (Calpurnia), Deborah Kerr (Portia), George Macready (Marullus), Michael Pate (Flavius), Richard Hale (Soothsayer).

Julius Caesar (Film, UK, 1970)

Director: Stuart Burge, Designer: Julia Trevelyan Oman, Cinematographer: Ken Higgins, Composer: Michael J. Lewis.

Cast: Charlton Heston (Marc Antony), Jason Robards (Brutus), John Gielgud (Julius Caesar), Richard Johnson (Cassius), Robert Vaughn (Casca), Richard Chamberlain (Octavius Caesar), Dianna Rigg (Portia), Christopher Lee (Artemidorus), Jill Bennett (Calpurnia), David Dodimead (Lepidus).

King Lear (Film, USSR, 1970)

Director: Grigori Kozinstev, Designer: Yevgeni Yenej, Cinematographer: Jonas Gritsius, Composer: Dmitri Shostakovich.

Cast: Regimantas Adomaitis (Edmund), Donatas Banionis (Albany), Juozas Budraitis (King of France), Oleg Dal (Fool), Jüri Järvet (King Lear), Aleksei Petrenko (Oswald), Elze Radzinya (Goneril), Karl Sebris (Gloster), Valentina Shendrikova (Cordelia), Aleksandr Vokach (Cornwall), Galina Volchek (Regan), Vladimir Yemelyanov (Kent).

King Lear (Film, UK, 1971)

Director: Peter Brook, Designer: Georges Wakhévitch, Cinematographer: Henning Kristiansen.

Cast: Cyril Cusack (Albany), Susan Engel (Regan), Tom Fleming (Kent), Anne-Lise Gabold (Cordelia), Ian Hogg (Edmund), Søren Elung Jensen (Duke of Burgundy), Robert Lloyd (Edgar), Jack MacGowran (Fool), Patrick Magee (Cornwall), Paul Scofield (King Lear), Barry Stanton (Oswald), Alan Webb (Gloucester), Irene Worth (Goneril).

King Lear (Television, USA, 1974)

Director: Edwin Sherin, Designer: Santo Loquasto, Composer: Charles Gross.

Cast: Tom Aldredge (Fool), Rene Auberjonois (Edgar), Rosalind Cash (Goneril), Lee Chamberlain (Cordelia), Frederick Coffin (Oswald), Ellen Holly (Regan), James Earl Jones (King Lear), Raul Julia (Edmund), Robert Lanchester (Cornwall), Lou Quinones (Burgundy), Paul Sorvino (Gloucester), Jean-Pierre Stewart (France), Douglass Watson (Kent).

King Lear (Television, UK, USA, 1998)

Director: Richard Eyre, Designer: Frank Walsh, Cinematographer: Roger Pratt, Composer: Dominic Muldowney.

Cast: Paul Rhys (Edgar), Finbar Lynch (Edmund), Timothy West (Gloucester), David Burke (Kent), Barbara Flynn (Goneril), Amanda Redman (Regan), Victoria Hamilton (Cordelia), David Lyon (Albany), Michael Simkins (Cornwall), Ian Holm (King Lear), Adrian Irvine (France), Nicholas R. Bailey (Burgundy), William Osborne (Oswald), Michael Bryant (Fool).

Looking for Richard (Film, USA, 1996)

Director: Al Pacino, Designer: Kevin Ritter, Cinematographer: Robert Leacock, Composer: Howard Shore.

Cast: Penelope Allen (Queen Elizabeth), Gordon MacDonald (Dorset), Madison Arnold (Rivers), Vincent Angell (Grey), Harris Yulin (King Edward), Alec Baldwin (Duke of Clarence), Al Pacino (Richard III), Timmy Prairie (Prince Edward), Kevin Conway (Hastings), Larry Bryggman (Lord Stanley), Kevin Spacey (Earl of Buckingham), Estelle Parsons (Margaret), Winona Ryder (Lady Anne).

Love's Labour's Lost (Film, UK, 1999)

Director: Kenneth Branagh, Designer: Tim Harvey, Cinematographer: Alex Thomson, Composer: Patrick Doyle.

Cast: Kenneth Branagh (Berowne), Richard Briers (Sir Nathaniel), Richard Clifford (Boyet), Carmen Ejogo (Maria), Daniel Hill (Mercade), Nathan Lane (Costard), Adrian Lester (Dumain), Matthew Lillard (Longaville), Natascha McElhone (Rosaline), Geraldine McEwan (Holofernia), Emily Mortimer (Katherine), Alessandro Nivola (King), Anthony O'Donnell (Moth), Stefania Rocca (Jaquenetta), Alicia Silverstone (Princess), Timothy Spall (Don Armado), Jimmy Yuill (Dull).

Macbeth (Film, UK, 1948)

Director: Orson Welles, Designer: Fred Ritter, Cinematographer: John L. Russell, Composer: Jacques Ibert.

Cast: Orson Welles (Macbeth), Jeanette Nolan (Lady Macbeth), Dan O'Herlihy (Macduff), Roddy McDowall (Malcolm), Edgar Barrier (Banquo), Erskine Sanford (Duncan), John Dierkes (Ross), Keene Curtis (Lennox), Peggy Webber (Lady Macduff/Witch), Lionel Braham (Siward), Archie Heugly (Young Siward), Jerry Farber (Fleance).

Macbeth (Film, UK, 1971)

Director: Roman Polanski, Designers: Wilfred Shingleton and Fred Carter, Cinematographer: Gilbert Taylor.

Cast: Jon Finch (Macbeth), Francesca Annis (Lady Macbeth), John Stride (Ross), Martin Shaw (Banquo), Nicholas Selby (Duncan), Stephen Chase (Malcolm), Paul Shelley (Donalbain), Terence Bayler (Macduff), Noelle

Rimmington (Young Witch), Maisie MacFarquhar (Blind Witch), Elsie Taylor (First Witch), Diane Fletcher (Lady Macduff), Richard Pearson (Doctor), Sidney Bromley (Porter).

Macbeth (Television, UK, 1979)

Directors: Philip Casson and Trevor Nunn, Designer: Mike Hall, Composer: Guy Woolfenden.

Cast: Ian McKellen (Macbeth), Judi Dench (Lady Macbeth), John Brown (Lennox), Greg Hicks (Donalbain and Seyton), Griffith Jones (Duncan), Bob Peck (Macduff), Duncan Preston (Angus), Roger Rees (Malcolm), John Woodvine (Banquo).

The Merchant of Venice (Film, USA, 2004)

Director: Michael Radford, Designer: Bruno Rubeo, Cinematographer: Benoit Delhomme, Composer: Jocelyn Pook.

Cast: Al Pacino (Shylock), Jeremy Irons (Antonio), Joseph Fiennes (Bassanio), Lynn Collins (Portia), Zuleikha Robinson (Jessica), Kris Marshall (Gratiano), Charlie Cox (Lorenzo), Heather Goldenhersh (Nerissa), Mackenzie Crook (Lancelot Gobbo), Ron Cook (Old Gobbo), John Sessions (Salerio), Gregor Fisher (Solanio), Allan Gorduner (Tubal), David Harewood (Prince of Morocco), Antonio Gil-Martinez (Aragon).

A Midsummer Night's Dream (Film, USA, 1935)

Directors: Max Reinhardt and William Dieterle, Designers: Anton Grot and Max Ree, Cinematographer: Hal Mohr, Composer: Felix Mendelssohn, music arranged by Erich Wolfgang Korngold.

Cast: Ian Hunter (Theseus), Verree Teasdale (Hippolyta), Hobart Cavanaugh (Philostrate), Grant Mitchell (Egeus), Victor Jory (Oberon), Anita Louise (Titania), Olivia de Havilland (Hermia), Jean Muir (Helena), Dick Powell (Lysander), Ross Alexander (Demetrius), James Cagney (Bottom), Mickey Rooney (Puck), Hugh Herbert (Snout), Joe E. Brown (Flute), Otis Harlan (Starveling), Dewey Robinson (Snug), Frank McHugh (Quince).

A Midsummer Night's Dream (Film, UK, 1968)

Director: Peter Hall, Designers: John Bury and Ann Curtis, Cinematographer: Peter Suschitzky, Composer: Guy Wolfenden.

Cast: Derek Godfrey (Theseus), Barbara Jefford (Hippolyta), Hugh Sullivan (Philostrate), Nicholas Selby (Egeus), Ian Richardson (Oberon), Judi Dench (Titania), Helen Mirren (Hermia), Diana Rigg (Helena), David Warner (Lysander), Michael Jayston (Demetrius), Paul Rogers (Bottom), Ian Holm (Puck), Bill Travers (Snout), John Normington (Flute), Donald Eccles (Starveling), Clive Swift (Snug), Sebastian Shaw (Quince).

A Midsummer Night's Dream (Film, UK, 1996)

Director: Adrian Noble, Designer: Anthony Ward, Cinematographer: Ian Wilson, Composer: Howard Blake.

Cast: Lindsay Duncan (Hippolyta/Titania), Alex Jennings (Theseus/Oberon), Desmond Barrit (Bottom), Finbar Lynch (Philostrate/Puck), Monica Dolan (Hermia), Emily Raymond (Helena), Alfred Burke (Egeus), Howard Crossley (Snout), Kevin Doyle (Demetrius), Daniel Evans (Lysander), Robert Gillespie (Starveling), John Kane (Quince), Kenn Sabberton (Snug).

A Midsummer Night's Dream (Film, USA, Italy, 1999)

Director: Michael Hoffman, Designer: Luciana Arrighi, Cinematographer: Oliver Stapleton, Composer: Simon Boswell.

Cast: Kevin Kline (Bottom), Michelle Pfeiffer (Titania), Rupert Everett (Oberon), Stanley Tucci (Puck), Calista Flockhart (Helena), Anna Friel (Hermia), Christian Bale (Demetrius), Dominic West (Lysander), David Strathairn (Theseus), Sophie Marceau (Hippolyta), Roger Rees (Peter Quince), Max Wright (Robin Starveling), Gregory Jbara (Snug), Bill Irwin (Tom Snout), Sam Rockwell (Francis Flute), Bernard Hill (Egeus).

Much Ado about Nothing (Television, USA, 1973)

Director: Nick Havinga, Designer: Ming Cho Lee, Composer: Peter Link.

Cast: Sam Waterston (Benedick), Kathleen Widdoes (Beatrice), Barnard Hughes (Dogberry), Frederick Coffin (Borachio), Arny Freeman (Antonio), Mark Hammer (Leonardo), Bette Henritze (Ursula), Jeanne Hepple (Margaret), Jerry Mayer (Don John), April Shawnham (Hero), Glenn Walken (Claudio), Douglas Watson (Don Pedro).

Much Ado about Nothing (Film, UK, Italy, 1993)

Director: Kenneth Branagh, Designer: Tim Harvey, Cinematographer: Roger Lanser, Composer: Patrick Doyle.

Cast: Richard Briers (Leonato), Kate Beckinsale (Hero), Imelda Staunton (Margaret), Jimmy Yuill (Friar Francis), Brian Blessed (Antonio), Phyllida Law (Ursula), Emma Thompson (Beatrice), Alex Lowe (Messenger), Denzel Washington (Don Pedro), Keanu Reeves (Don John), Richard Clifford (Conrade), Gerard Horan (Borachio), Robert Sean Leonard (Claudio), Kenneth Branagh (Benedick), Patrick Doyle (Balthasar), Michael Keaton (Dogberry), Ben Elton (Verges).

Othello (Film, Morocco, Italy, 1952)

Director: Orson Welles, Designers: Alexander Trauner and Luigi Schiaccianoce, Cinematographers: Anchise Brizzi, George Fanto, Obadan Troania, Roberto Fusi, and G. Araldo, Composer: Francesco Lavagnino and Alberto Barberi.

Cast: Orson Welles (Othello), Suzanne Cloutier (Desdemona), Micheál MacLiammóir (Iago), Michael Lawrence (Cassio), Fay Compton (Emilia), Hilton Edwards (Brabantio), Robert Coote (Roderigo), Nicholas Bruce (Lodovico), Jean Davis (Montano), Doris Dowling (Bianca).

Othello (Film, UK, 1965)

> Director: Stuart Burge, Designer: William Kellner, Cinematographer: Geoffrey Unsworth, Composer: Richard Hampton.
>
> Cast: Laurence Olivier (Othello), Maggie Smith (Desdemona), Joyce Redman (Emilia), Frank Finlay (Iago), Derek Jacobi (Cassio), Robert Lang (Roderigo), Kenneth MacKintosh (Lodovico), Anthony Nicholls (Brabantio), Sheila Reid (Bianca), Edward Hardwicke (Montano).

Othello (Television, UK, 1990)

> Director: Trevor Nunn, Designer: Bob Crowley, Composer: Guy Woolfenden.
>
> Cast: Michael Grandage (Roderigo), Ian McKellen (Iago), Clive Swift (Brabantio/Gratiano), Willard White (Othello), Sean Baker (Cassio), John Burgess (Duke of Venice/Lodovico), Philip Sully (Montano), Imogen Stubbs (Desdemona), Zoe Wanamaker (Emilia), Marsha Hunt (Bianca).

Othello (Film, UK, 1995)

> Director: Oliver Parker, Designer: Tim Harvey, Cinematographer: David Johnson, Composer: Charles Mole.
>
> Cast: Laurence Fishburne (Othello), Irene Jacob (Desdemona), Kenneth Branagh (Iago), Nathaniel Parker (Cassio), Michael Maloney (Roderigo), Anna Patrick (Emilia), Nicholas Farrell (Montano), Indra Ove (Bianca), Michael Sheen (Lodovico), Andre Oumansky (Gratiano), Gabriele Ferzetti (The Duke of Venice), Pierre Vaneck (Brabantio).

Prospero's Books (Film, UK, Netherlands, France, Italy, 1991)

> Director: Peter Greenaway, Designers: Ben van Os and Jan Roelfs, Cinematographer: Sacha Vierny, Composer: Michael Nyman.
>
> Cast: John Gielgud (Prospero), Michael Clark (Caliban), Michel Blanc (Alonso), Erland Josephson (Gonzalo), Isabelle Pasco (Miranda), Tom Bell (Antonio), Kenneth Cranham (Sebastian), Mark Rylance (Ferdinand), Gerard Thoolen (Adrian), Pierre Bokma (Francisco), Jim van der Woude (Trinculo), Michiel Romeyn (Stephano), Orpheo/Paul Russell/James Thiérrée/Emil Wolk (Ariel).

Ran (Film, Japan, 1985)

> Director: Akira Kurosawa, Designer: Shinobu Muraki and Yoshirô Muraki, Cinematographer: Asakazu Nakai, Takao Saitô and Masaharu Ueda, Composer: Tôru Takemitsu.
>
> Cast: Tatsuya Nakadai (Lord Hidetora Ichimonji), Akira Terao (Taro Takatora Ichimonji), Jinpachi Nezu (Jiro Masatora Ichimonji), Daisuke Ryu (Saburo Naotora Ichimonji), Mieko Harada (Lady Kaede), Yoshiko Miyazaki (Lady Sué), Hisashi Igawa (Shuri Kurogane), Peter (Kyoami), Masayuki Yui (Tango Hirayama), Kazuo Kato (Kageyu Ikoma), Norio Matsui (Shumenosuke Ogura).

Richard III (Film, USA, 1912)
> Director: M. B. Dudley and James Keane
> Cast: Robert Gemp (Edward IV), Frederick Warde (Richard III), Albert
>   Gardner (Prince Edward of Lancaster), James Keane (Earl of Richmond),
>   George Moss (Tressel), Howard Stuart (Edward), Virginia Rankin (York),
>   Violet Stuart (Lady Anne), Carey Lee (Queen Elizabeth), Carlotta De
>   Felice (Princess Elizabeth).

Richard III (Film, UK, 1955)
> Director: Laurence Olivier, Designer: Roger Furse, Cinematographer: Otto
>   Heller, Composer: William Walton.
> Cast: Cedric Hardwicke (Edward IV), Nicholas Hannen (Archbishop),
>   Laurence Olivier (Richard III), Ralph Richardson (Duke of Buckingham),
>   John Gielgud (Duke of Clarence), Pamela Brown (Jane Shore), Paul
>   Huson (Edward, Prince of Wales), Claire Bloom (Lady Anne), Clive
>   Morton (Lord Rivers), Norman Wooland (Catesby), Alec Clunes (Lord
>   Hastings), Dan Cunningham (Lord Grey), Douglas Wilmer (Lord
>   Dorset), Laurence Naismith (Lord Stanley).

Richard III (Film, UK, 1995)
> Director: Richard Loncraine, Designer: Tony Burrough, Cinematographer:
>   Peter Biziou, Composer: Trevor Jones.
> Cast: Ian McKellen (Richard III), Bill Paterson (Ratcliffe), Annette Bening
>   (Queen Elizabeth), John Wood (King Edward), Nigel Hawthorne
>   (Clarence), Maggie Smith (Duchess of York), Kate Steavenson-Payne
>   (Princess Elizabeth), Robert Downey Jr. (Rivers), Tim McInnerny
>   (Catesby), Jim Carter (Hastings), Roger Hammond (Archbishop), Jim
>   Broadbent (Buckingham), Edward Hardwicke (Stanley), Ryan Gilmore
>   (George Stanley), Dominic West (Richmond), Kristin Scott Thomas
>   (Lady Anne), Adrian Dunbar (Tyrell).

Romeo and Juliet (Film, USA, 1936)
> Director: George Cukor, Designer: Cedric Gibbons, Cinematographer:
>   William Daniels, Composer: Herbert Stothart and Edward Ward.
> Cast: Norma Shearer (Juliet), Leslie Howard (Romeo), John Barrymore
>   (Mercutio), Edna May Oliver (Nurse), Basil Rathbone (Tybalt), C.
>   Aubrey Smith (Lord Capulet), Henry Kolker (Friar Laurence), Virginia
>   Hammond (Lady Montague), Reginald Denny (Benvolio), Violet Kemble
>   Cooper (Lady Capulet).

Romeo and Juliet (Film, Italy, UK, 1968)
> Director: Franco Zeffirelli, Designer: Renzo Mongiardino, Cinematographer:
>   Pasqualino De Santis, Composer: Nino Rota.
> Cast: Leonard Whiting (Romeo), Olivia Hussey (Juliet), John McEnery
>   (Mercutio), Milo O'Shea (Friar Laurence), Pat Heywood (Nurse),
>   Michael York (Tybalt), Bruce Robinson (Benvolio), Paul Hardwick (Lord

Capulet), Natasha Parry (Lady Capulet), Antonio Pierfederici (Lord Montague), Esmeralda Ruspoli (Lady Montague).

William Shakespeare's Romeo +Juliet (Film, USA, 1996)

Director: Baz Luhrmann, Designer: Catherine Martin, Cinematographer: Donald McAlpine, Composers: Tim Atack and Nellee Hooper.

Cast: Leonardo DiCaprio (Romeo), Claire Danes (Juliet), Dash Mihok (Benvolio), Harold Perrineau (Mercutio), John Leguizamo (Tybalt), Jesse Bradford (Balthasar), Zak Orth (Gregory), Jamie Kennedy (Sampson), Pete Postlethwaite (Father Laurence), Miriam Margolyes (Nurse), Diane Venora (Gloria Capulet), Paul Sorvino (Fulgencio Capulet), Vondie Curtis-Hall (Captain Prince), Brian Dennehy (Ted Montague), Christina Pickles (Caroline Montague), Paul Rudd (Dave Paris), Edwina Moore (Anchorwoman).

The Taming of the Shrew (Film, USA, 1929)

Director: Sam Taylor, Designers: Laurence Irving and William Cameron Menzies, Cinematographer: Karl Struss.

Cast: Mary Pickford (Katherine), Douglas Fairbanks (Petruchio), Edwin Maxwell (Baptista), Joseph Cawthorn (Gremio), Clyde Cook (Grumio), Geoffrey Wardwell (Hortensio), Dorothy Jordan (Bianca), Charles Stevens (Servant).

The Taming of the Shrew (Film, USA, Italy, 1966)

Director: Franco Zeffirelli, Designers: John DeCuir and Renzo Mongiardino, Cinematographer: Oswald Morris, Composer: Nino Rota.

Cast: Elizabeth Taylor (Katharina), Richard Burton (Petruchio), Cyril Cusack (Grumio), Michael Hordern (Baptista), Alfred Lynch (Tranio), Alan Webb (Gremio), Giancarlo Cobelli (Priest), Vernon Dobtcheff (Pedant), Ken Parry (Tailor), Anthony Gardner (Haberdasher), Natasha Pyne (Bianca), Michael York (Lucentio), Victor Spinetti (Hortensio), Roy Holder (Biondello), Mark Dignam (Vincentio), Bice Valori (Widow).

The Tempest (Film, UK, 1980)

Director: Derek Jarman, Designer: Yolanda Sonnabend, Cinematographer: Peter Middleton, Composers: Brian Hodgson and John Lewis.

Cast: Peter Bull (Alonso), David Meyer (Ferdinand), Neil Cunningham (Sebastian), Heathcote Williams (Prospero), Toyah Willcox (Miranda), Richard Warwick (Antonio), Karl Johnson (Ariel), Jack Birkett (Caliban), Christopher Biggins (Stehphano), Peter Turner (Trinculo), Ken Campbell (Gonzalo).

Throne of Blood (*Kumonosu-jô*) (Film, Japan, 1957)

Director: Akira Kurosawa, Designer: Yoshirô Muraki, Cinematographer: Asakazu Nakai, Composer: Masaru Satô.

Cast: Toshirô Mifune (Taketori Washizu), Isuzu Yamada (Lady Asaji Washizu), Takashi Shimura (Noriyasu Odagura), Akira Kubo (Yoshiteru Miki), Hiroshi Tachikawa (Kunimaru Tsuzuki), Minoru Chiaki (Yoshiaki Miki), Takamaru Sasaki (Kuniharu Tsuzuki), Kokuten Kodo (Military Commander), Kichijiro Ueda (Washizu's workman).

Titus (Film, USA, Italy, 1999)

Director: Julie Taymor, Designer: Dante Ferretti, Cinematographer: Luciano Tovoli, Composer: Elliot Goldenthal.

Cast: Anthony Hopkins (Titus), Jessica Lange (Tamora), Alan Cumming (Saturninus), Harry Lennix (Aaron), Colm Feore (Marcus), Angus Macfadyen (Lucius), Jonathan Rhys Meyers (Chiron), Matthew Rhys (Demetrius), Laura Fraser (Lavinia), James Frain (Bassianus), Osheen Jones (Young Lucius).

Twelfth Night (Film, UK, 1995)

Director: Trevor Nunn, Designer: Sophie Becher, Cinematographer: Clive Tickner, Composer: Shaun Davey.

Cast: Imogen Stubbs (Viola), Sid Livingstone (Captain), Toby Stephens (Orsino), Alan Mitchell (Valentine), Imelda Staunton (Maria), Mel Smith (Sir Toby Belch), Richard E. Grant (Sir Andrew Aguecheek), Ben Kingsley (Feste), Nigel Hawthorne (Malvolio), Helena Bonham Carter (Olivia), Nicholas Farrell (Antonio), Stephen Mackintosh (Sebastian), Peter Gunn (Fabian).

Index

Page numbers in *italics* refer to illustrations.